JACK OF FABLES

The Bad Prince

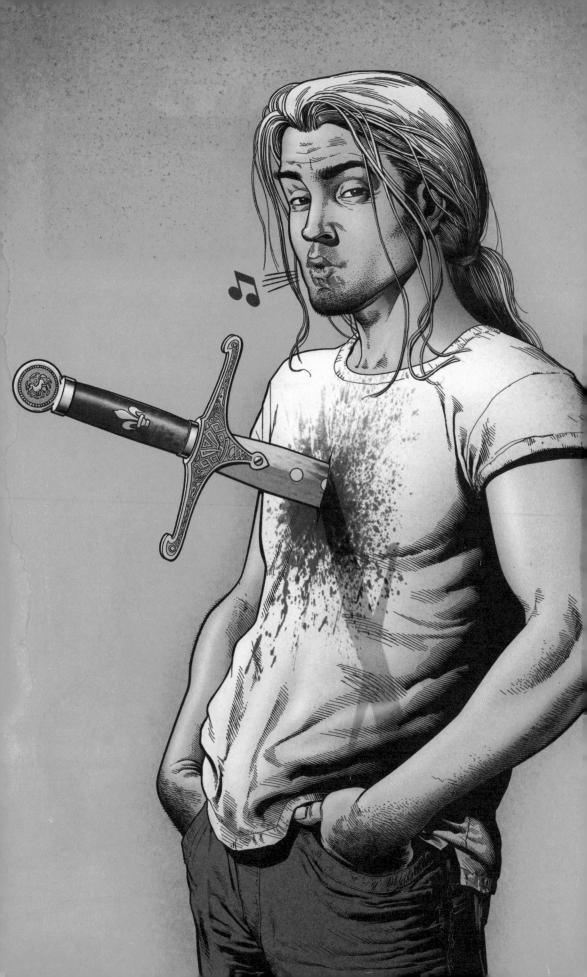

JACK
OF FABLES

The
Bad Prince

Bill **WILLINGHAM**   *Matthew* **STURGES**
Writers

Tony **AKINS**   *Russ* **BRAUN**
Andrew **ROBINSON**
Pencillers

Andrew **PEPOY**   *Andrew* **ROBINSON**
Bill **REINHOLD**
Inkers

Daniel **VOZZO**   *Lee* **LOUGHRIDGE**
Colorists

Todd **KLEIN**
Letterer

BRIAN BOLLAND Original Series Covers
Jack of Fables created by **BILL WILLINGHAM**

Cover illustration by Brian Bolland.
Logo design by James Jean.
Publication design by Brainchild Studios/NYC.

JACK OF FABLES: THE BAD PRINCE

Published by DC Comics. Cover and compilation
Copyright © 2008 DC Comics. All Rights Reserved.

Originally published in single magazine form as JACK
OF FABLES 12-16. Copyright © 2007 Bill Willingham
and DC Comics. All Rights Reserved. All characters,
their distinctive likenesses and related elements
featured in this publication are trademarks of Bill
Willingham. VERTIGO is a trademark of DC Comics.
The stories, characters and incidents featured in this
publication are entirely fictional. DC Comics does not
read or accept unsolicited submissions of ideas,
stories or artwork.

DC Comics, 1700 Broadway, New York, NY 10019
A Warner Bros. Entertainment Company.
Printed in Canada. First Printing.
ISBN: 978-1-4012-1854-6

Table of Contents

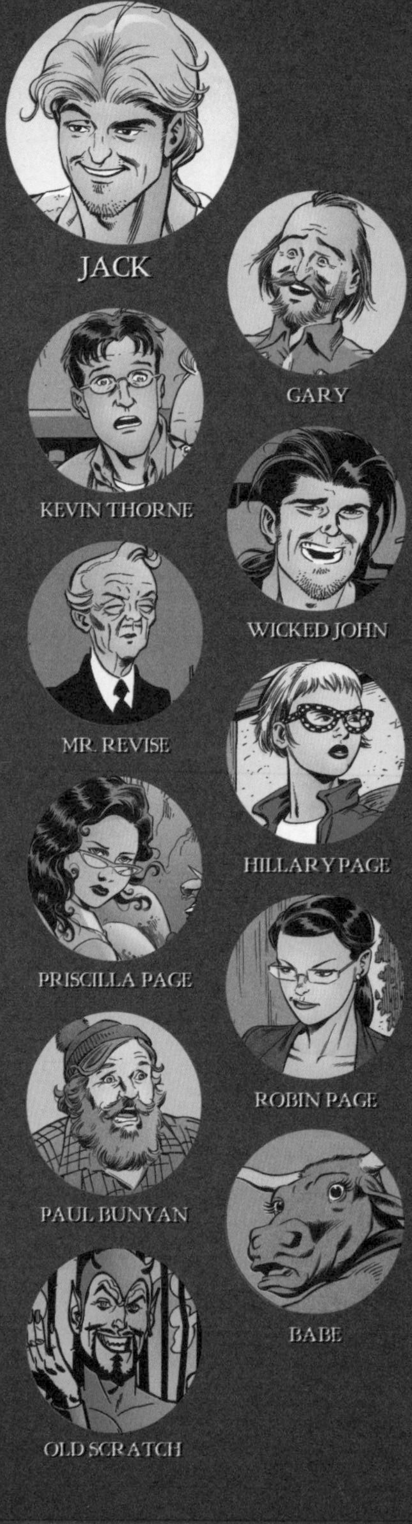
JACK
GARY
KEVIN THORNE
WICKED JOHN
MR. REVISE
HILLARY PAGE
PRISCILLA PAGE
ROBIN PAGE
PAUL BUNYAN
BABE
OLD SCRATCH

Dramatis Personae

Jack
Also known as Little Jack Horner, Jack B. Nimble, Jack the Giant Killer and countless other aliases, our hero Jack of Tales embodies the archetype of the lovable rogue (minus, according to many, the lovability).

Gary, the Pathetic Fallacy
A timid, impressionable and warm-hearted fellow whose power over inanimate objects is matched only by his love of Sousa marches.

Kevin Thorne
A curiously perceptive lawyer obsessed with proving that Fables live among us.

Wicked John
Except for his dark hair, he's the spitting image of Jack – right down to the insufferable air of superiority.

Mr. Revise
Jack's current nemesis, dedicated to trapping Fables and draining their power in pursuit of a magic-free world.

The Page Sisters
Right-hand women to Mr. Revise and the chief librarians at his Fable prison, the Golden Boughs Retirement Village.

Paul Bunyan
A giant of American history, now living in reduced circumstances.

Babe
A blue ox given to delusional musings.

Old Scratch
A sulphurous tempter.

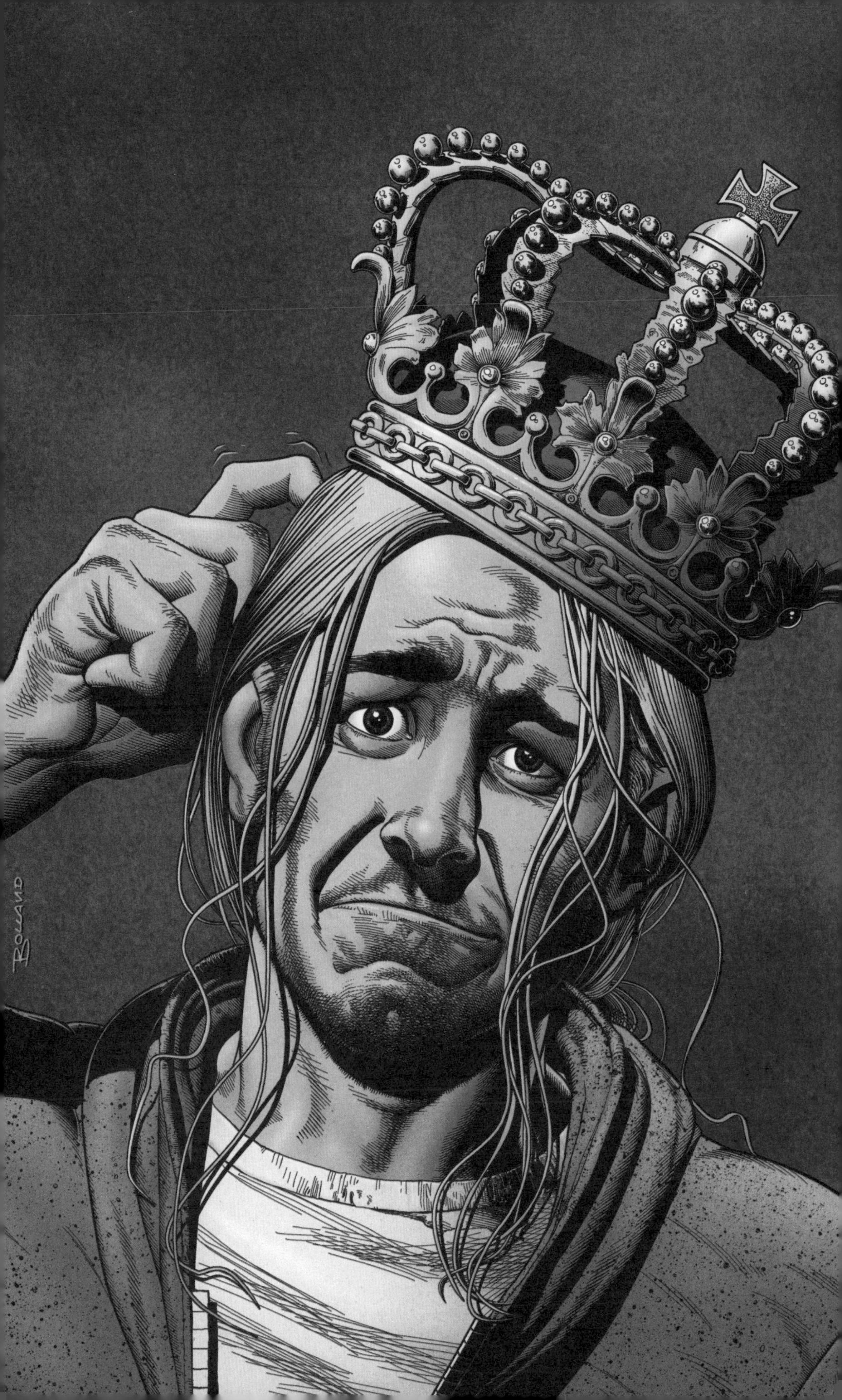
BOLLAND

"What's the use of
doing heroic things if nobody
can see you?"

Hit the Road, Jack

— Part One of THE BAD PRINCE —

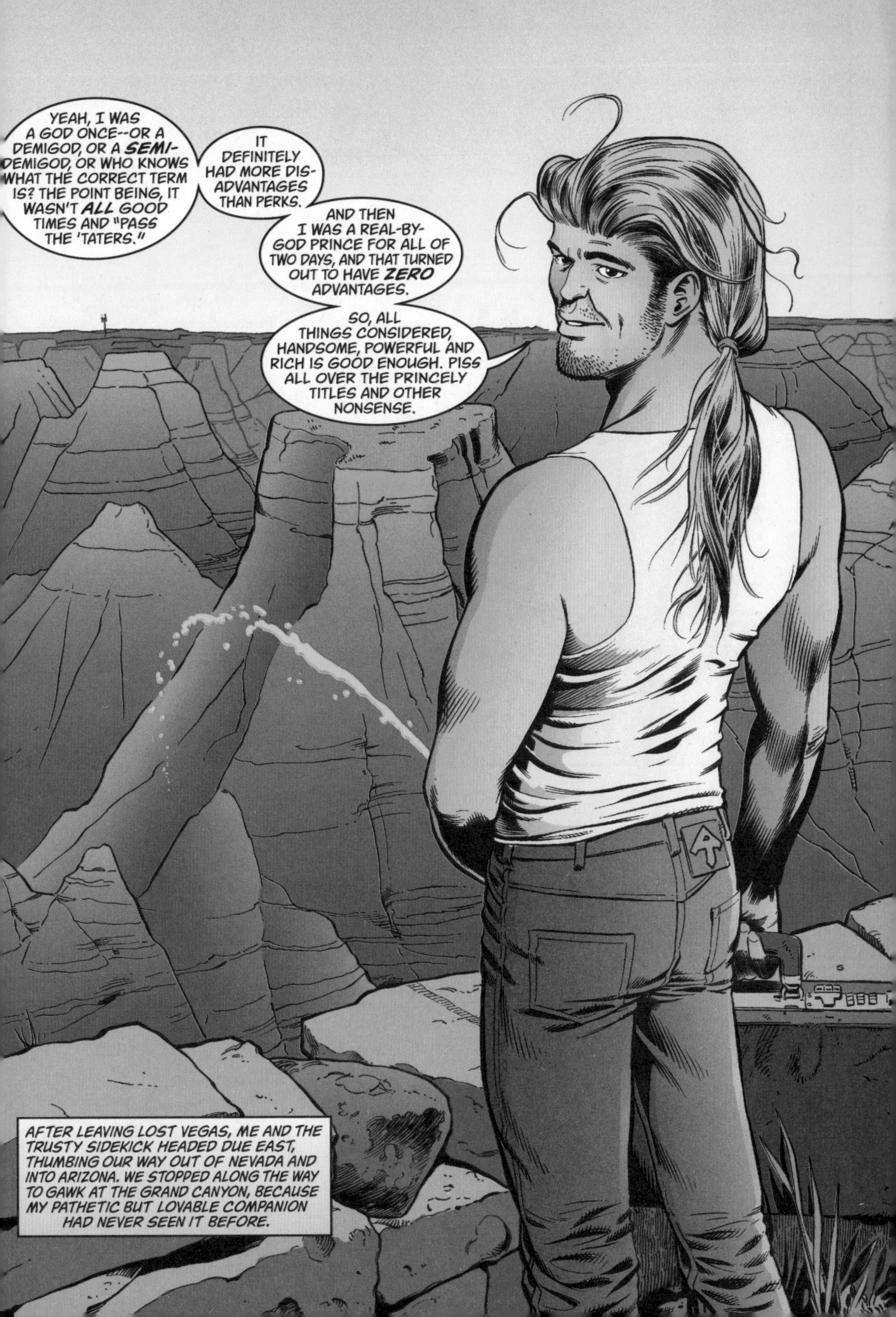
YEAH, I WAS A GOD ONCE--OR A DEMIGOD, OR A SEMI-DEMIGOD, OR WHO KNOWS WHAT THE CORRECT TERM IS? THE POINT BEING, IT WASN'T ALL GOOD TIMES AND "PASS THE 'TATERS."
IT DEFINITELY HAD MORE DIS-ADVANTAGES THAN PERKS.
AND THEN I WAS A REAL-BY-GOD PRINCE FOR ALL OF TWO DAYS, AND THAT TURNED OUT TO HAVE ZERO ADVANTAGES.
SO, ALL THINGS CONSIDERED, HANDSOME, POWERFUL AND RICH IS GOOD ENOUGH. PISS ALL OVER THE PRINCELY TITLES AND OTHER NONSENSE.
AFTER LEAVING LOST VEGAS, ME AND THE TRUSTY SIDEKICK HEADED DUE EAST, THUMBING OUR WAY OUT OF NEVADA AND INTO ARIZONA. WE STOPPED ALONG THE WAY TO GAWK AT THE GRAND CANYON, BECAUSE MY PATHETIC BUT LOVABLE COMPANION HAD NEVER SEEN IT BEFORE.

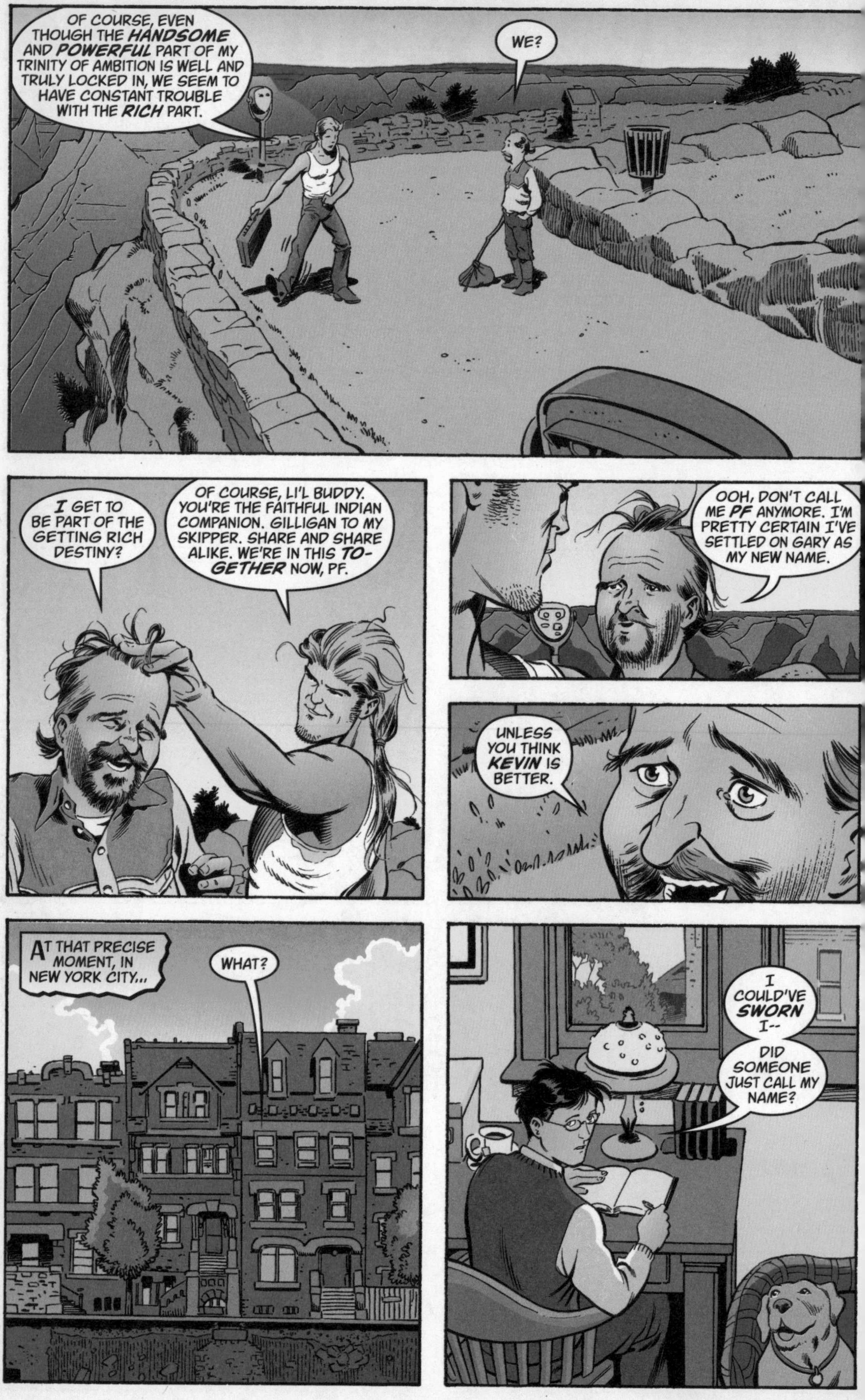

OF COURSE, EVEN THOUGH THE HANDSOME AND POWERFUL PART OF MY TRINITY OF AMBITION IS WELL AND TRULY LOCKED IN, WE SEEM TO HAVE CONSTANT TROUBLE WITH THE RICH PART.
WE?
I GET TO BE PART OF THE GETTING RICH DESTINY?
OF COURSE, LI'L BUDDY. YOU'RE THE FAITHFUL INDIAN COMPANION. GILLIGAN TO MY SKIPPER. SHARE AND SHARE ALIKE. WE'RE IN THIS TO-GETHER NOW, PF.
OOH, DON'T CALL ME PF ANYMORE. I'M PRETTY CERTAIN I'VE SETTLED ON GARY AS MY NEW NAME.
UNLESS YOU THINK KEVIN IS BETTER.
AT THAT PRECISE MOMENT, IN NEW YORK CITY...
WHAT?
I COULD'VE SWORN I--
DID SOMEONE JUST CALL MY NAME?

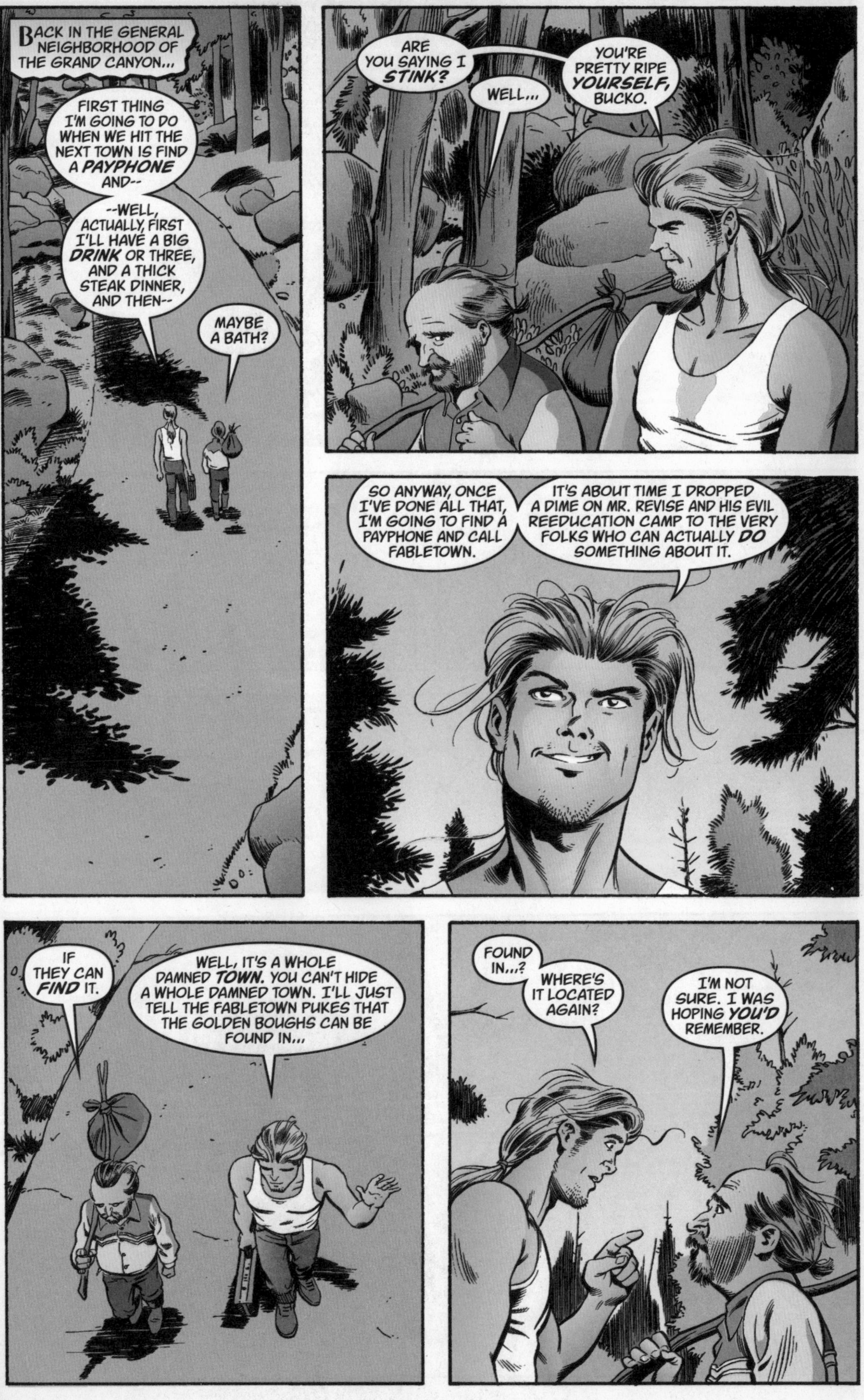
BACK IN THE GENERAL NEIGHBORHOOD OF THE GRAND CANYON...
FIRST THING I'M GOING TO DO WHEN WE HIT THE NEXT TOWN IS FIND A PAYPHONE AND--
--WELL, ACTUALLY, FIRST I'LL HAVE A BIG DRINK OR THREE, AND A THICK STEAK DINNER, AND THEN--
MAYBE A BATH?
ARE YOU SAYING I STINK?
WELL...
YOU'RE PRETTY RIPE YOURSELF, BUCKO.
SO ANYWAY, ONCE I'VE DONE ALL THAT, I'M GOING TO FIND A PAYPHONE AND CALL FABLETOWN.
IT'S ABOUT TIME I DROPPED A DIME ON MR. REVISE AND HIS EVIL REEDUCATION CAMP TO THE VERY FOLKS WHO CAN ACTUALLY DO SOMETHING ABOUT IT.
IF THEY CAN FIND IT.
WELL, IT'S A WHOLE DAMNED TOWN. YOU CAN'T HIDE A WHOLE DAMNED TOWN. I'LL JUST TELL THE FABLETOWN PUKES THAT THE GOLDEN BOUGHS CAN BE FOUND IN...
FOUND IN...?
WHERE'S IT LOCATED AGAIN?
I'M NOT SURE. I WAS HOPING YOU'D REMEMBER.

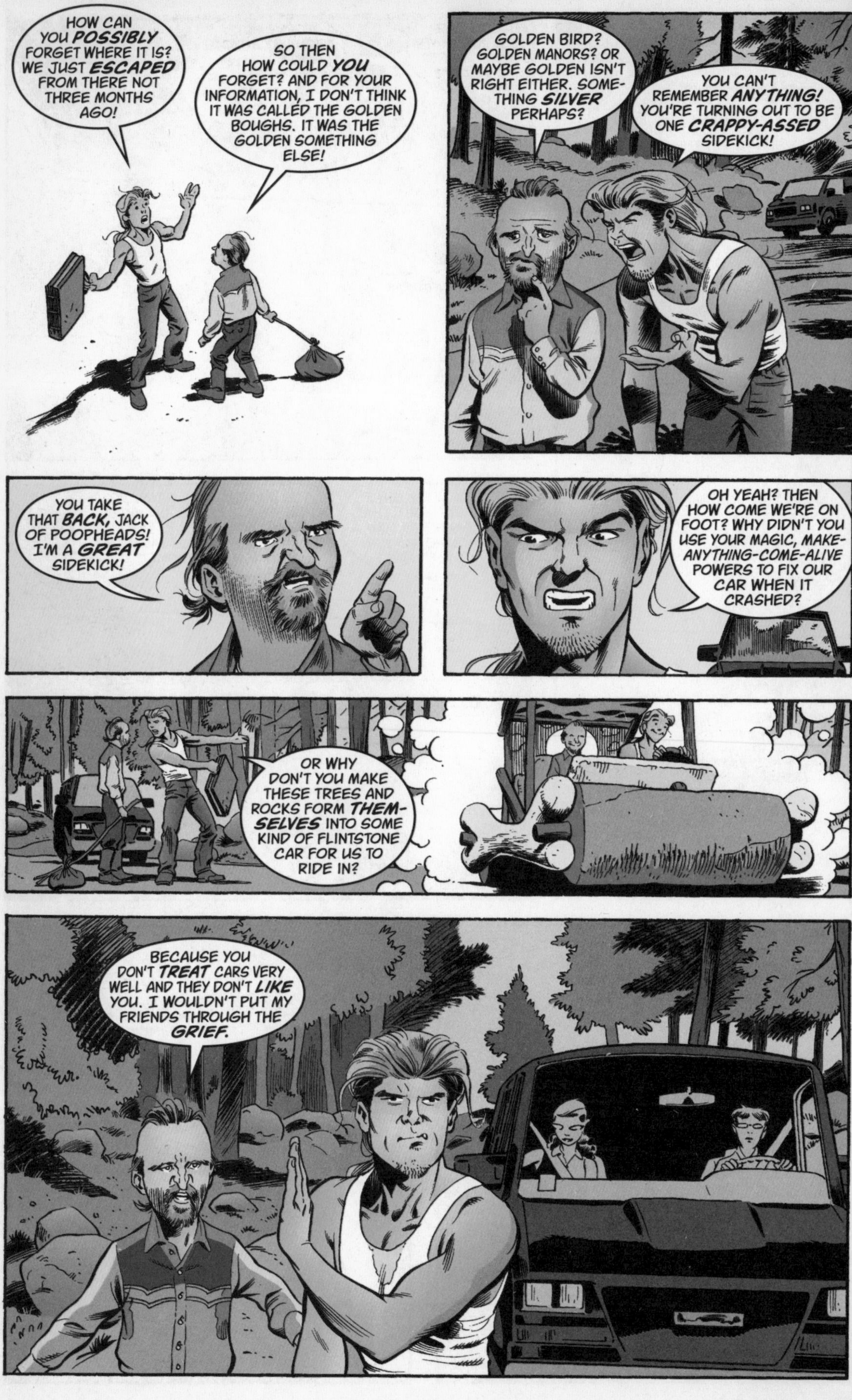
HOW CAN YOU POSSIBLY FORGET WHERE IT IS? WE JUST ESCAPED FROM THERE NOT THREE MONTHS AGO!
SO THEN HOW COULD YOU FORGET? AND FOR YOUR INFORMATION, I DON'T THINK IT WAS CALLED THE GOLDEN BOUGHS. IT WAS THE GOLDEN SOMETHING ELSE!
GOLDEN BIRD? GOLDEN MANORS? OR MAYBE GOLDEN ISN'T RIGHT EITHER. SOMETHING SILVER PERHAPS?
YOU CAN'T REMEMBER ANYTHING! YOU'RE TURNING OUT TO BE ONE CRAPPY-ASSED SIDEKICK!
YOU TAKE THAT BACK, JACK OF POOPHEADS! I'M A GREAT SIDEKICK!
OH YEAH? THEN HOW COME WE'RE ON FOOT? WHY DIDN'T YOU USE YOUR MAGIC, MAKE-ANYTHING-COME-ALIVE POWERS TO FIX OUR CAR WHEN IT CRASHED?
OR WHY DON'T YOU MAKE THESE TREES AND ROCKS FORM THEMSELVES INTO SOME KIND OF FLINTSTONE CAR FOR US TO RIDE IN?
BECAUSE YOU DON'T TREAT CARS VERY WELL AND THEY DON'T LIKE YOU. I WOULDN'T PUT MY FRIENDS THROUGH THE GRIEF.

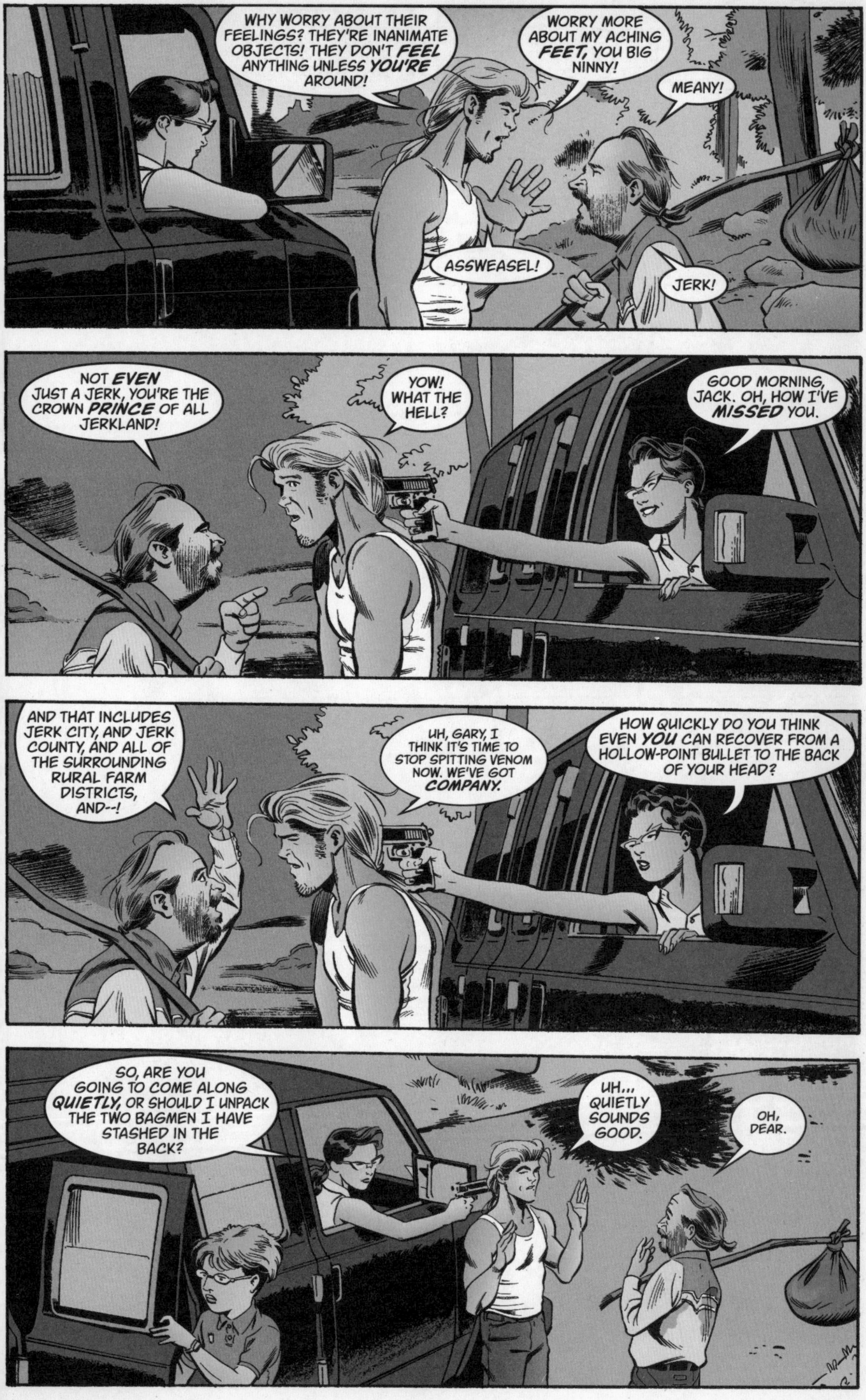

WHY WORRY ABOUT THEIR FEELINGS? THEY'RE INANIMATE OBJECTS! THEY DON'T *FEEL* ANYTHING UNLESS *YOU'RE* AROUND!
WORRY MORE ABOUT MY ACHING *FEET,* YOU BIG NINNY!
MEANY!
ASSWEASEL!
JERK!
NOT *EVEN* JUST A JERK, YOU'RE THE CROWN *PRINCE* OF ALL JERKLAND!
YOW! WHAT THE HELL?
GOOD MORNING, JACK. OH, HOW I'VE *MISSED* YOU.
AND THAT INCLUDES JERK CITY, AND JERK COUNTY, AND ALL OF THE SURROUNDING RURAL FARM DISTRICTS, AND--!
UH, GARY, I THINK IT'S TIME TO STOP SPITTING VENOM NOW. WE'VE GOT *COMPANY.*
HOW QUICKLY DO YOU THINK EVEN *YOU* CAN RECOVER FROM A HOLLOW-POINT BULLET TO THE BACK OF YOUR HEAD?
SO, ARE YOU GOING TO COME ALONG *QUIETLY,* OR SHOULD I UNPACK THE TWO BAGMEN I HAVE STASHED IN THE BACK?
UH... QUIETLY SOUNDS GOOD.
OH, DEAR.

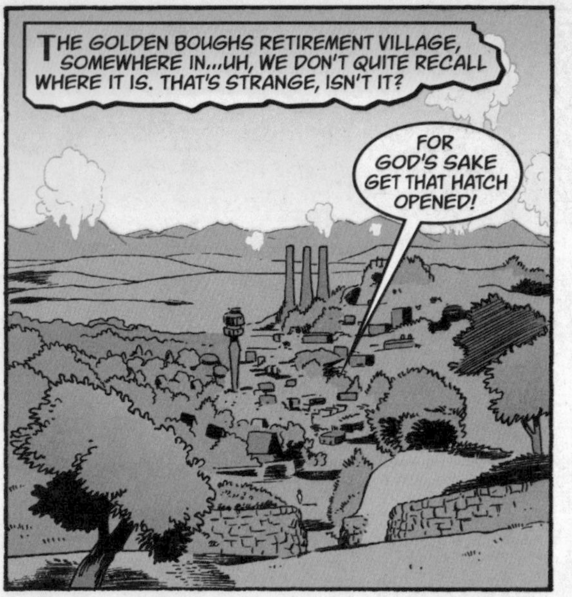
THE GOLDEN BOUGHS RETIREMENT VILLAGE, SOMEWHERE IN...UH, WE DON'T QUITE RECALL WHERE IT IS. THAT'S STRANGE, ISN'T IT?
FOR GOD'S SAKE GET THAT HATCH OPENED!

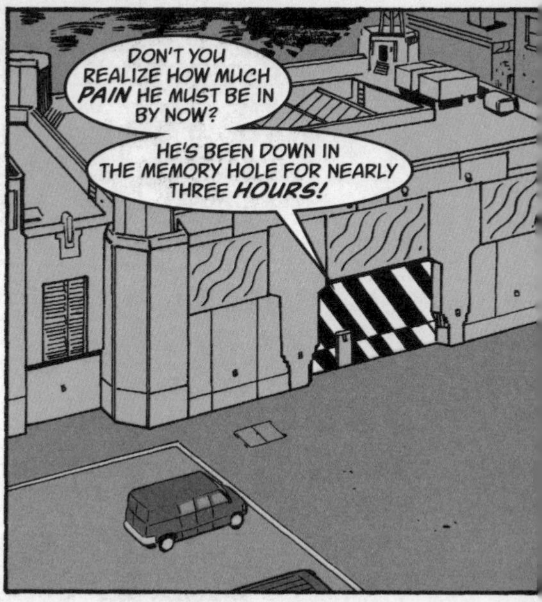
DON'T YOU REALIZE HOW MUCH PAIN HE MUST BE IN BY NOW?
HE'S BEEN DOWN IN THE MEMORY HOLE FOR NEARLY THREE HOURS!

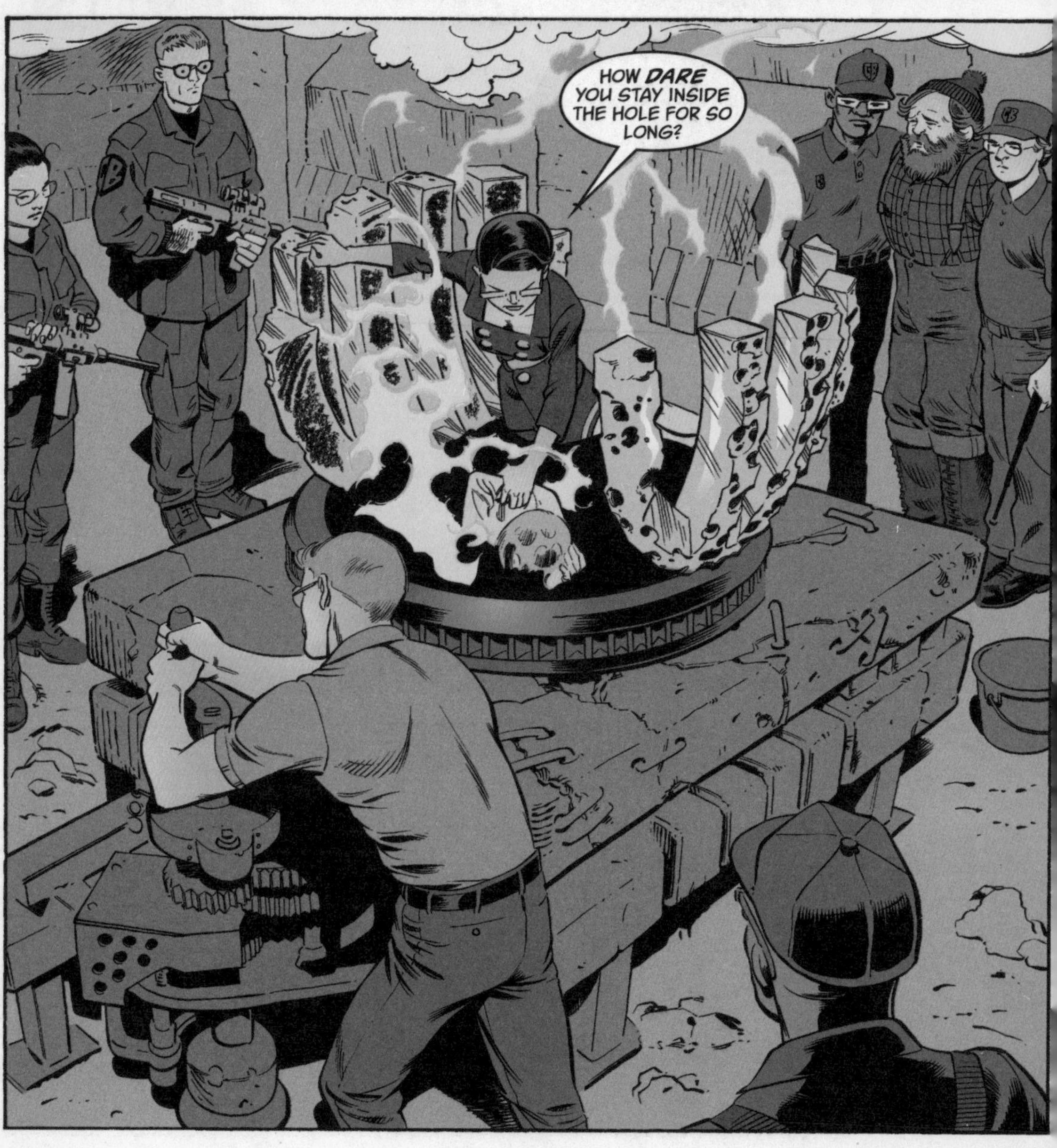
HOW DARE YOU STAY INSIDE THE HOLE FOR SO LONG?

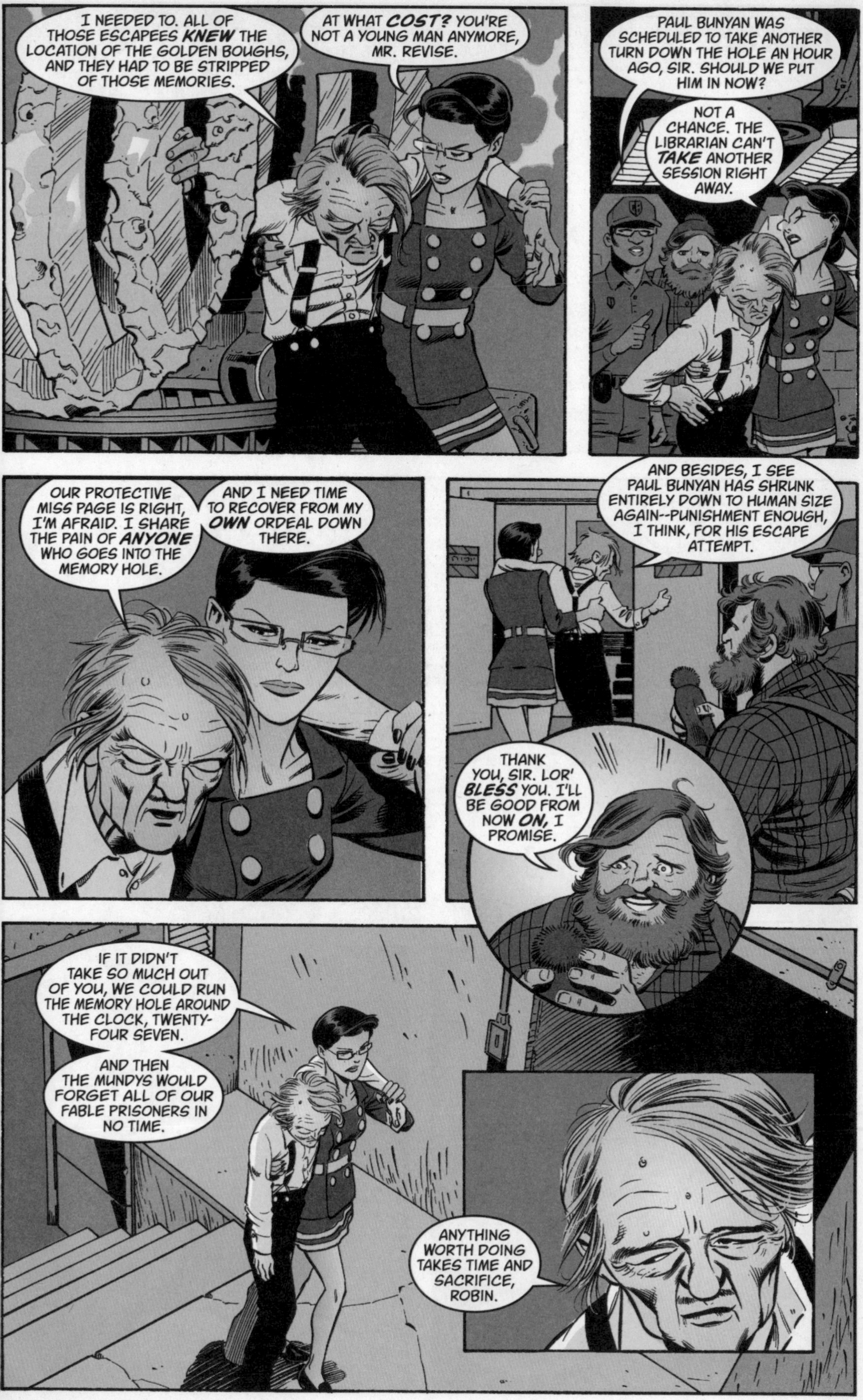

I NEEDED TO. ALL OF THOSE ESCAPEES KNEW THE LOCATION OF THE GOLDEN BOUGHS, AND THEY HAD TO BE STRIPPED OF THOSE MEMORIES.
AT WHAT COST? YOU'RE NOT A YOUNG MAN ANYMORE, MR. REVISE.
PAUL BUNYAN WAS SCHEDULED TO TAKE ANOTHER TURN DOWN THE HOLE AN HOUR AGO, SIR. SHOULD WE PUT HIM IN NOW?
NOT A CHANCE. THE LIBRARIAN CAN'T TAKE ANOTHER SESSION RIGHT AWAY.
OUR PROTECTIVE MISS PAGE IS RIGHT, I'M AFRAID. I SHARE THE PAIN OF ANYONE WHO GOES INTO THE MEMORY HOLE.
AND I NEED TIME TO RECOVER FROM MY OWN ORDEAL DOWN THERE.
AND BESIDES, I SEE PAUL BUNYAN HAS SHRUNK ENTIRELY DOWN TO HUMAN SIZE AGAIN--PUNISHMENT ENOUGH, I THINK, FOR HIS ESCAPE ATTEMPT.
THANK YOU, SIR. LOR' BLESS YOU. I'LL BE GOOD FROM NOW ON, I PROMISE.
IF IT DIDN'T TAKE SO MUCH OUT OF YOU, WE COULD RUN THE MEMORY HOLE AROUND THE CLOCK, TWENTY-FOUR SEVEN.
AND THEN THE MUNDYS WOULD FORGET ALL OF OUR FABLE PRISONERS IN NO TIME.
ANYTHING WORTH DOING TAKES TIME AND SACRIFICE, ROBIN.

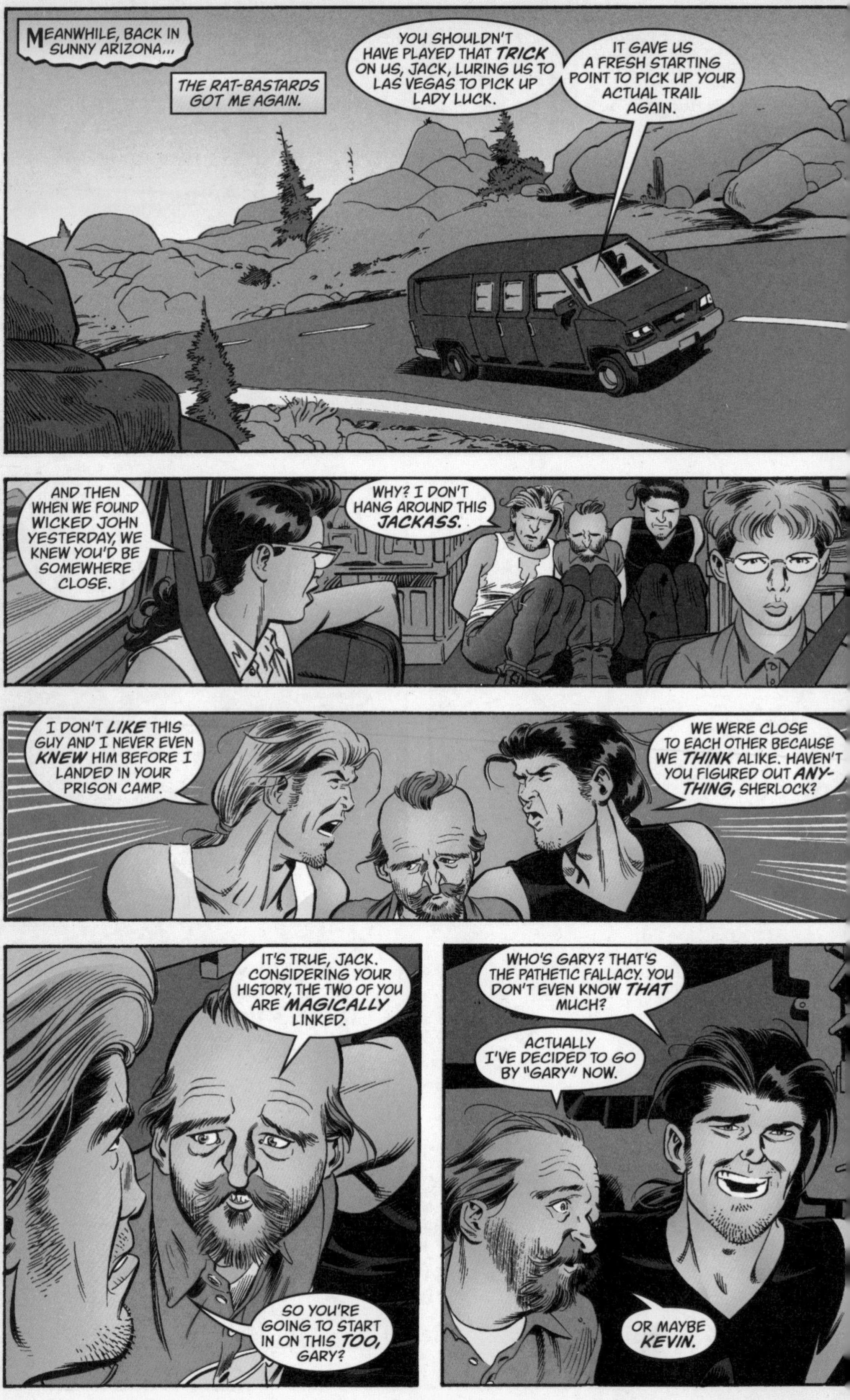
MEANWHILE, BACK IN SUNNY ARIZONA...
THE RAT-BASTARDS GOT ME AGAIN.
YOU SHOULDN'T HAVE PLAYED THAT TRICK ON US, JACK, LURING US TO LAS VEGAS TO PICK UP LADY LUCK.
IT GAVE US A FRESH STARTING POINT TO PICK UP YOUR ACTUAL TRAIL AGAIN.
AND THEN WHEN WE FOUND WICKED JOHN YESTERDAY, WE KNEW YOU'D BE SOMEWHERE CLOSE.
WHY? I DON'T HANG AROUND THIS JACKASS.
I DON'T LIKE THIS GUY AND I NEVER EVEN KNEW HIM BEFORE I LANDED IN YOUR PRISON CAMP.
WE WERE CLOSE TO EACH OTHER BECAUSE WE THINK ALIKE. HAVEN'T YOU FIGURED OUT ANYTHING, SHERLOCK?
IT'S TRUE, JACK. CONSIDERING YOUR HISTORY, THE TWO OF YOU ARE MAGICALLY LINKED.
SO YOU'RE GOING TO START IN ON THIS TOO, GARY?
WHO'S GARY? THAT'S THE PATHETIC FALLACY. YOU DON'T EVEN KNOW THAT MUCH?
ACTUALLY I'VE DECIDED TO GO BY "GARY" NOW.
OR MAYBE KEVIN.

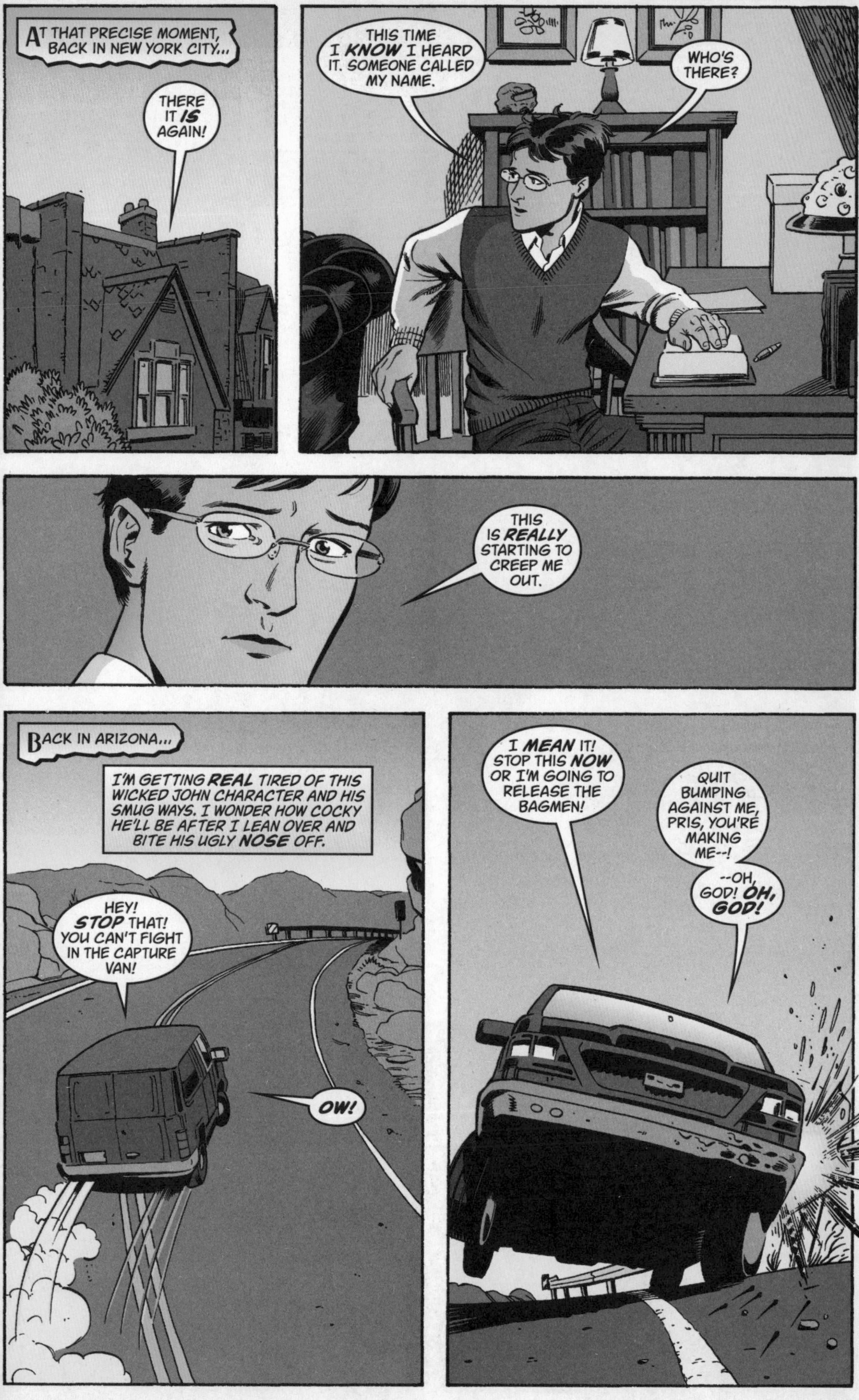
AT THAT PRECISE MOMENT, BACK IN NEW YORK CITY...
THERE IT IS AGAIN!
THIS TIME I KNOW I HEARD IT. SOMEONE CALLED MY NAME.
WHO'S THERE?
THIS IS REALLY STARTING TO CREEP ME OUT.
BACK IN ARIZONA...
I'M GETTING REAL TIRED OF THIS WICKED JOHN CHARACTER AND HIS SMUG WAYS. I WONDER HOW COCKY HE'LL BE AFTER I LEAN OVER AND BITE HIS UGLY NOSE OFF.
HEY! STOP THAT! YOU CAN'T FIGHT IN THE CAPTURE VAN!
OW!
I MEAN IT! STOP THIS NOW OR I'M GOING TO RELEASE THE BAGMEN!
QUIT BUMPING AGAINST ME, PRIS, YOU'RE MAKING ME--!
--OH, GOD! OH, GOD!

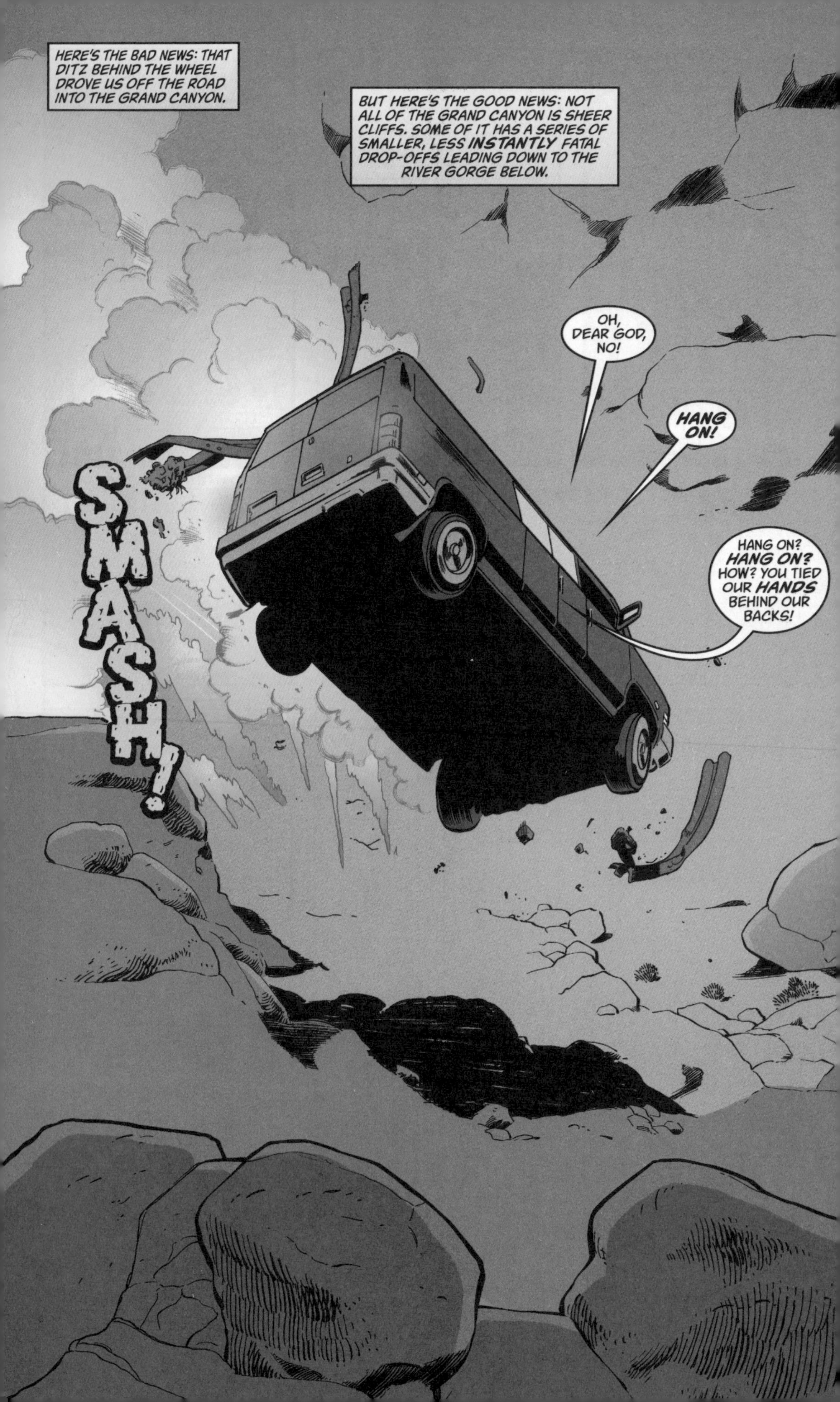

HERE'S THE BAD NEWS: THAT DITZ BEHIND THE WHEEL DROVE US OFF THE ROAD INTO THE GRAND CANYON.
BUT HERE'S THE GOOD NEWS: NOT ALL OF THE GRAND CANYON IS SHEER CLIFFS. SOME OF IT HAS A SERIES OF SMALLER, LESS INSTANTLY FATAL DROP-OFFS LEADING DOWN TO THE RIVER GORGE BELOW.
SMASH!
OH, DEAR GOD, NO!
HANG ON!
HANG ON? HANG ON? HOW? YOU TIED OUR HANDS BEHIND OUR BACKS!

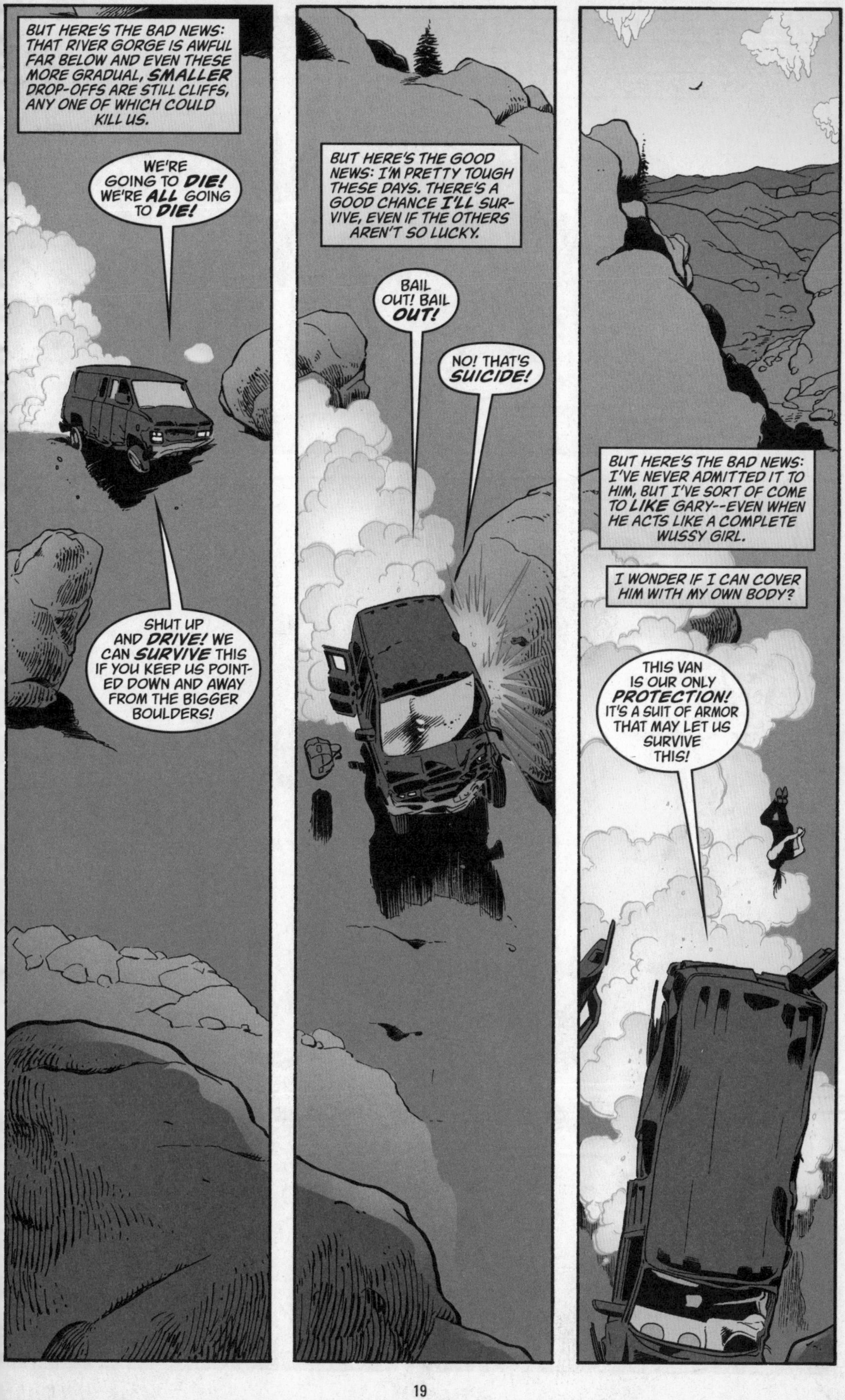
BUT HERE'S THE BAD NEWS: THAT RIVER GORGE IS AWFUL FAR BELOW AND EVEN THESE MORE GRADUAL, SMALLER DROP-OFFS ARE STILL CLIFFS, ANY ONE OF WHICH COULD KILL US.
WE'RE GOING TO DIE! WE'RE ALL GOING TO DIE!
SHUT UP AND DRIVE! WE CAN SURVIVE THIS IF YOU KEEP US POINTED DOWN AND AWAY FROM THE BIGGER BOULDERS!
BUT HERE'S THE GOOD NEWS: I'M PRETTY TOUGH THESE DAYS. THERE'S A GOOD CHANCE I'LL SURVIVE, EVEN IF THE OTHERS AREN'T SO LUCKY.
BAIL OUT! BAIL OUT!
NO! THAT'S SUICIDE!
BUT HERE'S THE BAD NEWS: I'VE NEVER ADMITTED IT TO HIM, BUT I'VE SORT OF COME TO LIKE GARY--EVEN WHEN HE ACTS LIKE A COMPLETE WUSSY GIRL.
I WONDER IF I CAN COVER HIM WITH MY OWN BODY?
THIS VAN IS OUR ONLY PROTECTION! IT'S A SUIT OF ARMOR THAT MAY LET US SURVIVE THIS!

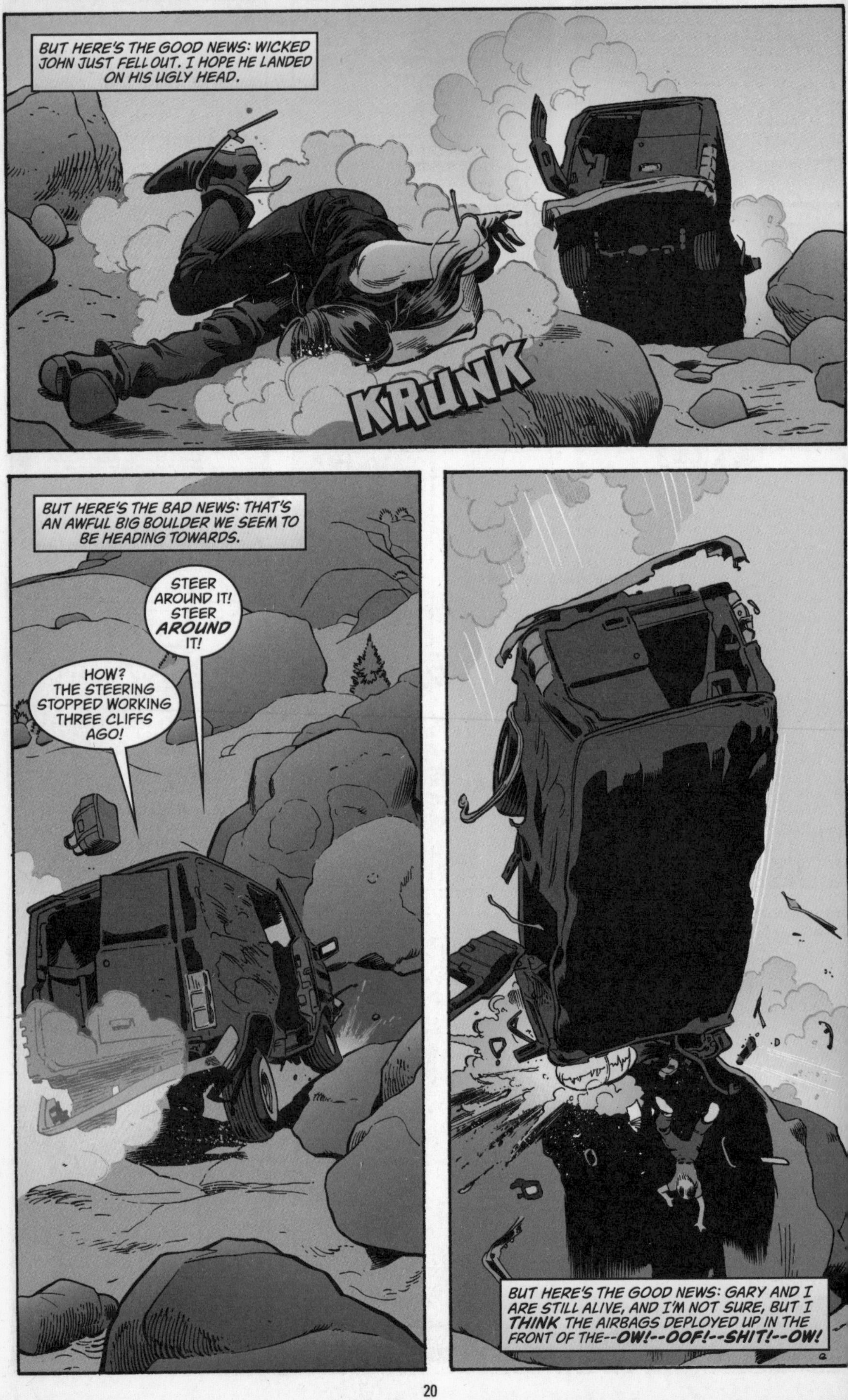
BUT HERE'S THE GOOD NEWS: WICKED JOHN JUST FELL OUT. I HOPE HE LANDED ON HIS UGLY HEAD.
KRUNK
BUT HERE'S THE BAD NEWS: THAT'S AN AWFUL BIG BOULDER WE SEEM TO BE HEADING TOWARDS.
STEER AROUND IT! STEER **AROUND** IT!
HOW? THE STEERING STOPPED WORKING THREE CLIFFS AGO!
BUT HERE'S THE GOOD NEWS: GARY AND I ARE STILL ALIVE, AND I'M NOT SURE, BUT I **THINK** THE AIRBAGS DEPLOYED UP IN THE FRONT OF THE--**OW!**--**OOF!**--**SHIT!**--**OW!**

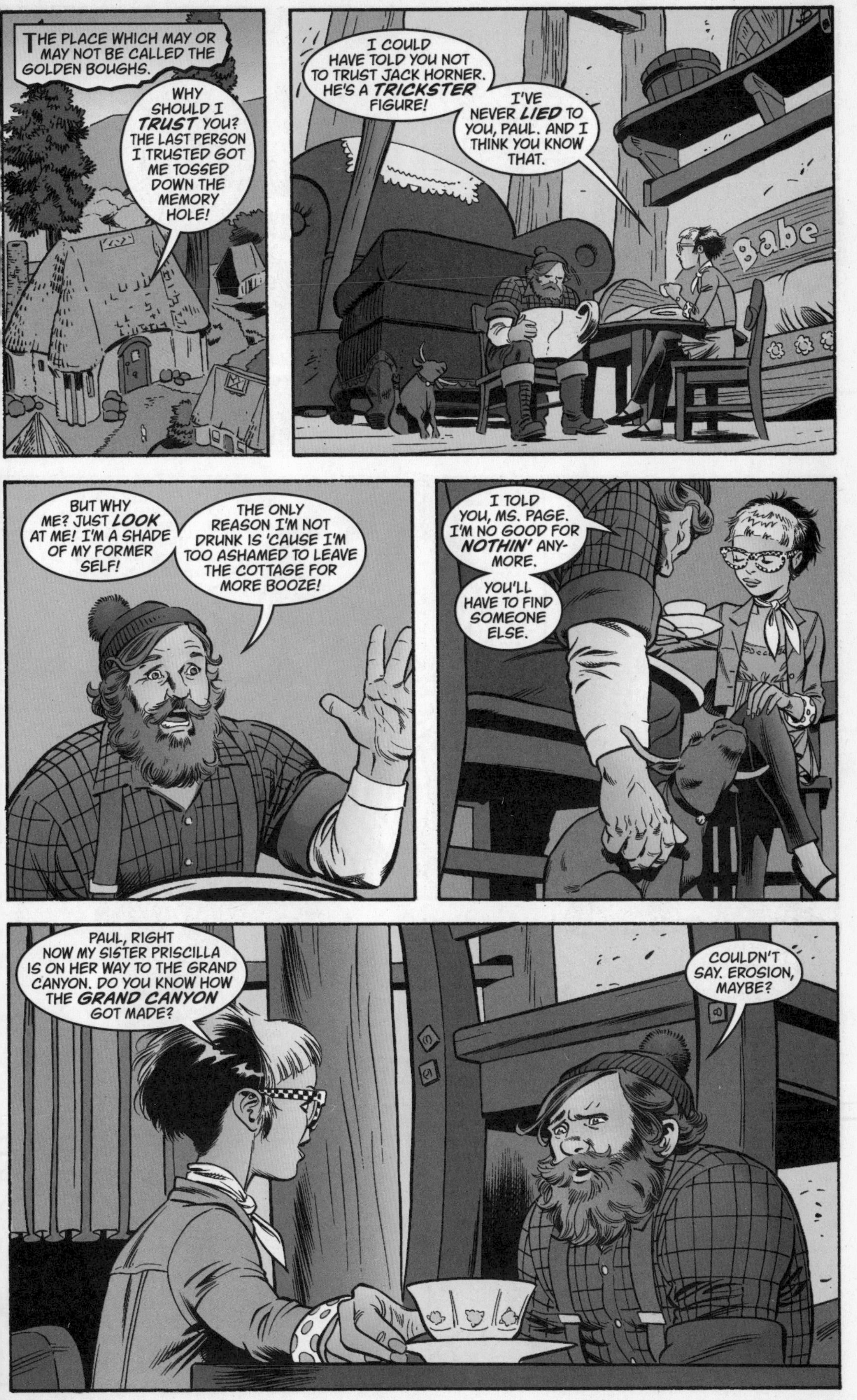
THE PLACE WHICH MAY OR MAY NOT BE CALLED THE GOLDEN BOUGHS.
WHY SHOULD I TRUST YOU? THE LAST PERSON I TRUSTED GOT ME TOSSED DOWN THE MEMORY HOLE!
I COULD HAVE TOLD YOU NOT TO TRUST JACK HORNER. HE'S A TRICKSTER FIGURE!
I'VE NEVER LIED TO YOU, PAUL. AND I THINK YOU KNOW THAT.
Babe
BUT WHY ME? JUST LOOK AT ME! I'M A SHADE OF MY FORMER SELF!
THE ONLY REASON I'M NOT DRUNK IS 'CAUSE I'M TOO ASHAMED TO LEAVE THE COTTAGE FOR MORE BOOZE!
I TOLD YOU, MS. PAGE. I'M NO GOOD FOR NOTHIN' ANY-MORE.
YOU'LL HAVE TO FIND SOMEONE ELSE.
PAUL, RIGHT NOW MY SISTER PRISCILLA IS ON HER WAY TO THE GRAND CANYON. DO YOU KNOW HOW THE GRAND CANYON GOT MADE?
COULDN'T SAY. EROSION, MAYBE?

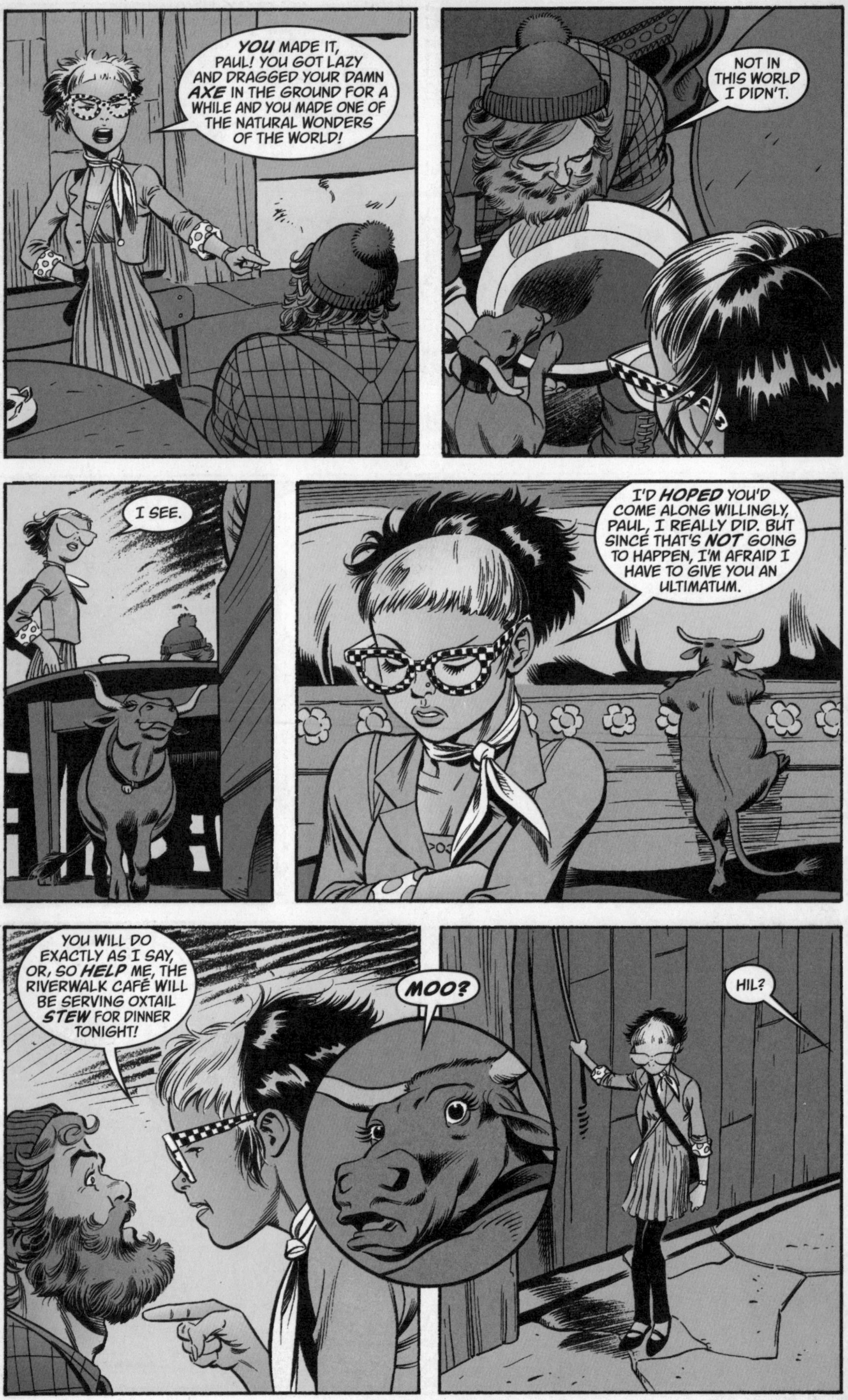
YOU MADE IT, PAUL! YOU GOT LAZY AND DRAGGED YOUR DAMN AXE IN THE GROUND FOR A WHILE AND YOU MADE ONE OF THE NATURAL WONDERS OF THE WORLD!
NOT IN THIS WORLD I DIDN'T.
I SEE.
I'D HOPED YOU'D COME ALONG WILLINGLY, PAUL, I REALLY DID. BUT SINCE THAT'S NOT GOING TO HAPPEN, I'M AFRAID I HAVE TO GIVE YOU AN ULTIMATUM.
YOU WILL DO EXACTLY AS I SAY, OR, SO HELP ME, THE RIVERWALK CAFÉ WILL BE SERVING OXTAIL STEW FOR DINNER TONIGHT!
MOO?
HIL?

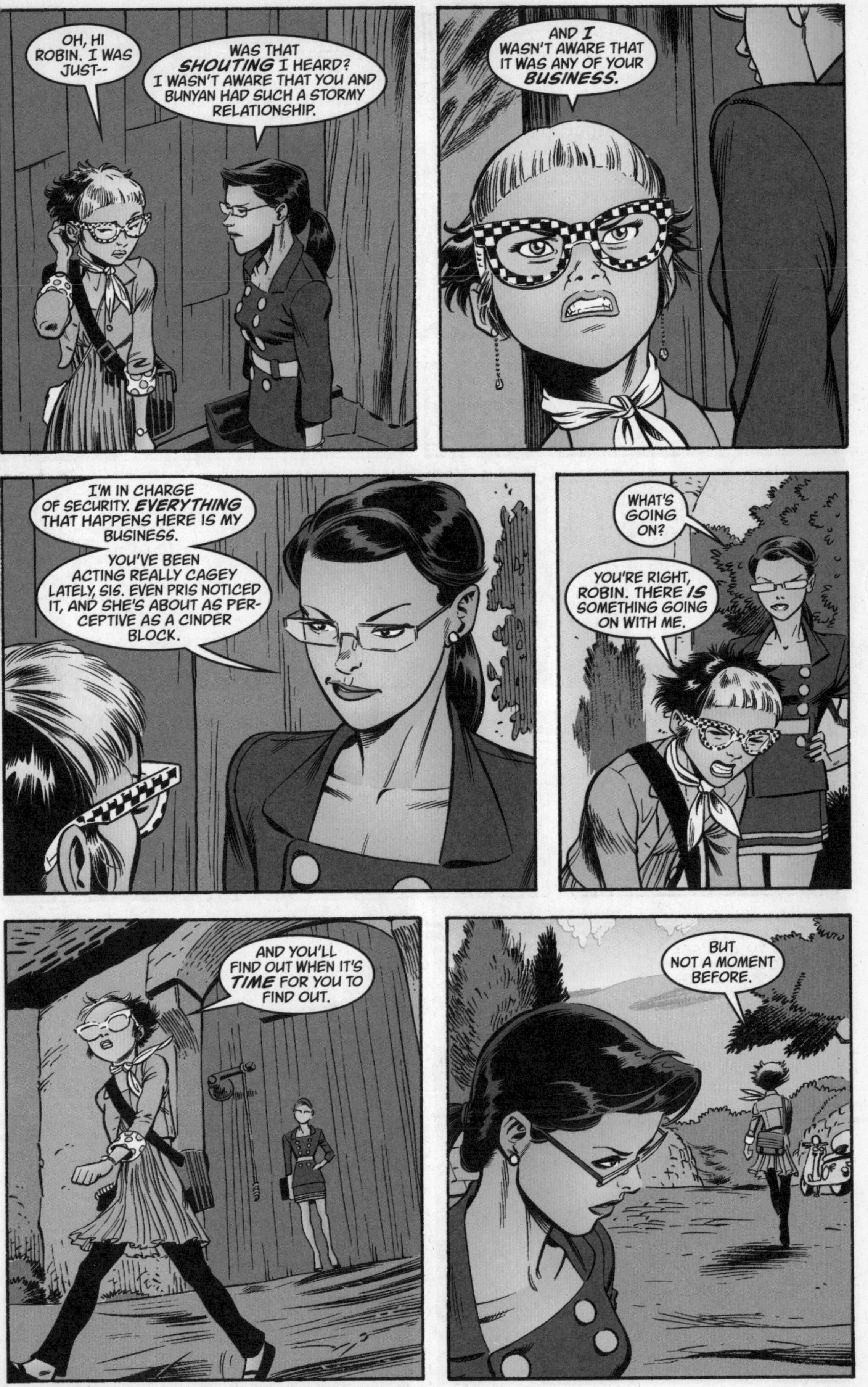
OH, HI ROBIN. I WAS JUST--
WAS THAT SHOUTING I HEARD? I WASN'T AWARE THAT YOU AND BUNYAN HAD SUCH A STORMY RELATIONSHIP.
AND I WASN'T AWARE THAT IT WAS ANY OF YOUR BUSINESS.
I'M IN CHARGE OF SECURITY. EVERYTHING THAT HAPPENS HERE IS MY BUSINESS.
YOU'VE BEEN ACTING REALLY CAGEY LATELY, SIS. EVEN PRIS NOTICED IT, AND SHE'S ABOUT AS PERCEPTIVE AS A CINDER BLOCK.
WHAT'S GOING ON?
YOU'RE RIGHT, ROBIN. THERE IS SOMETHING GOING ON WITH ME.
AND YOU'LL FIND OUT WHEN IT'S TIME FOR YOU TO FIND OUT.
BUT NOT A MOMENT BEFORE.

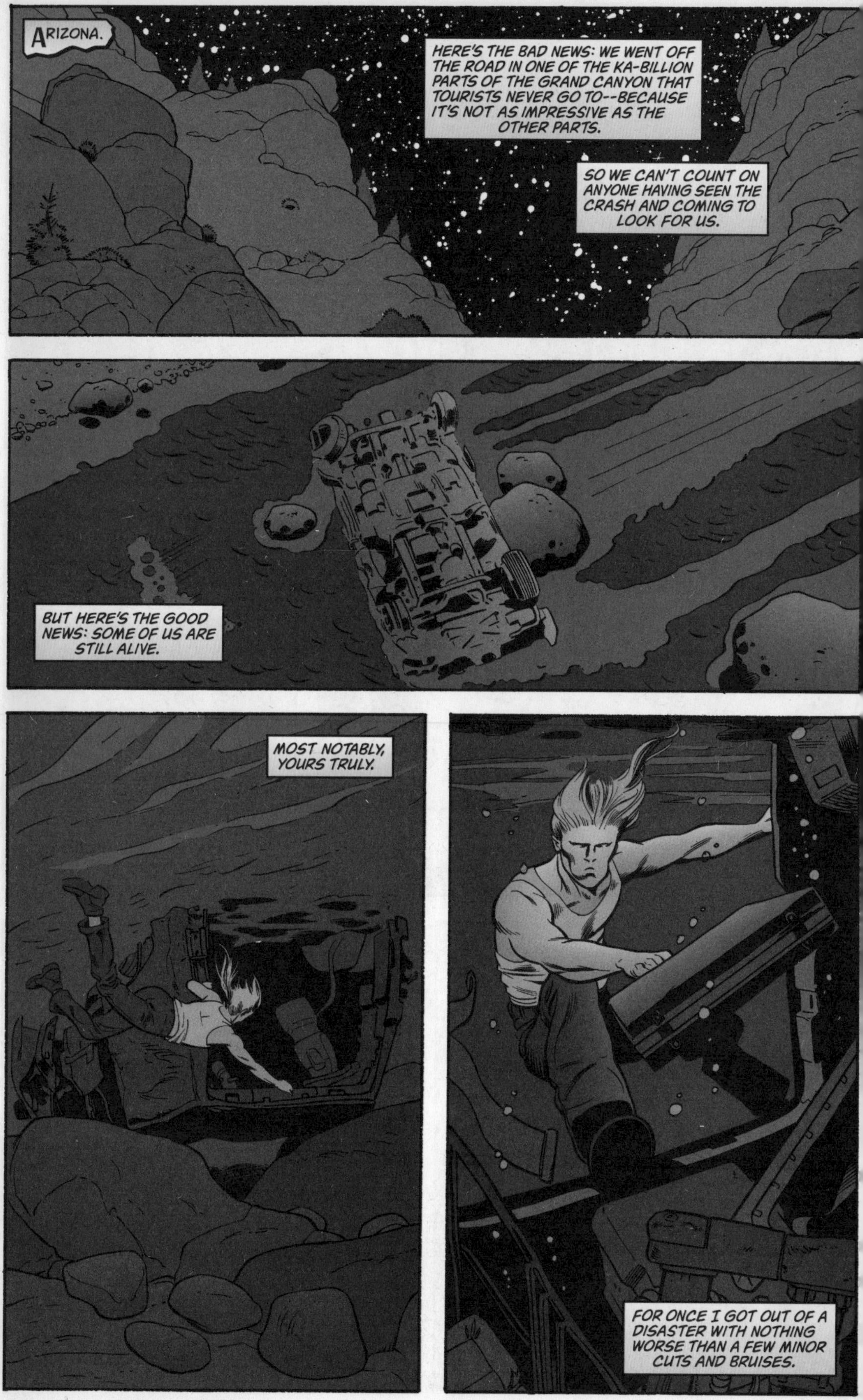
ARIZONA.
HERE'S THE BAD NEWS: WE WENT OFF THE ROAD IN ONE OF THE KA-BILLION PARTS OF THE GRAND CANYON THAT TOURISTS NEVER GO TO--BECAUSE IT'S NOT AS IMPRESSIVE AS THE OTHER PARTS.
SO WE CAN'T COUNT ON ANYONE HAVING SEEN THE CRASH AND COMING TO LOOK FOR US.
BUT HERE'S THE GOOD NEWS: SOME OF US ARE STILL ALIVE.
MOST NOTABLY, YOURS TRULY.
FOR ONCE I GOT OUT OF A DISASTER WITH NOTHING WORSE THAN A FEW MINOR CUTS AND BRUISES.

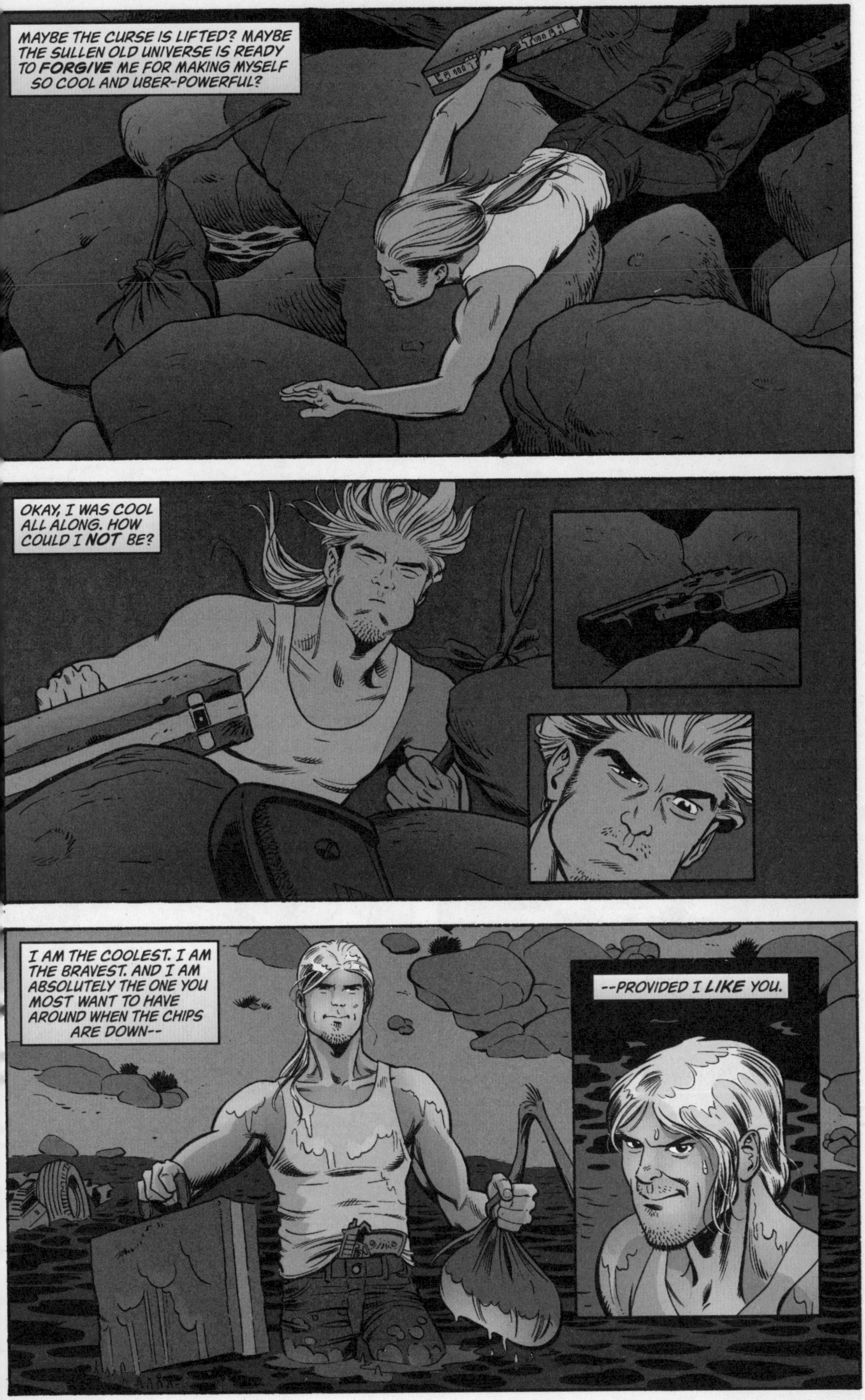
MAYBE THE CURSE IS LIFTED? MAYBE THE SULLEN OLD UNIVERSE IS READY TO FORGIVE ME FOR MAKING MYSELF SO COOL AND UBER-POWERFUL?
OKAY, I WAS COOL ALL ALONG. HOW COULD I NOT BE?
I AM THE COOLEST. I AM THE BRAVEST. AND I AM ABSOLUTELY THE ONE YOU MOST WANT TO HAVE AROUND WHEN THE CHIPS ARE DOWN--
--PROVIDED I LIKE YOU.

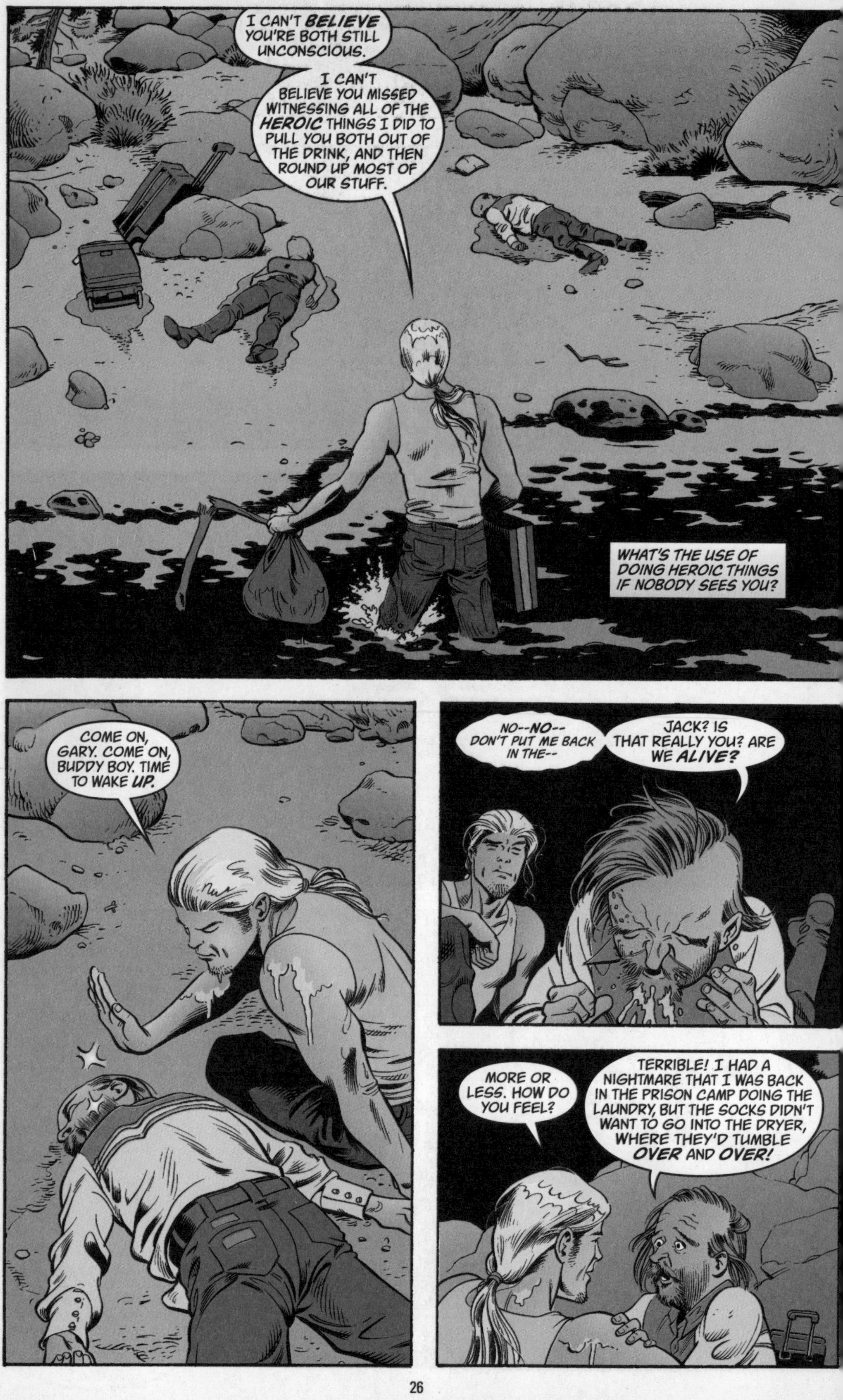

I CAN'T BELIEVE YOU'RE BOTH STILL UNCONSCIOUS.
I CAN'T BELIEVE YOU MISSED WITNESSING ALL OF THE HEROIC THINGS I DID TO PULL YOU BOTH OUT OF THE DRINK, AND THEN ROUND UP MOST OF OUR STUFF.
WHAT'S THE USE OF DOING HEROIC THINGS IF NOBODY SEES YOU?
COME ON, GARY. COME ON, BUDDY BOY. TIME TO WAKE UP.
NO--NO-- DON'T PUT ME BACK IN THE--
JACK? IS THAT REALLY YOU? ARE WE ALIVE?
MORE OR LESS. HOW DO YOU FEEL?
TERRIBLE! I HAD A NIGHTMARE THAT I WAS BACK IN THE PRISON CAMP DOING THE LAUNDRY, BUT THE SOCKS DIDN'T WANT TO GO INTO THE DRYER, WHERE THEY'D TUMBLE OVER AND OVER!

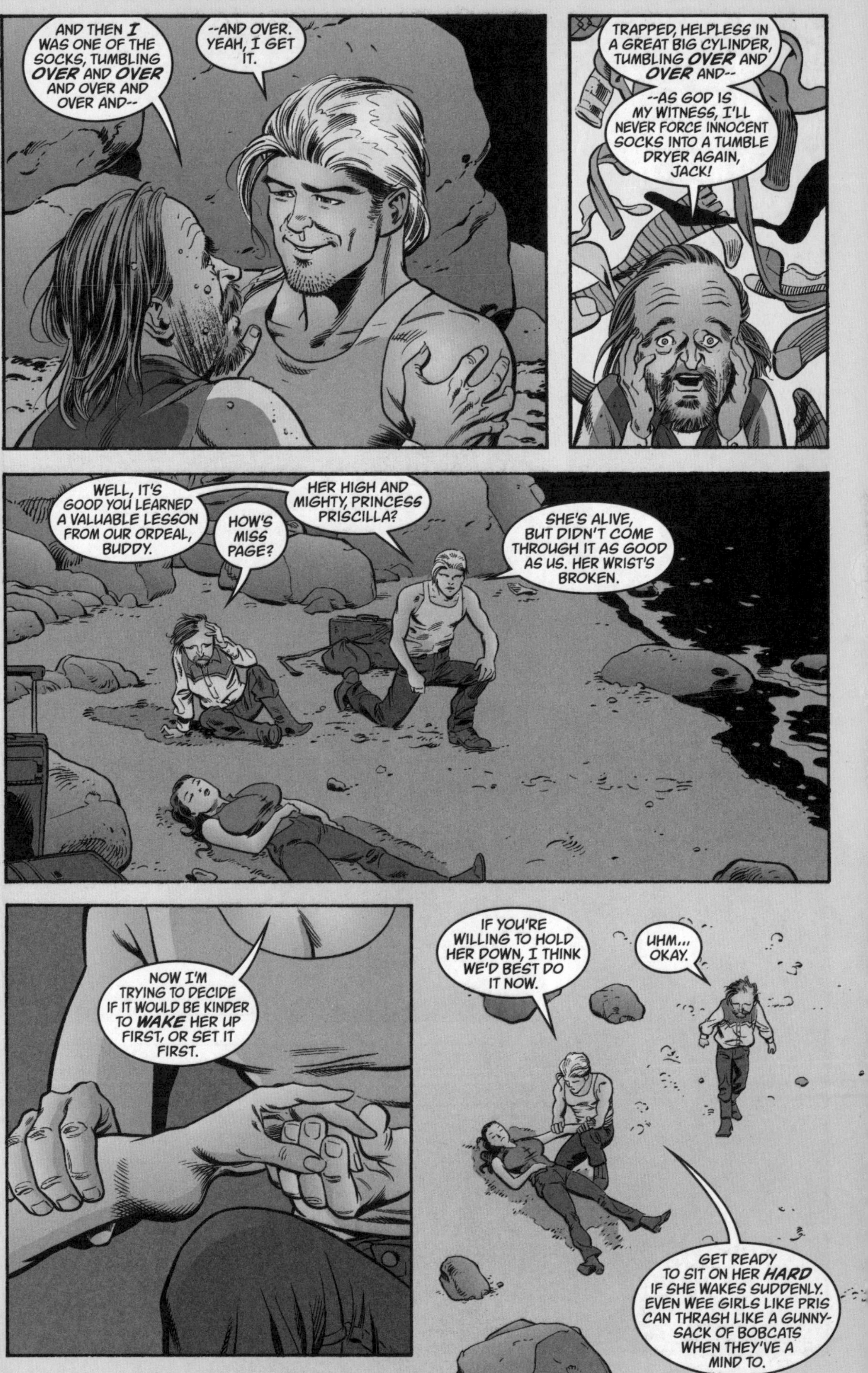
AND THEN I WAS ONE OF THE SOCKS, TUMBLING OVER AND OVER AND OVER AND OVER AND--
--AND OVER. YEAH, I GET IT.
TRAPPED, HELPLESS IN A GREAT BIG CYLINDER, TUMBLING OVER AND OVER AND--
--AS GOD IS MY WITNESS, I'LL NEVER FORCE INNOCENT SOCKS INTO A TUMBLE DRYER AGAIN, JACK!
WELL, IT'S GOOD YOU LEARNED A VALUABLE LESSON FROM OUR ORDEAL, BUDDY.
HOW'S MISS PAGE?
HER HIGH AND MIGHTY, PRINCESS PRISCILLA?
SHE'S ALIVE, BUT DIDN'T COME THROUGH IT AS GOOD AS US. HER WRIST'S BROKEN.
NOW I'M TRYING TO DECIDE IF IT WOULD BE KINDER TO WAKE HER UP FIRST, OR SET IT FIRST.
IF YOU'RE WILLING TO HOLD HER DOWN, I THINK WE'D BEST DO IT NOW.
UHM... OKAY.
GET READY TO SIT ON HER HARD IF SHE WAKES SUDDENLY. EVEN WEE GIRLS LIKE PRIS CAN THRASH LIKE A GUNNY-SACK OF BOBCATS WHEN THEY'VE A MIND TO.

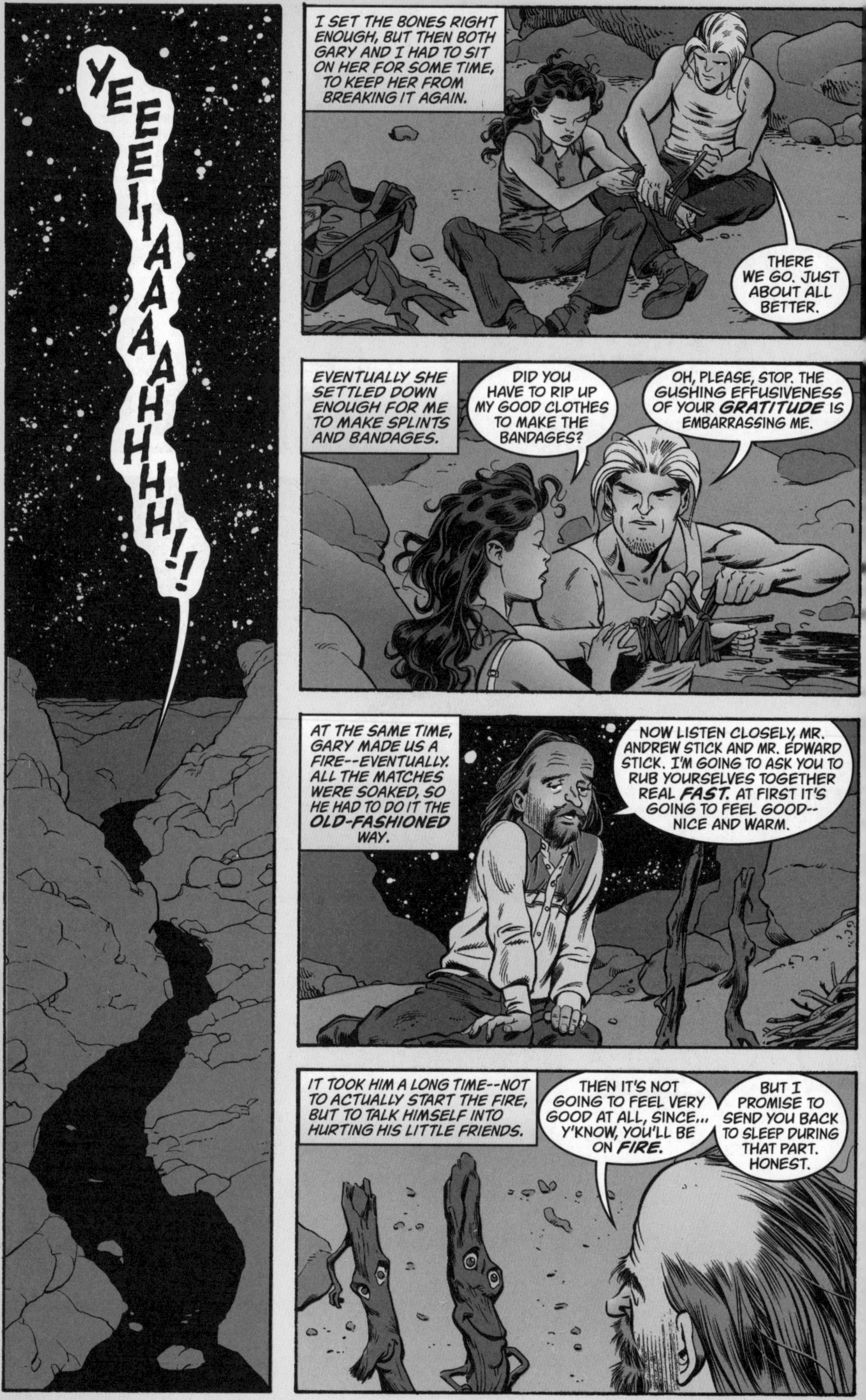
YEEEIIAAAAAHHHH!!
I SET THE BONES RIGHT ENOUGH, BUT THEN BOTH GARY AND I HAD TO SIT ON HER FOR SOME TIME, TO KEEP HER FROM BREAKING IT AGAIN.
THERE WE GO. JUST ABOUT ALL BETTER.
EVENTUALLY SHE SETTLED DOWN ENOUGH FOR ME TO MAKE SPLINTS AND BANDAGES.
DID YOU HAVE TO RIP UP MY GOOD CLOTHES TO MAKE THE BANDAGES?
OH, PLEASE, STOP. THE GUSHING EFFUSIVENESS OF YOUR GRATITUDE IS EMBARRASSING ME.
AT THE SAME TIME, GARY MADE US A FIRE--EVENTUALLY. ALL THE MATCHES WERE SOAKED, SO HE HAD TO DO IT THE OLD-FASHIONED WAY.
NOW LISTEN CLOSELY, MR. ANDREW STICK AND MR. EDWARD STICK. I'M GOING TO ASK YOU TO RUB YOURSELVES TOGETHER REAL FAST. AT FIRST IT'S GOING TO FEEL GOOD--NICE AND WARM.
IT TOOK HIM A LONG TIME--NOT TO ACTUALLY START THE FIRE, BUT TO TALK HIMSELF INTO HURTING HIS LITTLE FRIENDS.
THEN IT'S NOT GOING TO FEEL VERY GOOD AT ALL, SINCE... Y'KNOW, YOU'LL BE ON FIRE.
BUT I PROMISE TO SEND YOU BACK TO SLEEP DURING THAT PART. HONEST.

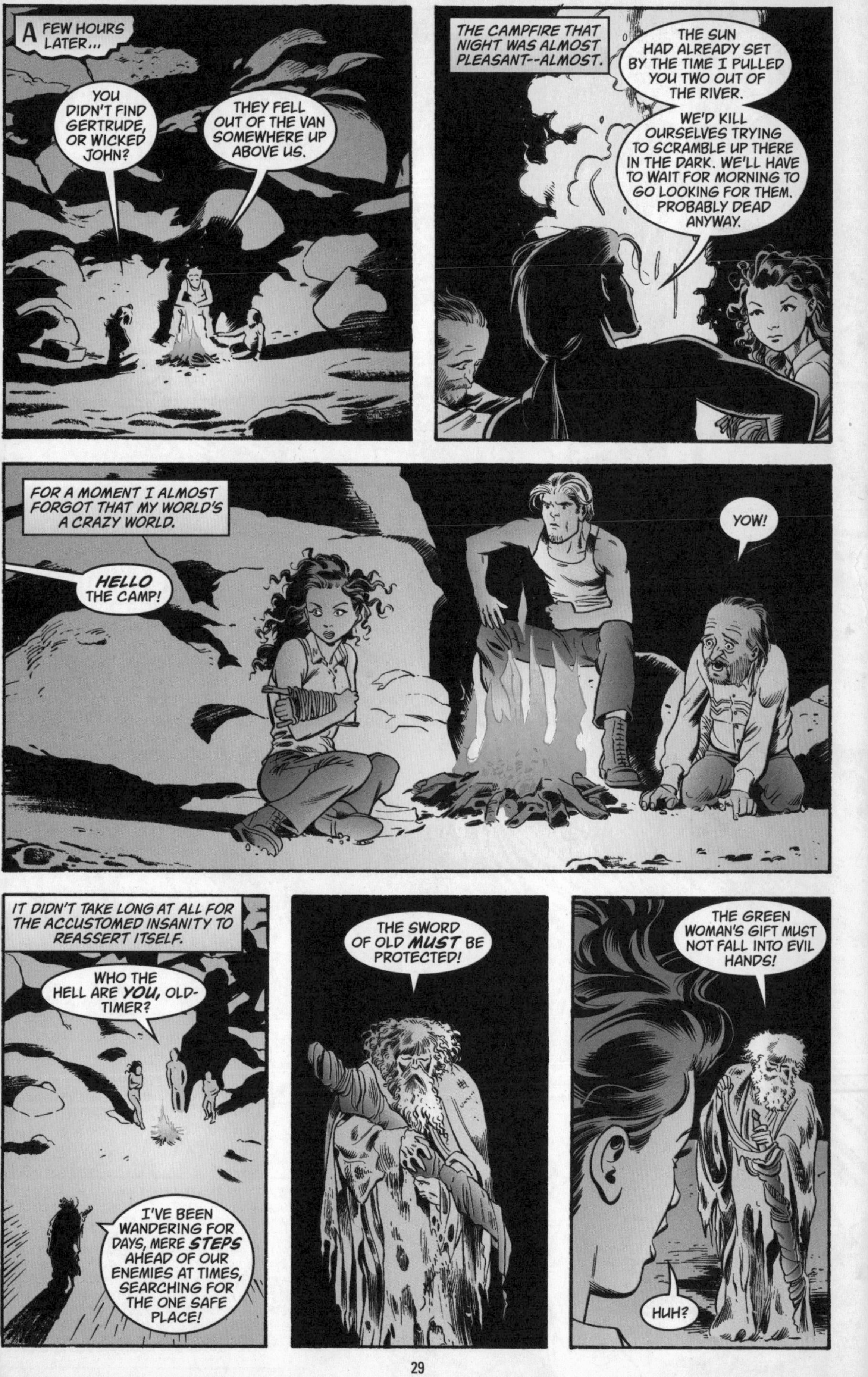

A FEW HOURS LATER...
YOU DIDN'T FIND GERTRUDE, OR WICKED JOHN?
THEY FELL OUT OF THE VAN SOMEWHERE UP ABOVE US.
THE CAMPFIRE THAT NIGHT WAS ALMOST PLEASANT--ALMOST.
THE SUN HAD ALREADY SET BY THE TIME I PULLED YOU TWO OUT OF THE RIVER.
WE'D KILL OURSELVES TRYING TO SCRAMBLE UP THERE IN THE DARK. WE'LL HAVE TO WAIT FOR MORNING TO GO LOOKING FOR THEM. PROBABLY DEAD ANYWAY.
FOR A MOMENT I ALMOST FORGOT THAT MY WORLD'S A CRAZY WORLD.
HELLO THE CAMP!
YOW!
IT DIDN'T TAKE LONG AT ALL FOR THE ACCUSTOMED INSANITY TO REASSERT ITSELF.
WHO THE HELL ARE YOU, OLD-TIMER?
I'VE BEEN WANDERING FOR DAYS, MERE STEPS AHEAD OF OUR ENEMIES AT TIMES, SEARCHING FOR THE ONE SAFE PLACE!
THE SWORD OF OLD MUST BE PROTECTED!
THE GREEN WOMAN'S GIFT MUST NOT FALL INTO EVIL HANDS!
HUH?

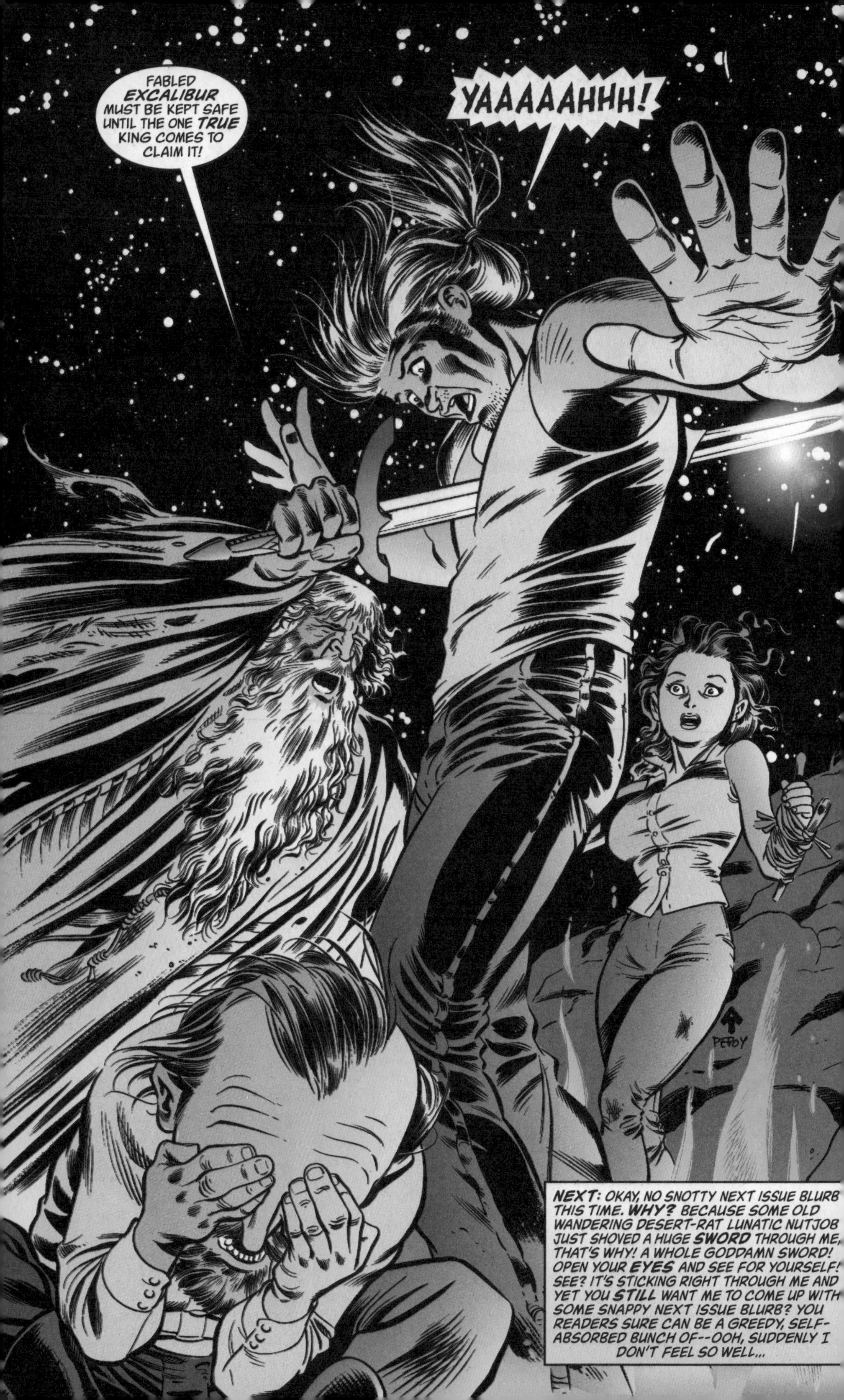
FABLED EXCALIBUR MUST BE KEPT SAFE UNTIL THE ONE TRUE KING COMES TO CLAIM IT!
YAAAAAHHH!
PEPOY
NEXT: OKAY, NO SNOTTY NEXT ISSUE BLURB THIS TIME. WHY? BECAUSE SOME OLD WANDERING DESERT-RAT LUNATIC NUTJOB JUST SHOVED A HUGE SWORD THROUGH ME, THAT'S WHY! A WHOLE GODDAMN SWORD! OPEN YOUR EYES AND SEE FOR YOURSELF! SEE? IT'S STICKING RIGHT THROUGH ME AND YET YOU STILL WANT ME TO COME UP WITH SOME SNAPPY NEXT ISSUE BLURB? YOU READERS SURE CAN BE A GREEDY, SELF-ABSORBED BUNCH OF--OOH, SUDDENLY I DON'T FEEL SO WELL...

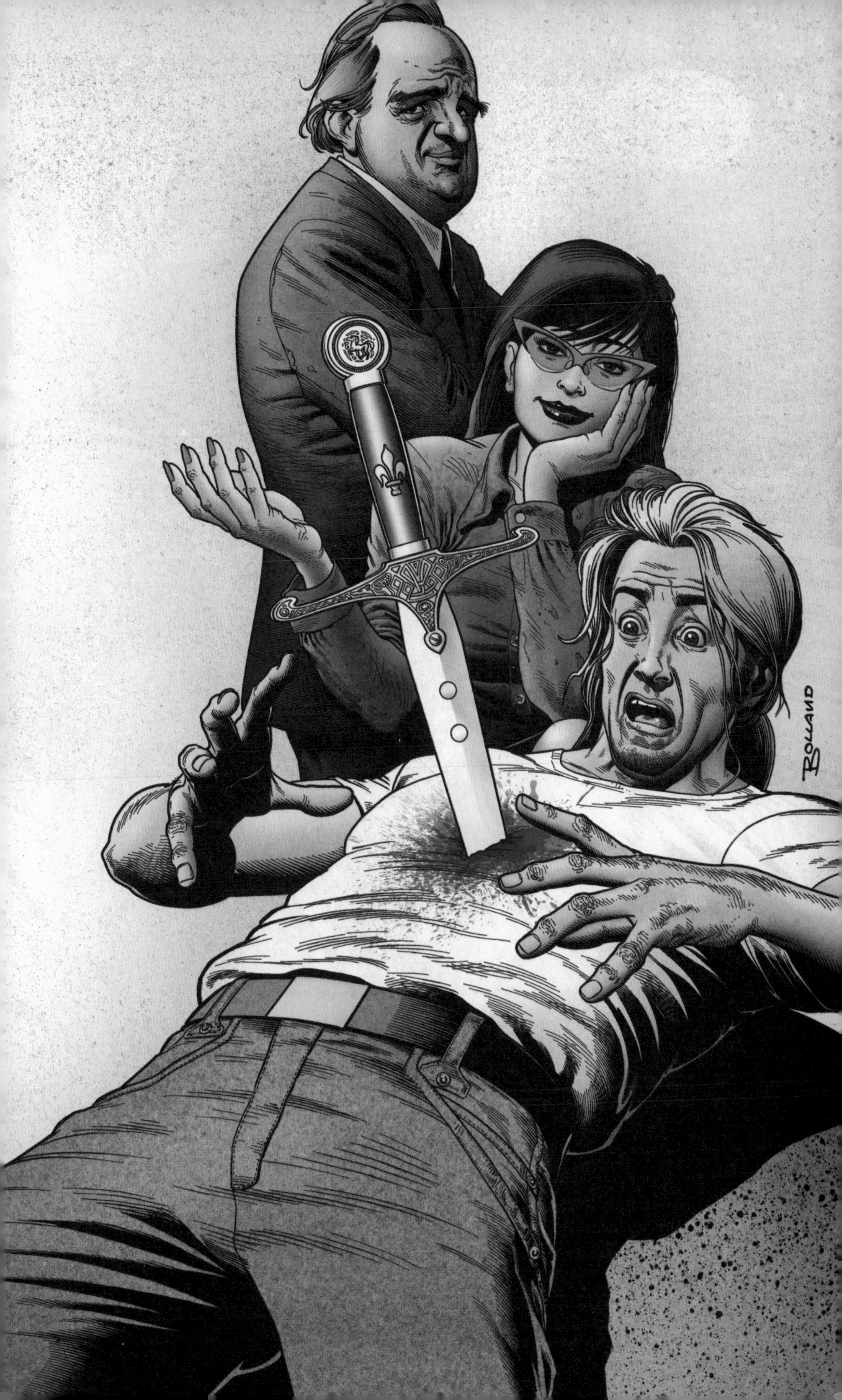
BOLLAND

"Okay, fine.
I yield to the ridiculous and
yet impossible truth."

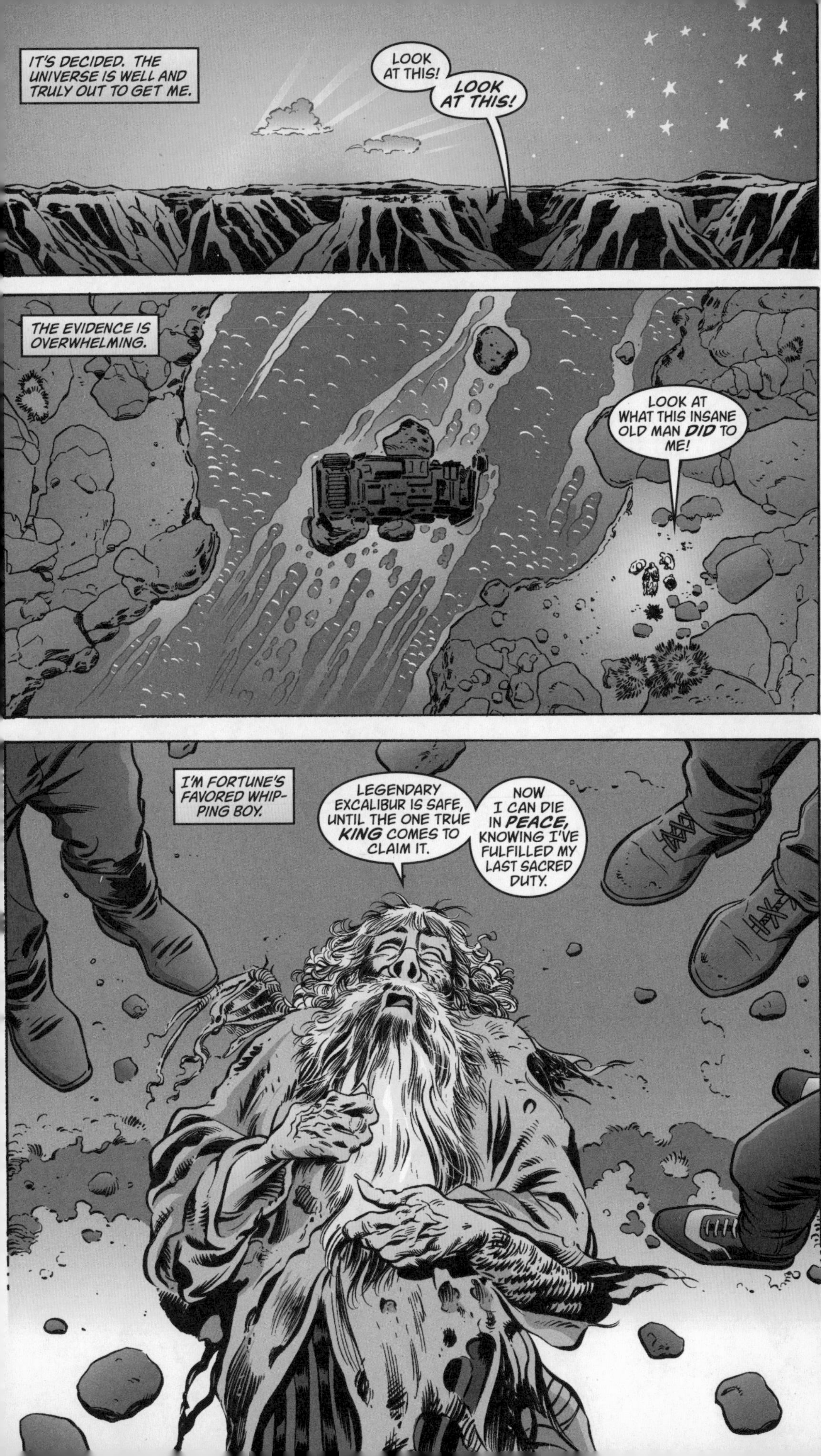
IT'S DECIDED. THE UNIVERSE IS WELL AND TRULY OUT TO GET ME.
LOOK AT THIS!
LOOK AT THIS!
THE EVIDENCE IS OVERWHELMING.
LOOK AT WHAT THIS INSANE OLD MAN DID TO ME!
I'M FORTUNE'S FAVORED WHIPPING BOY.
LEGENDARY EXCALIBUR IS SAFE, UNTIL THE ONE TRUE KING COMES TO CLAIM IT.
NOW I CAN DIE IN PEACE, KNOWING I'VE FULFILLED MY LAST SACRED DUTY.

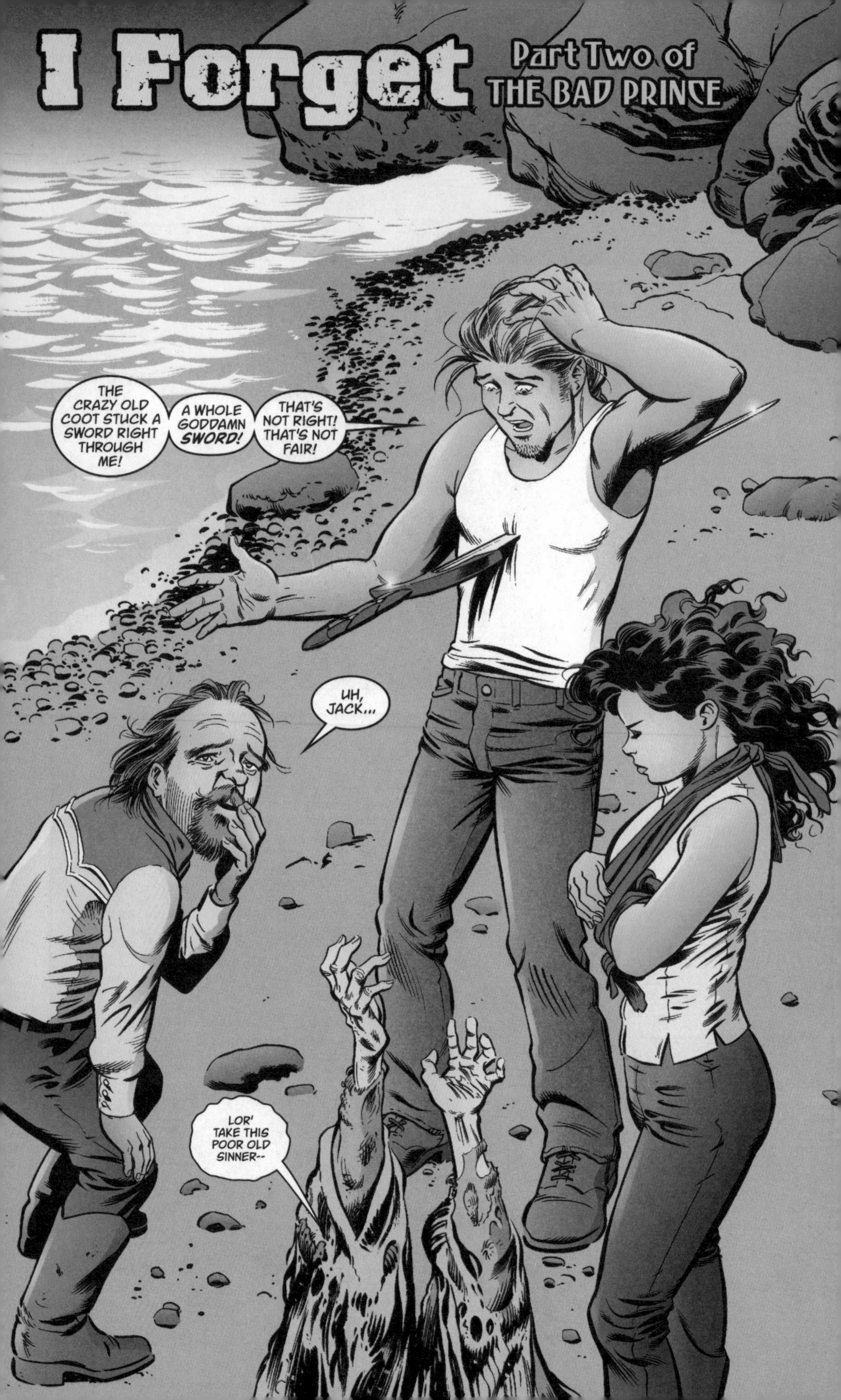

I Forget
Part Two of THE BAD PRINCE
THE CRAZY OLD COOT STUCK A SWORD RIGHT THROUGH ME!
A WHOLE GODDAMN SWORD!
THAT'S NOT RIGHT! THAT'S NOT FAIR!
UH, JACK...
LOR' TAKE THIS POOR OLD SINNER--

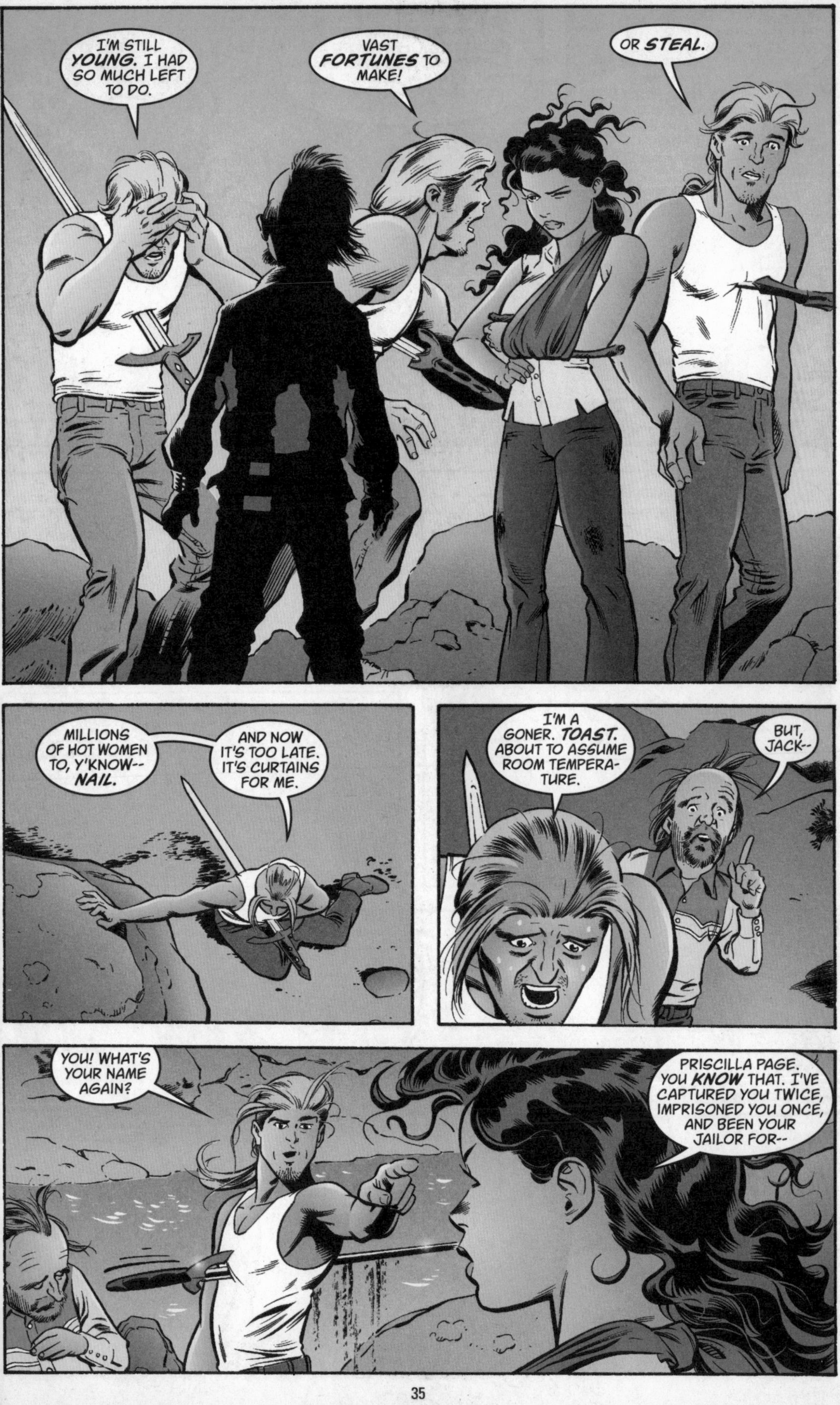
I'M STILL YOUNG. I HAD SO MUCH LEFT TO DO.
VAST FORTUNES TO MAKE!
OR STEAL.
MILLIONS OF HOT WOMEN TO, Y'KNOW-- NAIL.
AND NOW IT'S TOO LATE. IT'S CURTAINS FOR ME.
I'M A GONER. TOAST. ABOUT TO ASSUME ROOM TEMPERA-TURE.
BUT, JACK--
YOU! WHAT'S YOUR NAME AGAIN?
PRISCILLA PAGE. YOU KNOW THAT. I'VE CAPTURED YOU TWICE, IMPRISONED YOU ONCE, AND BEEN YOUR JAILOR FOR--

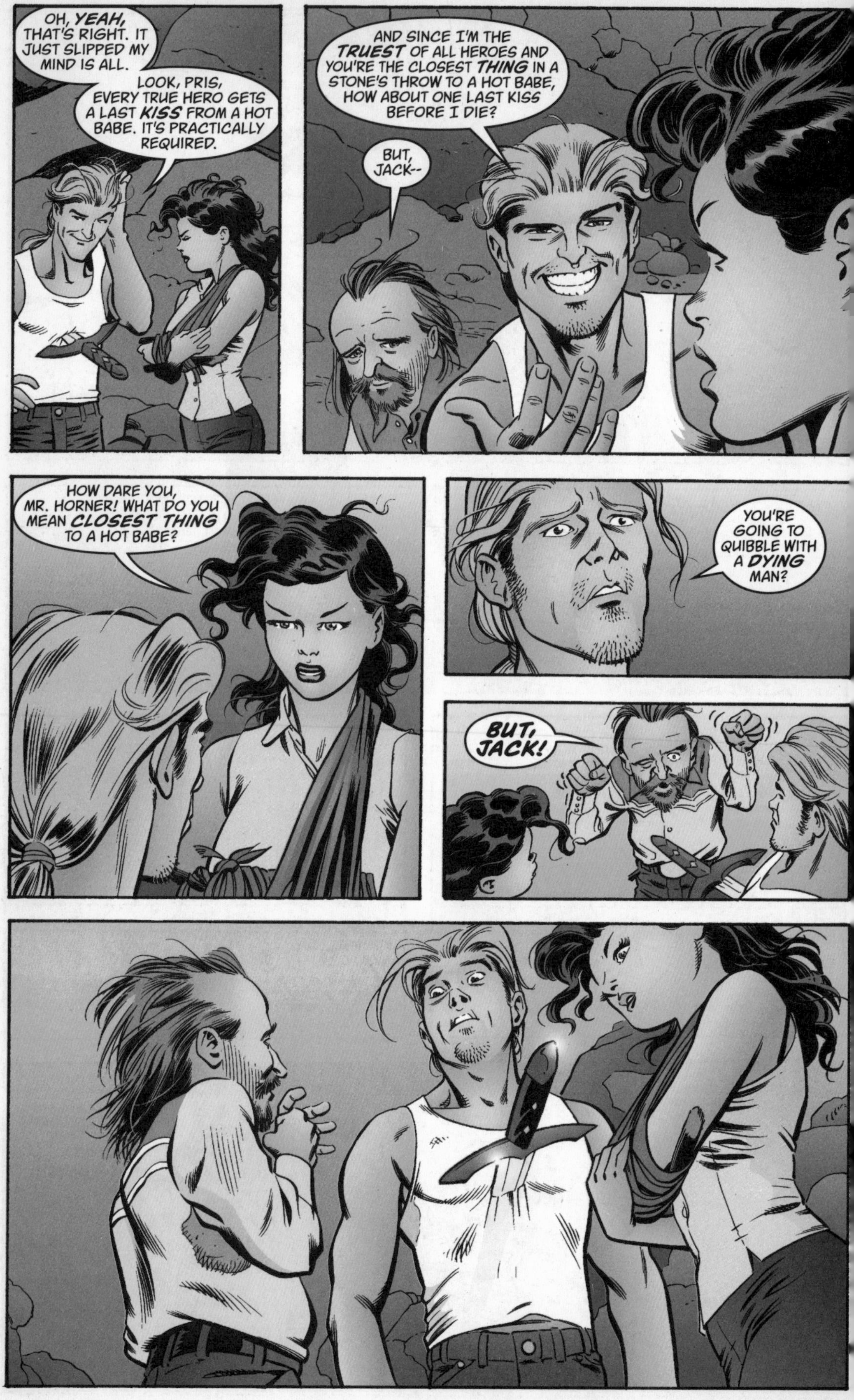
OH, YEAH, THAT'S RIGHT. IT JUST SLIPPED MY MIND IS ALL.
LOOK, PRIS, EVERY TRUE HERO GETS A LAST KISS FROM A HOT BABE. IT'S PRACTICALLY REQUIRED.
AND SINCE I'M THE TRUEST OF ALL HEROES AND YOU'RE THE CLOSEST THING IN A STONE'S THROW TO A HOT BABE, HOW ABOUT ONE LAST KISS BEFORE I DIE?
BUT, JACK--
HOW DARE YOU, MR. HORNER! WHAT DO YOU MEAN CLOSEST THING TO A HOT BABE?
YOU'RE GOING TO QUIBBLE WITH A DYING MAN?
BUT, JACK!

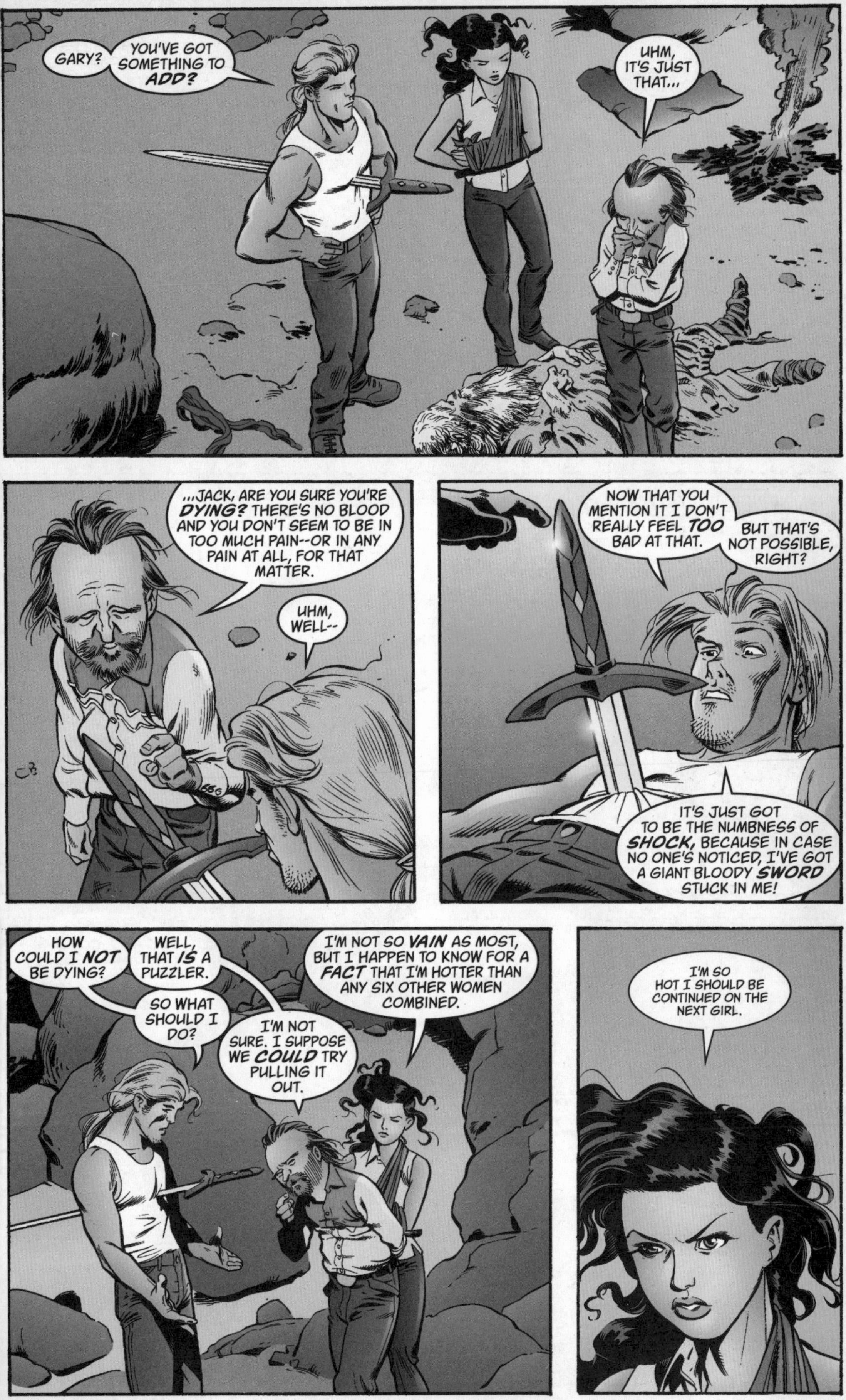
GARY?
YOU'VE GOT SOMETHING TO ADD?
UHM, IT'S JUST THAT...
...JACK, ARE YOU SURE YOU'RE DYING? THERE'S NO BLOOD AND YOU DON'T SEEM TO BE IN TOO MUCH PAIN--OR IN ANY PAIN AT ALL, FOR THAT MATTER.
UHM, WELL--
NOW THAT YOU MENTION IT I DON'T REALLY FEEL TOO BAD AT THAT.
BUT THAT'S NOT POSSIBLE, RIGHT?
IT'S JUST GOT TO BE THE NUMBNESS OF SHOCK, BECAUSE IN CASE NO ONE'S NOTICED, I'VE GOT A GIANT BLOODY SWORD STUCK IN ME!
HOW COULD I NOT BE DYING?
WELL, THAT IS A PUZZLER.
SO WHAT SHOULD I DO?
I'M NOT SURE. I SUPPOSE WE COULD TRY PULLING IT OUT.
I'M NOT SO VAIN AS MOST, BUT I HAPPEN TO KNOW FOR A FACT THAT I'M HOTTER THAN ANY SIX OTHER WOMEN COMBINED.
I'M SO HOT I SHOULD BE CONTINUED ON THE NEXT GIRL.

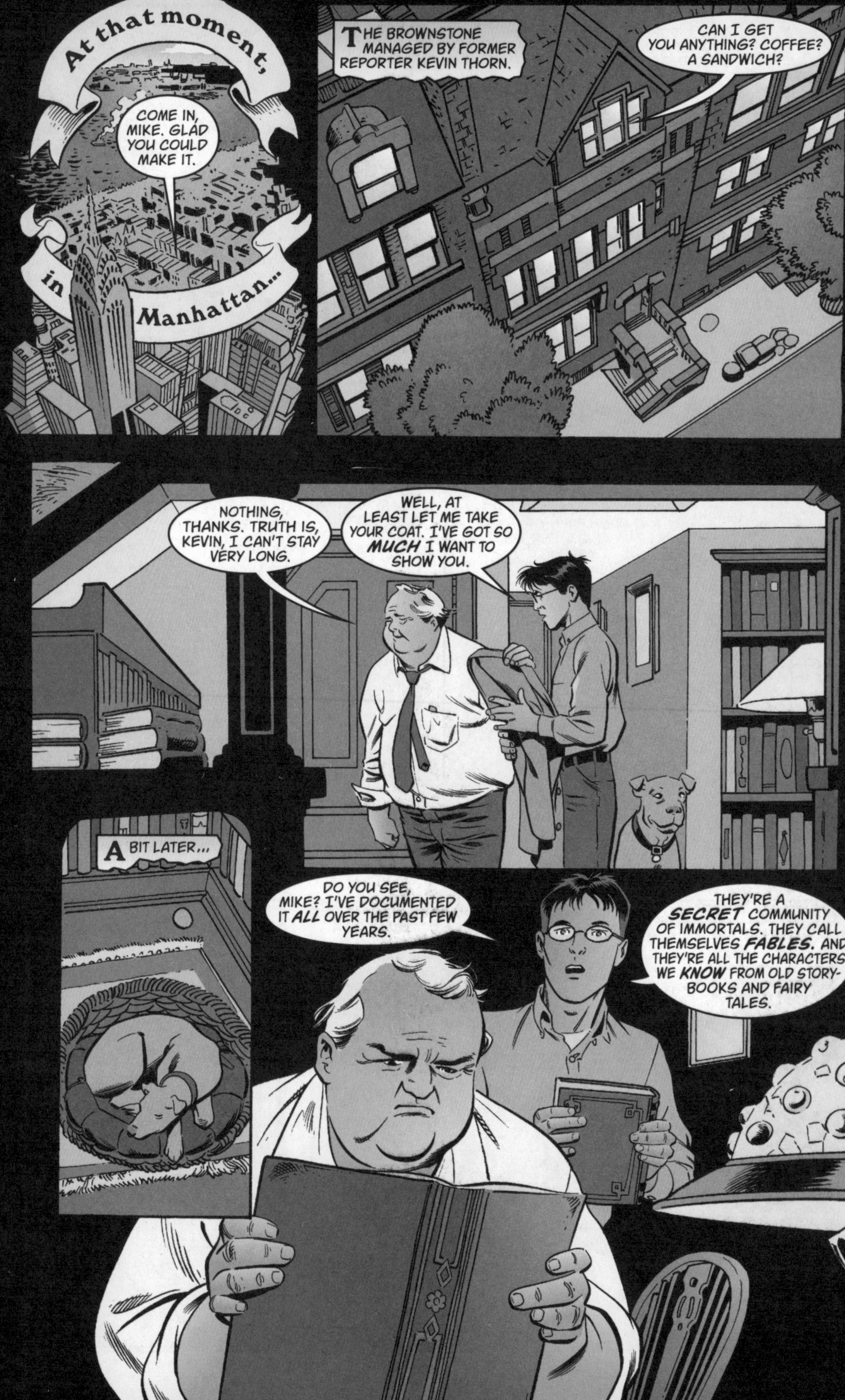
At that moment, in Manhattan...
COME IN, MIKE. GLAD YOU COULD MAKE IT.
THE BROWNSTONE MANAGED BY FORMER REPORTER KEVIN THORN.
CAN I GET YOU ANYTHING? COFFEE? A SANDWICH?
NOTHING, THANKS. TRUTH IS, KEVIN, I CAN'T STAY VERY LONG.
WELL, AT LEAST LET ME TAKE YOUR COAT. I'VE GOT SO MUCH I WANT TO SHOW YOU.
A BIT LATER...
DO YOU SEE, MIKE? I'VE DOCUMENTED IT ALL OVER THE PAST FEW YEARS.
THEY'RE A SECRET COMMUNITY OF IMMORTALS. THEY CALL THEMSELVES FABLES. AND THEY'RE ALL THE CHARACTERS WE KNOW FROM OLD STORYBOOKS AND FAIRY TALES.

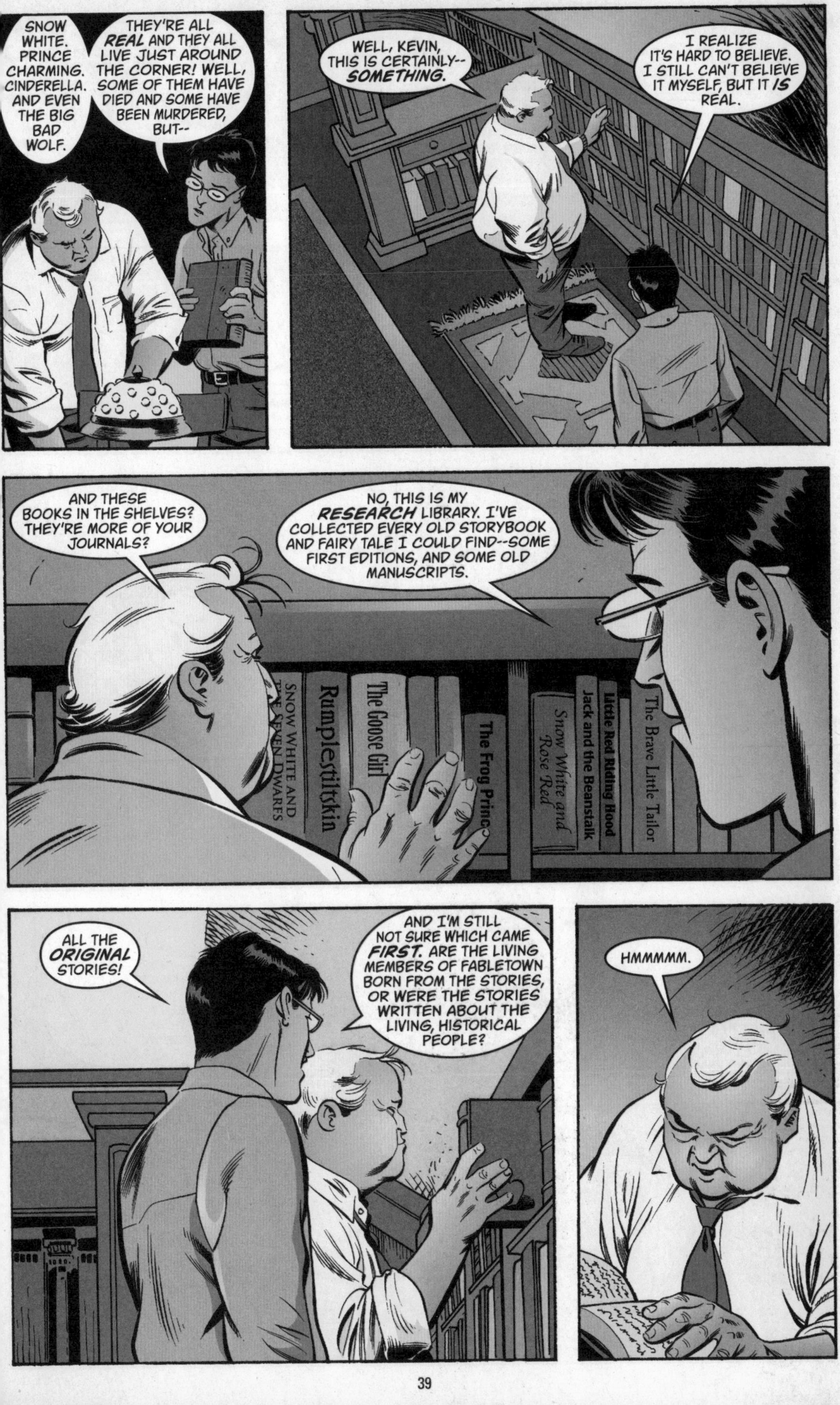
SNOW WHITE. PRINCE CHARMING. CINDERELLA. AND EVEN THE BIG BAD WOLF.
THEY'RE ALL REAL AND THEY ALL LIVE JUST AROUND THE CORNER! WELL, SOME OF THEM HAVE DIED AND SOME HAVE BEEN MURDERED, BUT--
WELL, KEVIN, THIS IS CERTAINLY-- SOMETHING.
I REALIZE IT'S HARD TO BELIEVE. I STILL CAN'T BELIEVE IT MYSELF, BUT IT IS REAL.
AND THESE BOOKS IN THE SHELVES? THEY'RE MORE OF YOUR JOURNALS?
NO, THIS IS MY RESEARCH LIBRARY. I'VE COLLECTED EVERY OLD STORYBOOK AND FAIRY TALE I COULD FIND--SOME FIRST EDITIONS, AND SOME OLD MANUSCRIPTS.
Rumplestiltskin
The Goose Girl
The Frog Princ
Snow White and Rose Red
Jack and the Beanstalk
Little Red Riding Hood
The Brave Little Tailor
ALL THE ORIGINAL STORIES!
AND I'M STILL NOT SURE WHICH CAME FIRST. ARE THE LIVING MEMBERS OF FABLETOWN BORN FROM THE STORIES, OR WERE THE STORIES WRITTEN ABOUT THE LIVING, HISTORICAL PEOPLE?
HMMMMM.

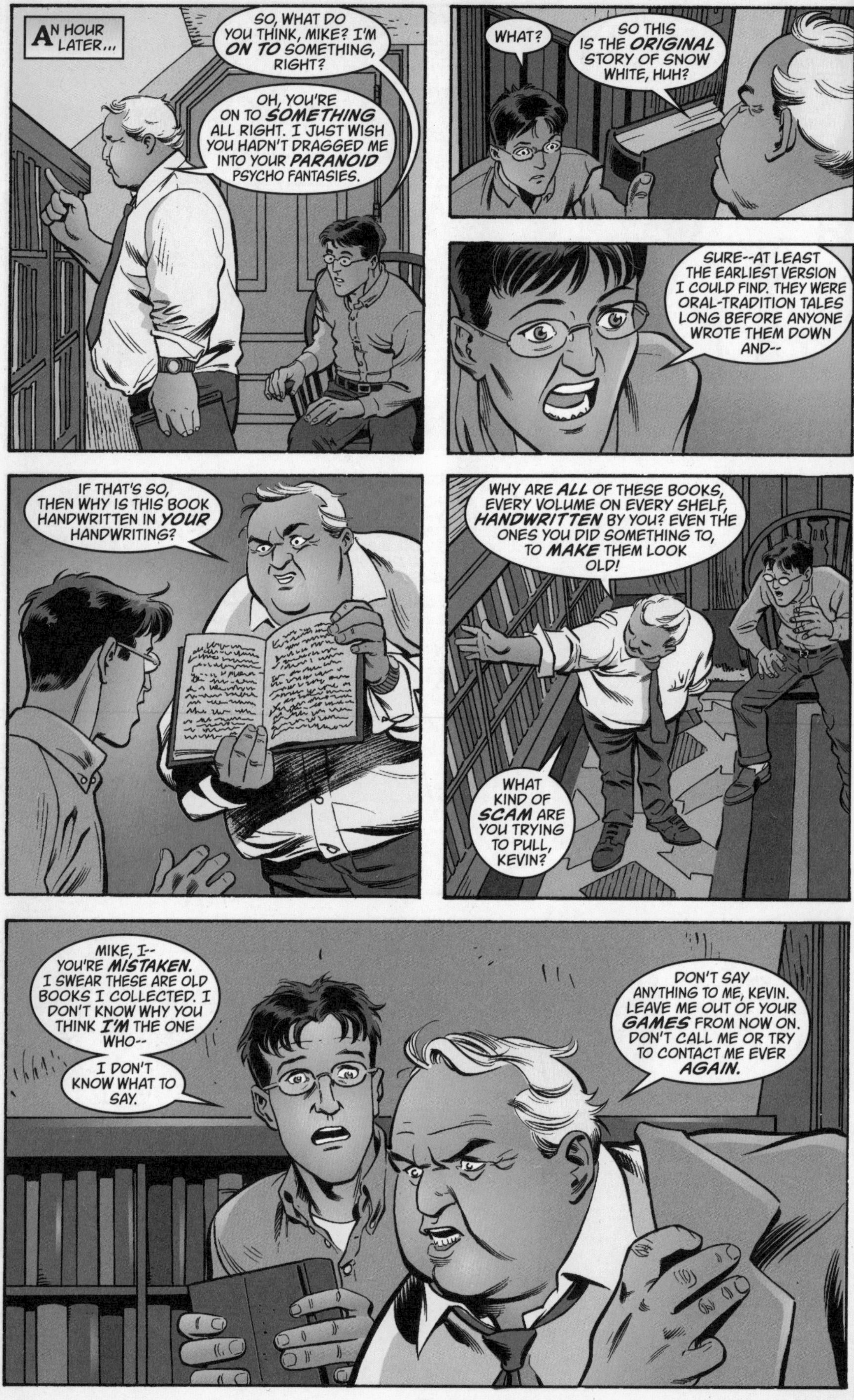
AN HOUR LATER...
SO, WHAT DO YOU THINK, MIKE? I'M ON TO SOMETHING, RIGHT?
OH, YOU'RE ON TO SOMETHING ALL RIGHT. I JUST WISH YOU HADN'T DRAGGED ME INTO YOUR PARANOID PSYCHO FANTASIES.
WHAT?
SO THIS IS THE ORIGINAL STORY OF SNOW WHITE, HUH?
SURE--AT LEAST THE EARLIEST VERSION I COULD FIND. THEY WERE ORAL-TRADITION TALES LONG BEFORE ANYONE WROTE THEM DOWN AND--
IF THAT'S SO, THEN WHY IS THIS BOOK HANDWRITTEN IN YOUR HANDWRITING?
WHY ARE ALL OF THESE BOOKS, EVERY VOLUME ON EVERY SHELF, HANDWRITTEN BY YOU? EVEN THE ONES YOU DID SOMETHING TO, TO MAKE THEM LOOK OLD!
WHAT KIND OF SCAM ARE YOU TRYING TO PULL, KEVIN?
MIKE, I-- YOU'RE MISTAKEN. I SWEAR THESE ARE OLD BOOKS I COLLECTED. I DON'T KNOW WHY YOU THINK I'M THE ONE WHO--
I DON'T KNOW WHAT TO SAY.
DON'T SAY ANYTHING TO ME, KEVIN. LEAVE ME OUT OF YOUR GAMES FROM NOW ON. DON'T CALL ME OR TRY TO CONTACT ME EVER AGAIN.

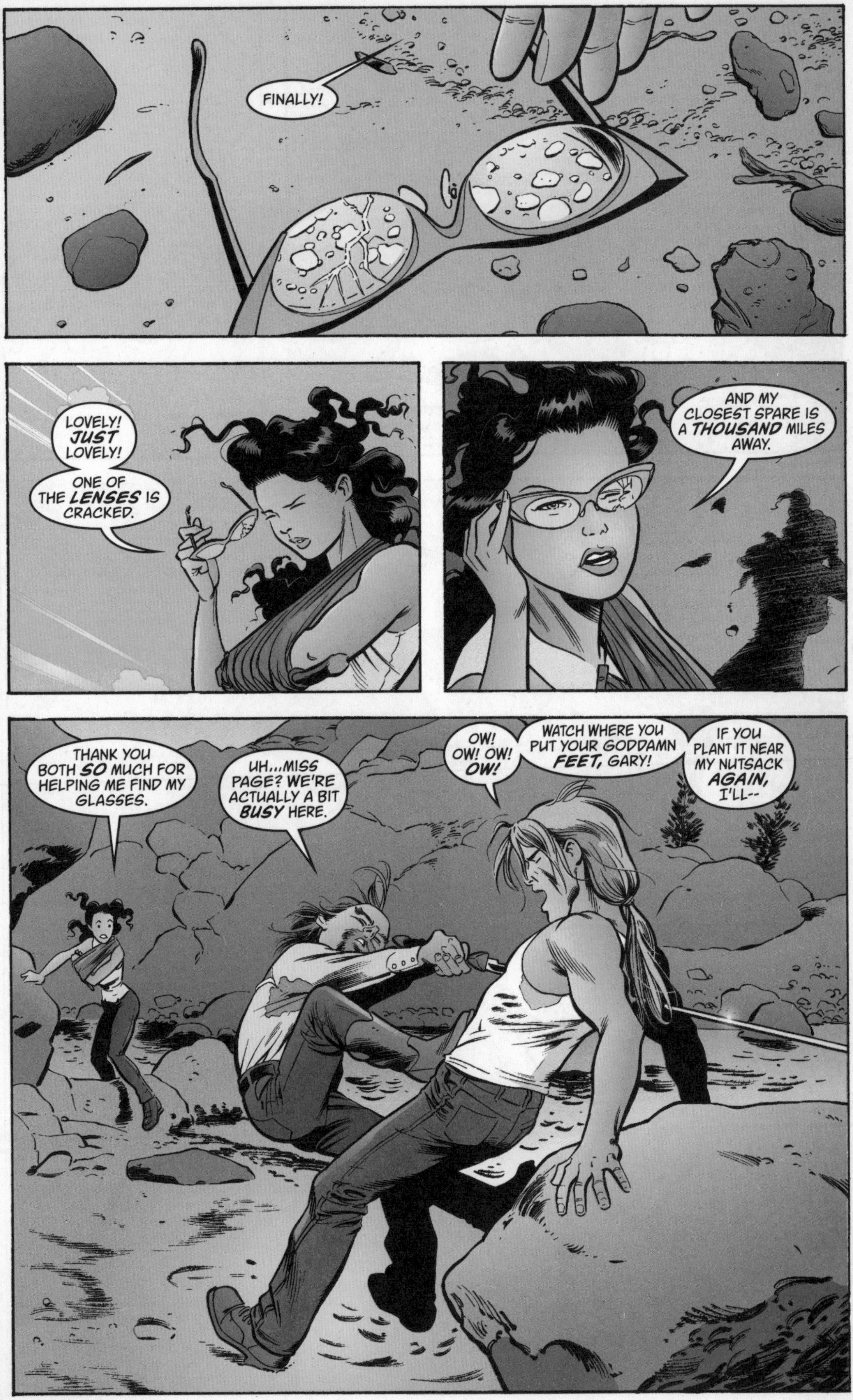
FINALLY!
LOVELY! JUST LOVELY!
ONE OF THE LENSES IS CRACKED.
AND MY CLOSEST SPARE IS A THOUSAND MILES AWAY.
THANK YOU BOTH SO MUCH FOR HELPING ME FIND MY GLASSES.
UH...MISS PAGE? WE'RE ACTUALLY A BIT BUSY HERE.
OW! OW! OW! OW!
WATCH WHERE YOU PUT YOUR GODDAMN FEET, GARY!
IF YOU PLANT IT NEAR MY NUTSACK AGAIN, I'LL--

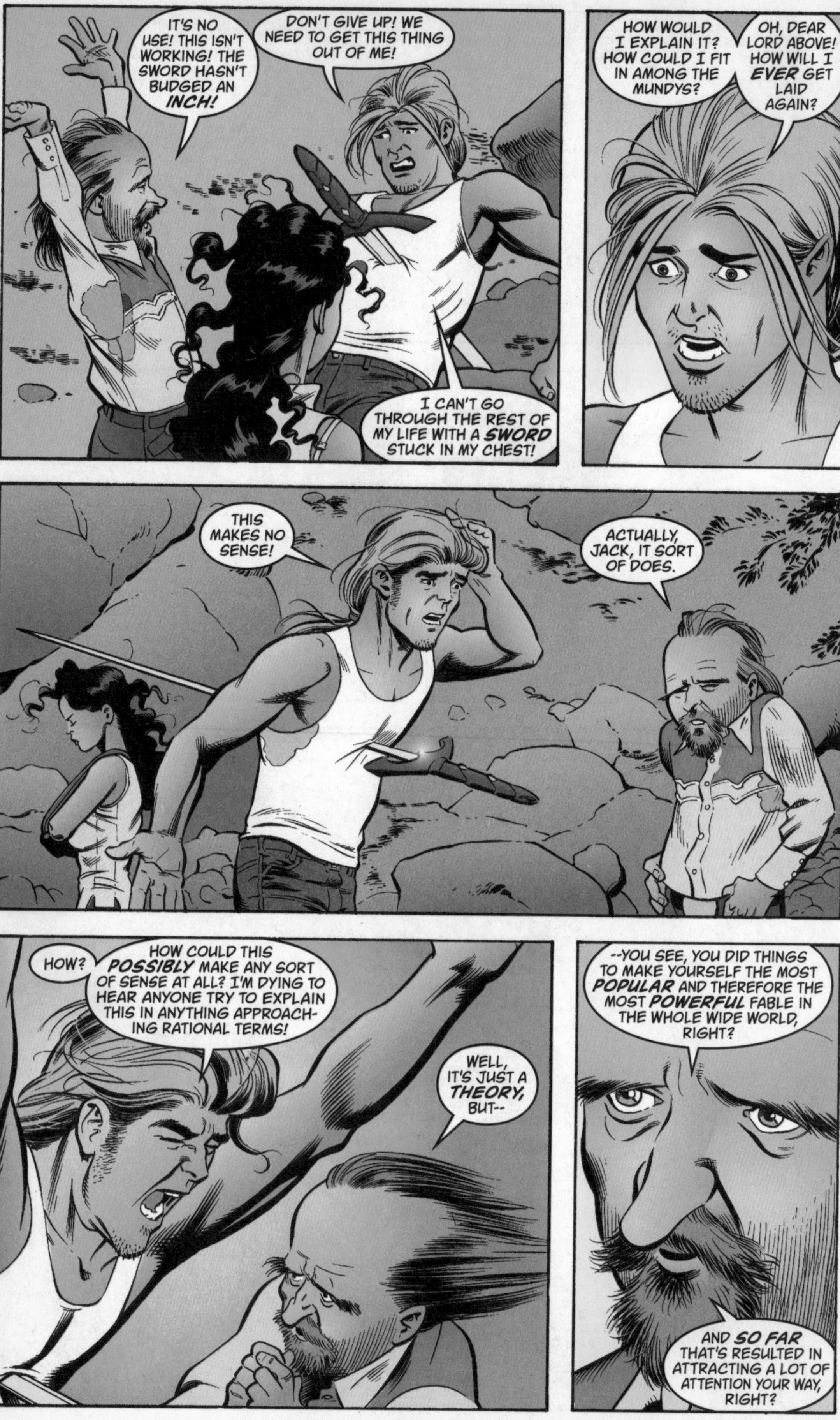
IT'S NO USE! THIS ISN'T WORKING! THE SWORD HASN'T BUDGED AN *INCH!*
DON'T GIVE UP! WE NEED TO GET THIS THING OUT OF ME!
I CAN'T GO THROUGH THE REST OF MY LIFE WITH A *SWORD* STUCK IN MY CHEST!
HOW WOULD I EXPLAIN IT? HOW COULD I FIT IN AMONG THE MUNDYS?
OH, DEAR LORD ABOVE! HOW WILL I *EVER* GET LAID AGAIN?
THIS MAKES NO SENSE!
ACTUALLY, JACK, IT SORT OF DOES.
HOW?
HOW COULD THIS *POSSIBLY* MAKE ANY SORT OF SENSE AT ALL? I'M DYING TO HEAR ANYONE TRY TO EXPLAIN THIS IN ANYTHING APPROACHING RATIONAL TERMS!
WELL, IT'S JUST A *THEORY,* BUT--
--YOU SEE, YOU DID THINGS TO MAKE YOURSELF THE MOST *POPULAR* AND THEREFORE THE MOST *POWERFUL* FABLE IN THE WHOLE WIDE WORLD, RIGHT?
AND *SO FAR* THAT'S RESULTED IN ATTRACTING A LOT OF ATTENTION YOUR WAY, RIGHT?

NOT THE GOOD KIND OF ATTENTION!

I'VE BEEN BUSTED UP, *MASHED*, MOOSHED, MUTILATED, AND *NOW* I HAVE A SWORD IN ME!

EXACTLY. YOU MADE YOURSELF *HARD* TO KILL, SO THE UNIVERSE RESPONDED BY TRYING TO KILL YOU WITH *GUSTO* AND ALARMING REGULARITY.

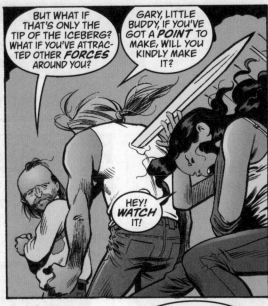

BUT WHAT IF THAT'S ONLY THE TIP OF THE ICEBERG? WHAT IF YOU'VE ATTRACTED OTHER *FORCES* AROUND YOU?

GARY, LITTLE BUDDY, IF YOU'VE GOT A *POINT* TO MAKE, WILL YOU KINDLY MAKE IT?

HEY! *WATCH* IT!

JACK, I THINK YOU'VE MANAGED TO MAKE YOURSELF A LIVING STORY-MAGNET. YOU'VE DOOMED YOURSELF TO BE THE *CENTER* OF EVERY GREAT TALE, OR ADVENTURE, OR WHAT-HAVE-YOU.

AND HOW DOES THIS TURN OF EVENTS TELL YOU *THAT?* WHAT'S A GODAWFUL BLOODY TOAD-STICKER IN MY *CHEST* HAVE TO DO WITH--

WATCH THE DAMN BLADE, JACK!

IT'S ONE OF THE REALLY BIG RECURRING STORIES--*THE SWORD IN THE STONE.*

I THINK SOMEHOW, SOMEWHERE, THE EXCALIBUR LEGEND HAS BECOME, OR IS ABOUT TO BECOME *IMPORTANT* AGAIN...

...AND WHAT HAPPENED *HERE* REFLECTS THAT.

ONE COULD REASONABLY ARGUE THAT THE VERY CENTER OF THE STORY IS THE *STONE*-- AND I THINK THAT'S YOU NOW.

I'M THE STONE?

EXACTLY.

WELL, THAT'S APT.

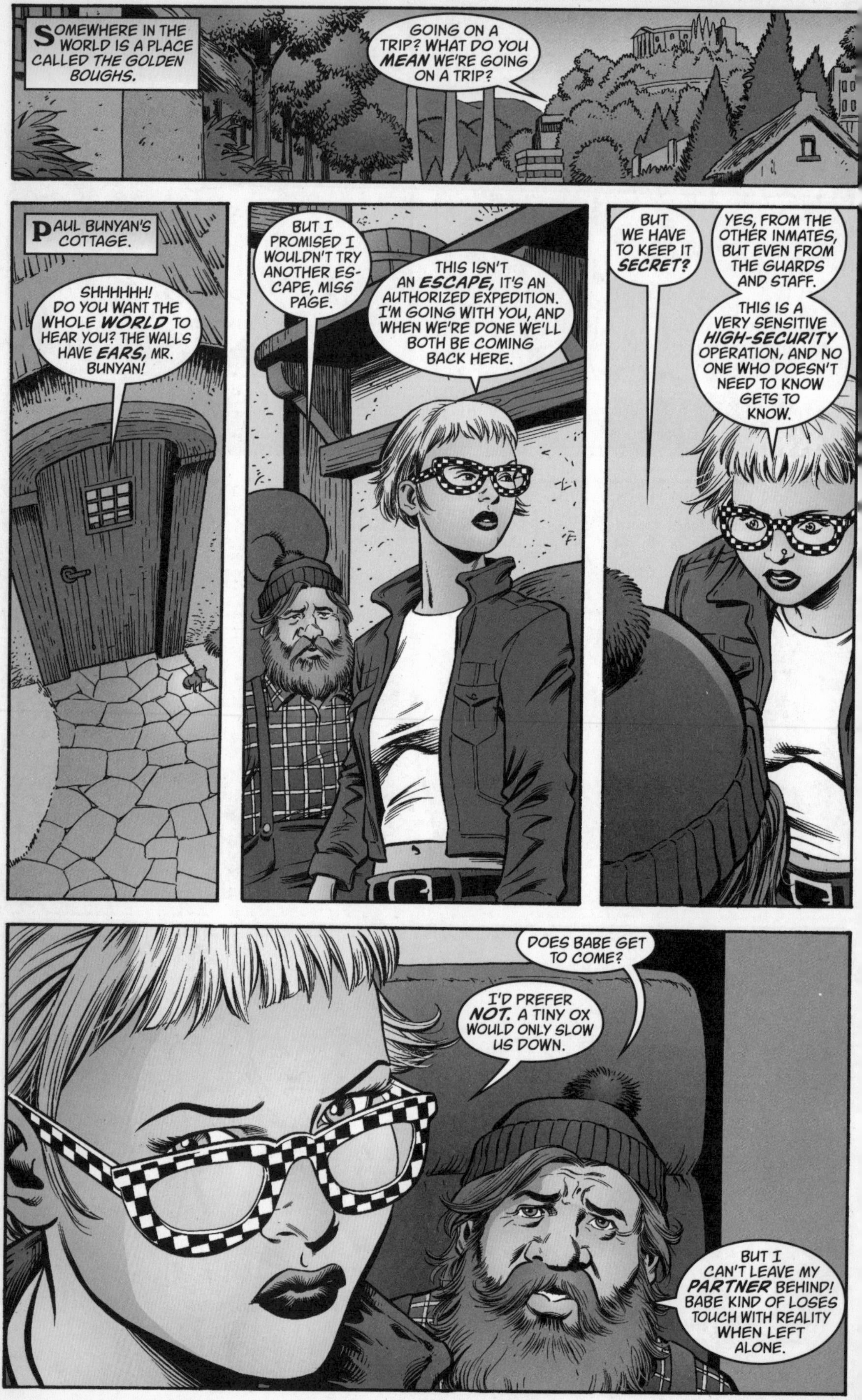

SOMEWHERE IN THE WORLD IS A PLACE CALLED THE GOLDEN BOUGHS.
GOING ON A TRIP? WHAT DO YOU MEAN WE'RE GOING ON A TRIP?
PAUL BUNYAN'S COTTAGE.
SHHHHHH! DO YOU WANT THE WHOLE WORLD TO HEAR YOU? THE WALLS HAVE EARS, MR. BUNYAN!
BUT I PROMISED I WOULDN'T TRY ANOTHER ES-CAPE, MISS PAGE.
THIS ISN'T AN ESCAPE, IT'S AN AUTHORIZED EXPEDITION. I'M GOING WITH YOU, AND WHEN WE'RE DONE WE'LL BOTH BE COMING BACK HERE.
BUT WE HAVE TO KEEP IT SECRET?
YES, FROM THE OTHER INMATES, BUT EVEN FROM THE GUARDS AND STAFF.
THIS IS A VERY SENSITIVE HIGH-SECURITY OPERATION, AND NO ONE WHO DOESN'T NEED TO KNOW GETS TO KNOW.
DOES BABE GET TO COME?
I'D PREFER NOT. A TINY OX WOULD ONLY SLOW US DOWN.
BUT I CAN'T LEAVE MY PARTNER BEHIND! BABE KIND OF LOSES TOUCH WITH REALITY WHEN LEFT ALONE.

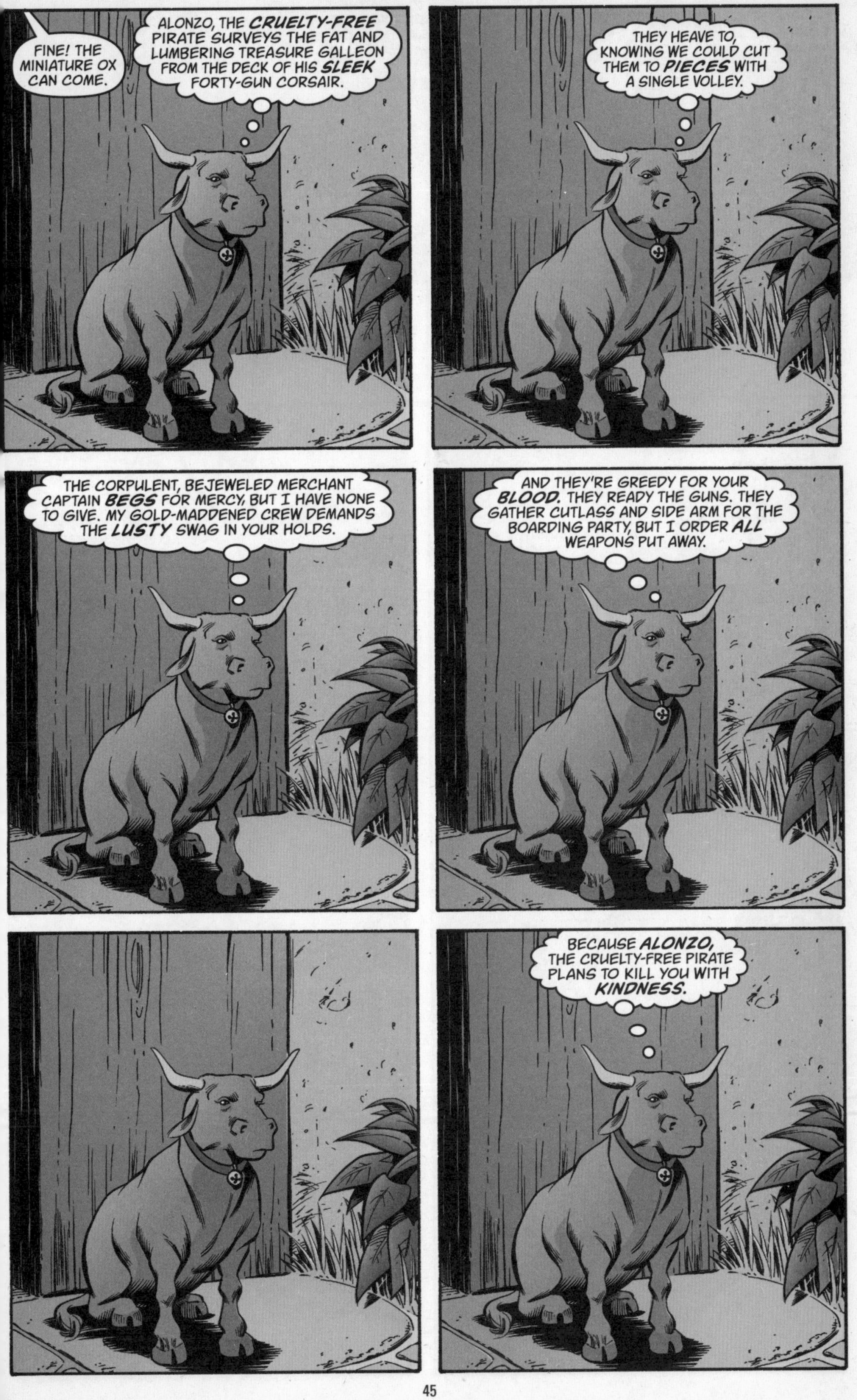
FINE! THE MINIATURE OX CAN COME.
ALONZO, THE CRUELTY-FREE PIRATE SURVEYS THE FAT AND LUMBERING TREASURE GALLEON FROM THE DECK OF HIS SLEEK FORTY-GUN CORSAIR.
THEY HEAVE TO, KNOWING WE COULD CUT THEM TO PIECES WITH A SINGLE VOLLEY.
THE CORPULENT, BEJEWELED MERCHANT CAPTAIN BEGS FOR MERCY, BUT I HAVE NONE TO GIVE. MY GOLD-MADDENED CREW DEMANDS THE LUSTY SWAG IN YOUR HOLDS.
AND THEY'RE GREEDY FOR YOUR BLOOD. THEY READY THE GUNS. THEY GATHER CUTLASS AND SIDE ARM FOR THE BOARDING PARTY, BUT I ORDER ALL WEAPONS PUT AWAY.
BECAUSE ALONZO, THE CRUELTY-FREE PIRATE PLANS TO KILL YOU WITH KINDNESS.

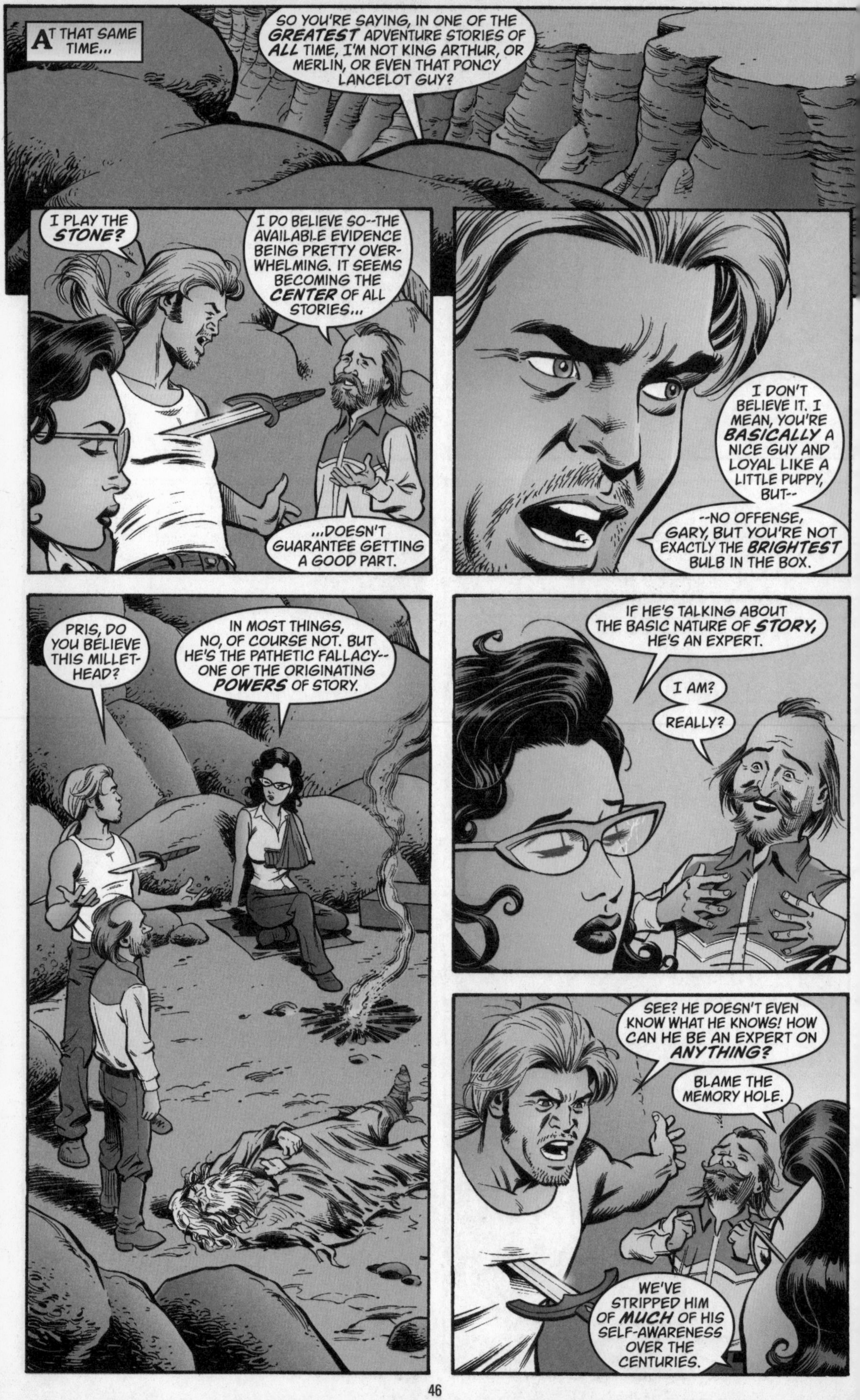
AT THAT SAME TIME...
SO YOU'RE SAYING, IN ONE OF THE GREATEST ADVENTURE STORIES OF ALL TIME, I'M NOT KING ARTHUR, OR MERLIN, OR EVEN THAT PONCY LANCELOT GUY?
I PLAY THE STONE?
I DO BELIEVE SO--THE AVAILABLE EVIDENCE BEING PRETTY OVERWHELMING. IT SEEMS BECOMING THE CENTER OF ALL STORIES...
...DOESN'T GUARANTEE GETTING A GOOD PART.
I DON'T BELIEVE IT. I MEAN, YOU'RE BASICALLY A NICE GUY AND LOYAL LIKE A LITTLE PUPPY, BUT--
--NO OFFENSE, GARY, BUT YOU'RE NOT EXACTLY THE BRIGHTEST BULB IN THE BOX.
PRIS, DO YOU BELIEVE THIS MILLET-HEAD?
IN MOST THINGS, NO, OF COURSE NOT. BUT HE'S THE PATHETIC FALLACY--ONE OF THE ORIGINATING POWERS OF STORY.
IF HE'S TALKING ABOUT THE BASIC NATURE OF STORY, HE'S AN EXPERT.
I AM?
REALLY?
SEE? HE DOESN'T EVEN KNOW WHAT HE KNOWS! HOW CAN HE BE AN EXPERT ON ANYTHING?
BLAME THE MEMORY HOLE.
WE'VE STRIPPED HIM OF MUCH OF HIS SELF-AWARENESS OVER THE CENTURIES.

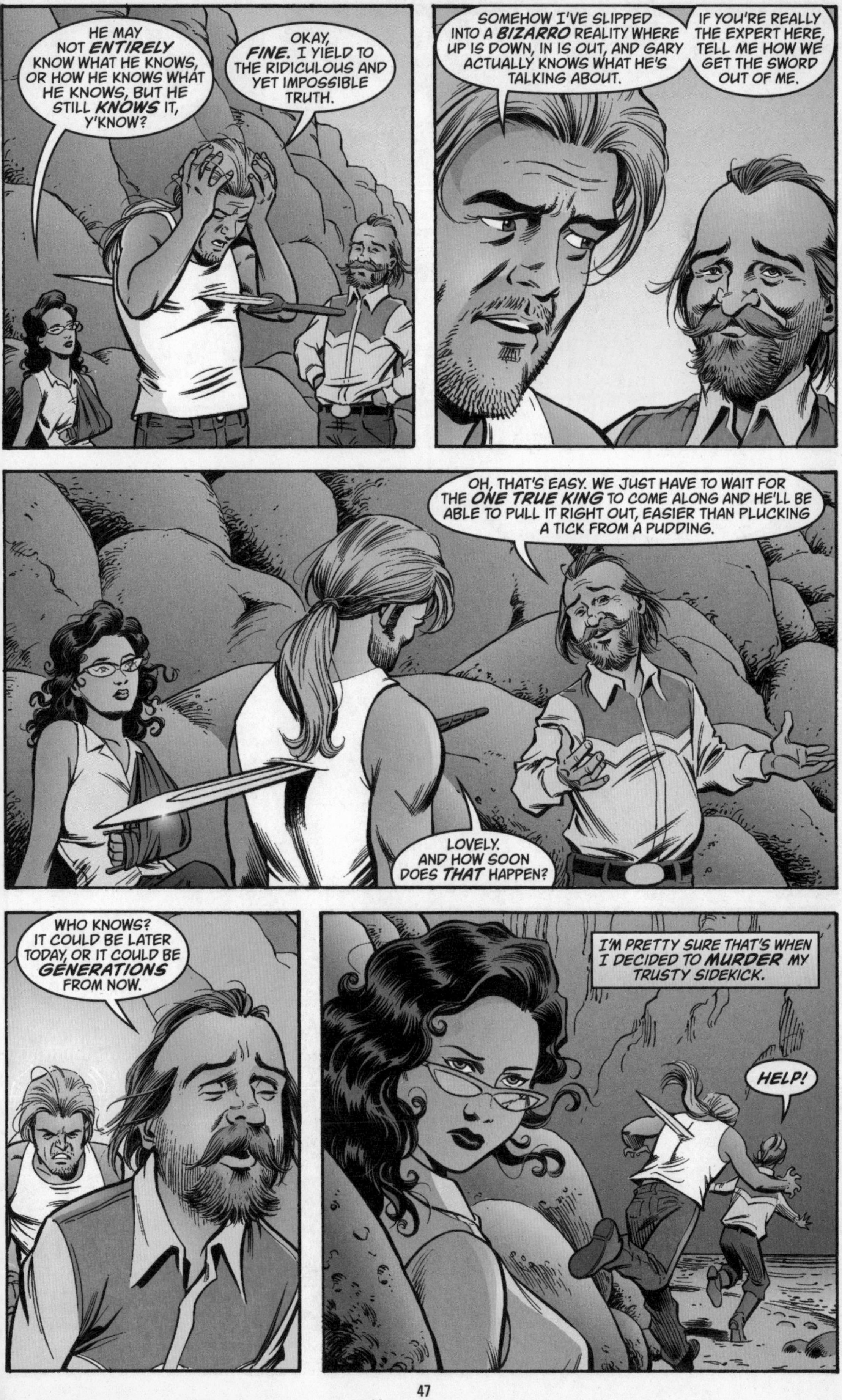
HE MAY NOT ENTIRELY KNOW WHAT HE KNOWS, OR HOW HE KNOWS WHAT HE KNOWS, BUT HE STILL KNOWS IT, Y'KNOW?
OKAY, FINE. I YIELD TO THE RIDICULOUS AND YET IMPOSSIBLE TRUTH.
SOMEHOW I'VE SLIPPED INTO A BIZARRO REALITY WHERE UP IS DOWN, IN IS OUT, AND GARY ACTUALLY KNOWS WHAT HE'S TALKING ABOUT.
IF YOU'RE REALLY THE EXPERT HERE, TELL ME HOW WE GET THE SWORD OUT OF ME.
OH, THAT'S EASY. WE JUST HAVE TO WAIT FOR THE ONE TRUE KING TO COME ALONG AND HE'LL BE ABLE TO PULL IT RIGHT OUT, EASIER THAN PLUCKING A TICK FROM A PUDDING.
LOVELY. AND HOW SOON DOES THAT HAPPEN?
WHO KNOWS? IT COULD BE LATER TODAY, OR IT COULD BE GENERATIONS FROM NOW.
I'M PRETTY SURE THAT'S WHEN I DECIDED TO MURDER MY TRUSTY SIDEKICK.
HELP!

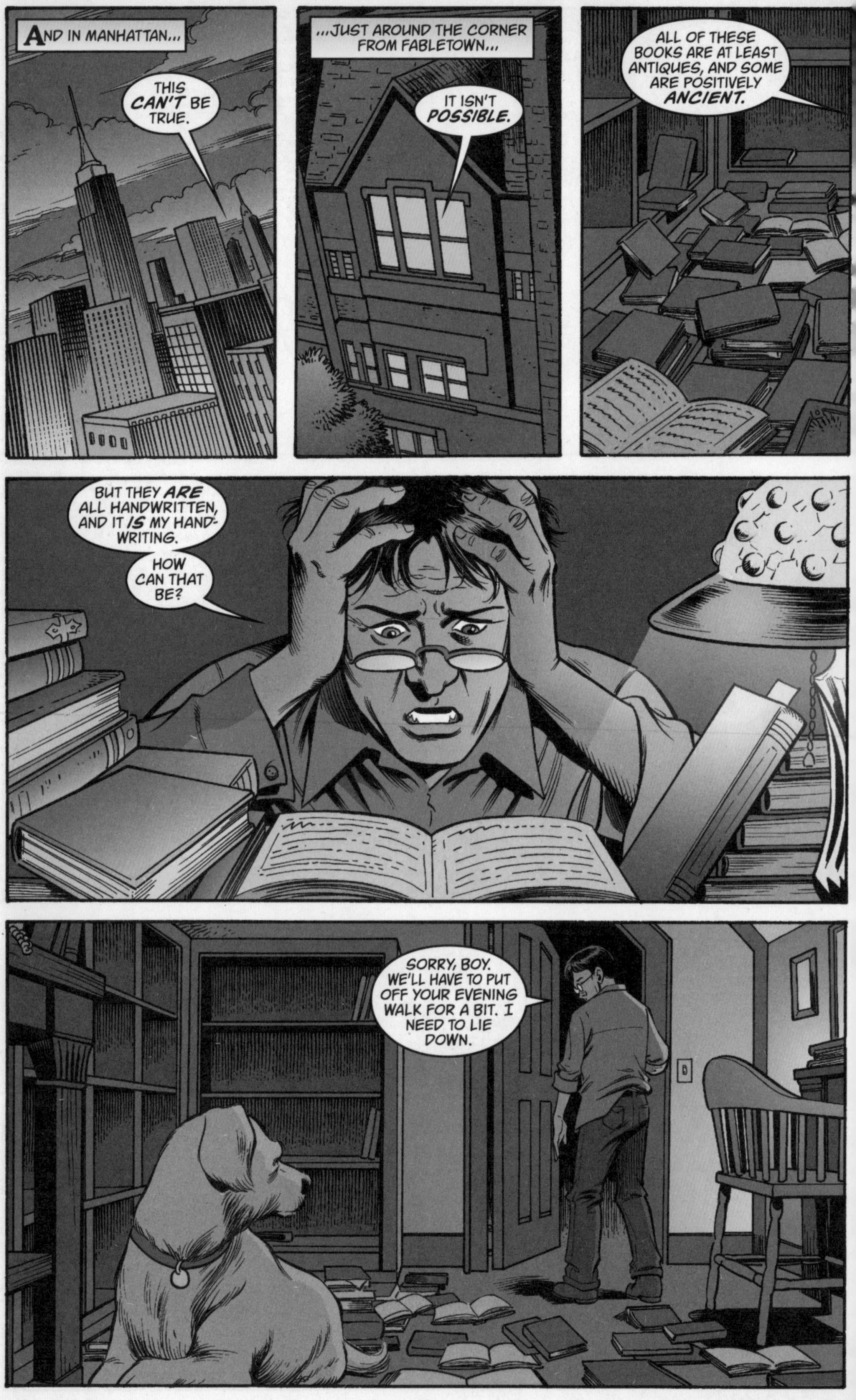
AND IN MANHATTAN...
THIS CAN'T BE TRUE.
...JUST AROUND THE CORNER FROM FABLETOWN...
IT ISN'T POSSIBLE.
ALL OF THESE BOOKS ARE AT LEAST ANTIQUES, AND SOME ARE POSITIVELY ANCIENT.
BUT THEY ARE ALL HANDWRITTEN, AND IT IS MY HANDWRITING.
HOW CAN THAT BE?
SORRY, BOY. WE'LL HAVE TO PUT OFF YOUR EVENING WALK FOR A BIT. I NEED TO LIE DOWN.

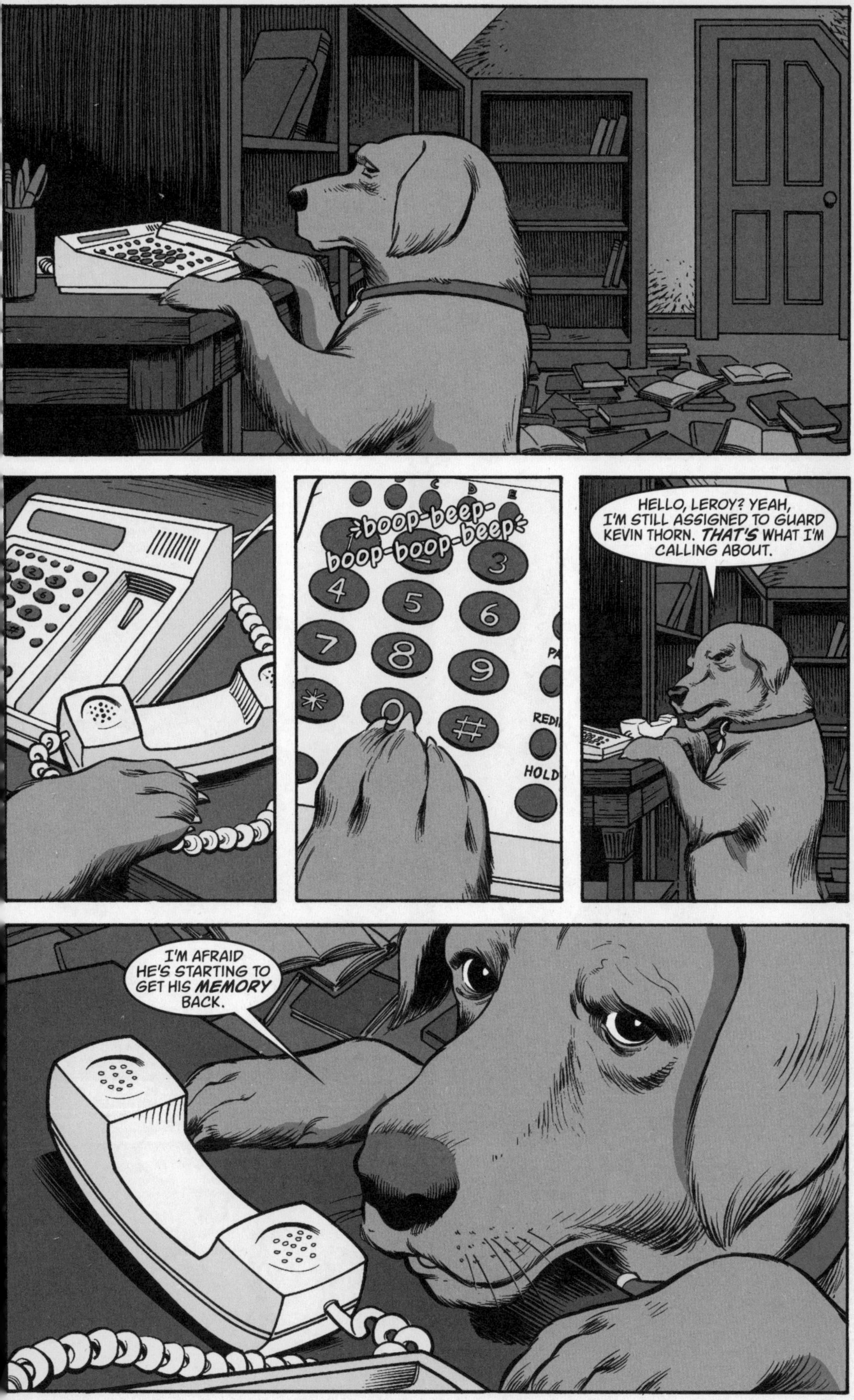
boop-beep-
boop-boop-beep
HELLO, LEROY? YEAH, I'M STILL ASSIGNED TO GUARD KEVIN THORN. *THAT'S* WHAT I'M CALLING ABOUT.
I'M AFRAID HE'S STARTING TO GET HIS *MEMORY* BACK.

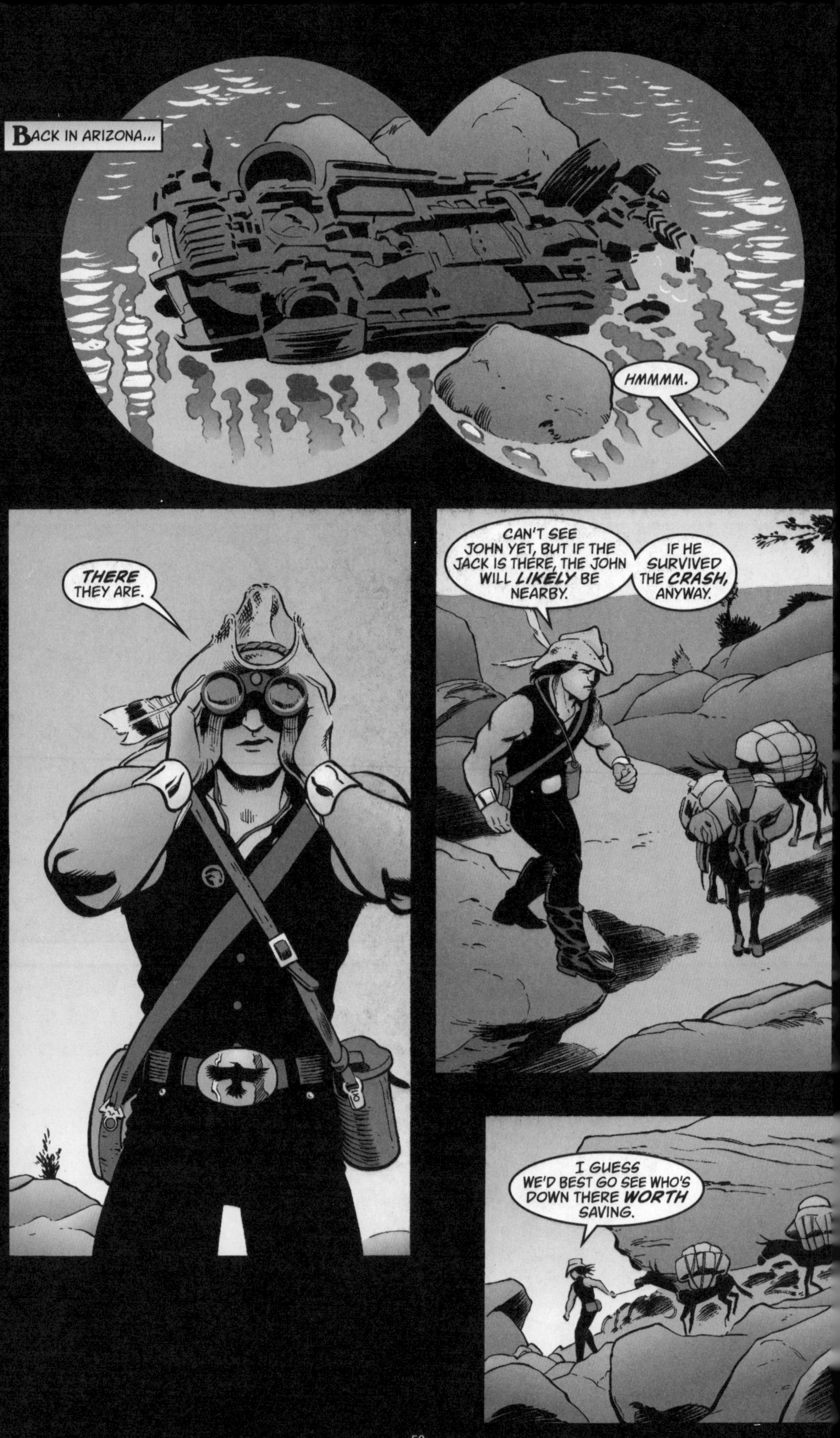
BACK IN ARIZONA...
HMMMM.
THERE THEY ARE.
CAN'T SEE JOHN YET, BUT IF THE JACK IS THERE, THE JOHN WILL LIKELY BE NEARBY.
IF HE SURVIVED THE CRASH, ANYWAY.
I GUESS WE'D BEST GO SEE WHO'S DOWN THERE WORTH SAVING.

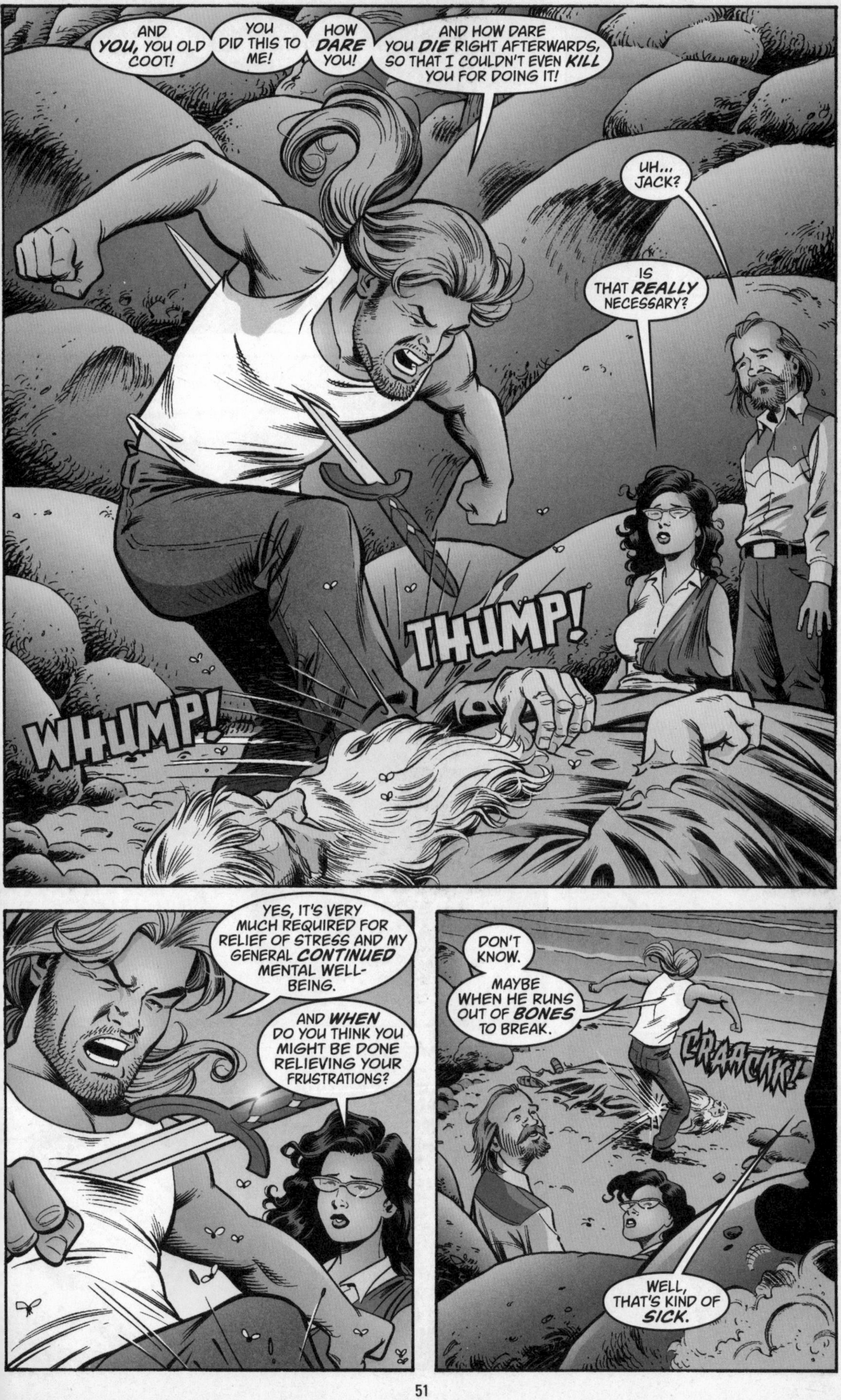

AND YOU, YOU OLD COOT!
YOU DID THIS TO ME!
HOW DARE YOU!
AND HOW DARE YOU DIE RIGHT AFTERWARDS, SO THAT I COULDN'T EVEN KILL YOU FOR DOING IT!
UH... JACK?
IS THAT REALLY NECESSARY?
THUMP!
WHUMP!
YES, IT'S VERY MUCH REQUIRED FOR RELIEF OF STRESS AND MY GENERAL CONTINUED MENTAL WELL-BEING.
AND WHEN DO YOU THINK YOU MIGHT BE DONE RELIEVING YOUR FRUSTRATIONS?
DON'T KNOW.
MAYBE WHEN HE RUNS OUT OF BONES TO BREAK.
CRAAACKK!
WELL, THAT'S KIND OF SICK.

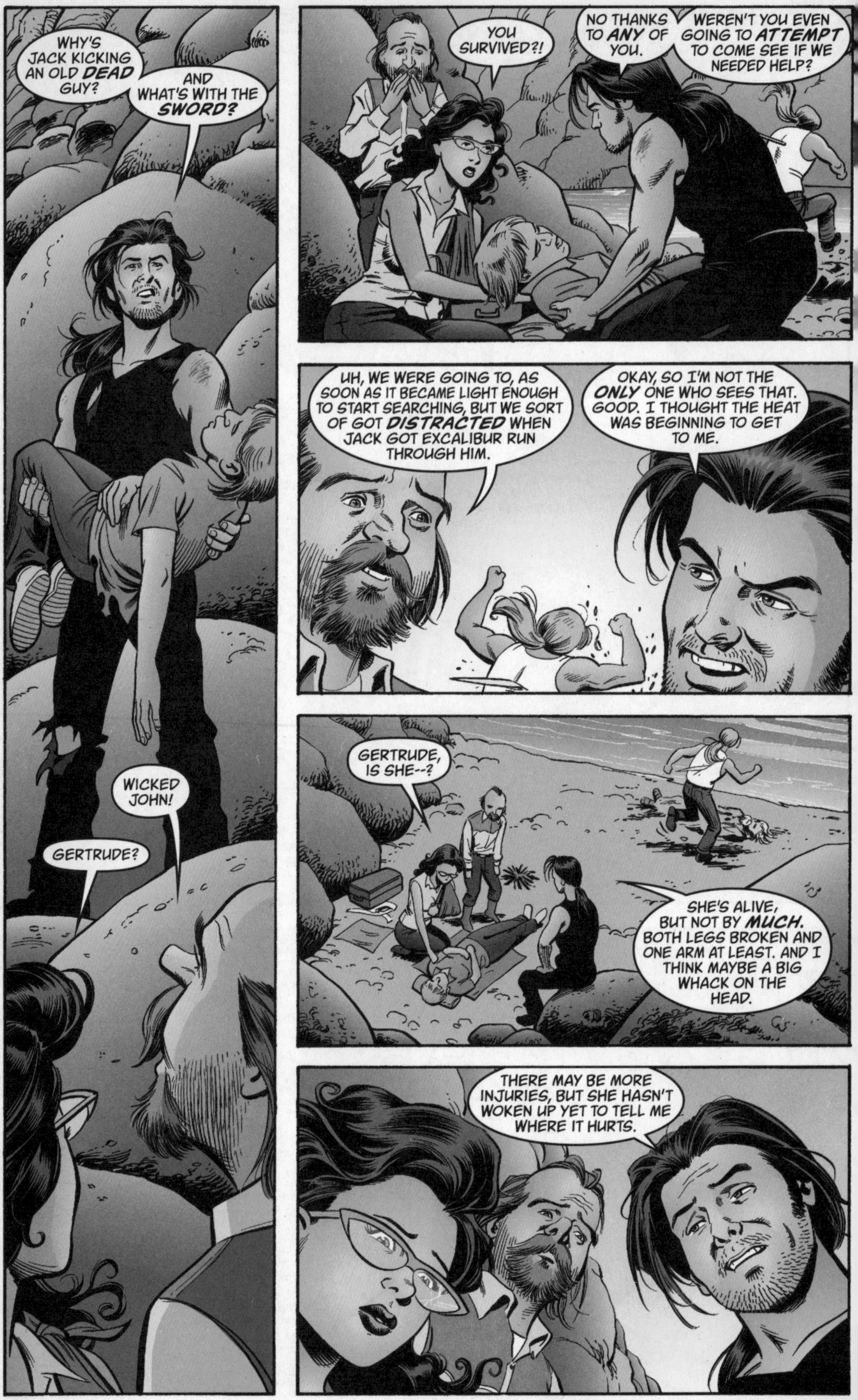
WHY'S JACK KICKING AN OLD DEAD GUY?
AND WHAT'S WITH THE SWORD?
WICKED JOHN!
GERTRUDE?
YOU SURVIVED?!
NO THANKS TO ANY OF YOU.
WEREN'T YOU EVEN GOING TO ATTEMPT TO COME SEE IF WE NEEDED HELP?
UH, WE WERE GOING TO, AS SOON AS IT BECAME LIGHT ENOUGH TO START SEARCHING, BUT WE SORT OF GOT DISTRACTED WHEN JACK GOT EXCALIBUR RUN THROUGH HIM.
OKAY, SO I'M NOT THE ONLY ONE WHO SEES THAT. GOOD. I THOUGHT THE HEAT WAS BEGINNING TO GET TO ME.
GERTRUDE, IS SHE--?
SHE'S ALIVE, BUT NOT BY MUCH. BOTH LEGS BROKEN AND ONE ARM AT LEAST. AND I THINK MAYBE A BIG WHACK ON THE HEAD.
THERE MAY BE MORE INJURIES, BUT SHE HASN'T WOKEN UP YET TO TELL ME WHERE IT HURTS.

WE NEED TO GET HER TO A HOSPITAL *RIGHT* AWAY.

GOOD LUCK WITH *THAT.* I TRIED CARRYING HER UP THE HILL, BEFORE I SETTLED FOR CARRYING HER DOWN HERE. TOO STEEP.

SO WE'RE GOING TO HAVE TO WALK ALONG THE RIVER, UNTIL WE FIND AN EASIER SLOPE.

OR MAYBE RUN INTO ONE OF THE *INDIAN TRIBES* WHO STILL LIVE DOWN HERE.

I'D REALLY LIKE TO SEE SOME *REAL* INDIANS-- YOU KNOW, THE KIND THAT *AREN'T* RUNNING CASINOS NOW.

WOW, BUDDY, WAS THAT AN *ACTUAL* SNARKY REMARK? FROM YOU? HANGING OUT WITH JACKASS HORNER'S REALLY HAD A LOOSENING EFFECT ON YOU.

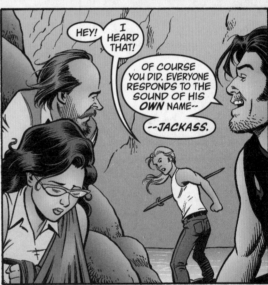

HEY! I HEARD THAT!

OF COURSE YOU DID. EVERYONE RESPONDS TO THE SOUND OF HIS *OWN* NAME--

--JACKASS.

Y'KNOW, I'VE ALREADY HAD A PRETTY BAD DAY, AND I DON'T NEED *YOU* SHOWING UP TO MAKE IT *WORSE!*

53

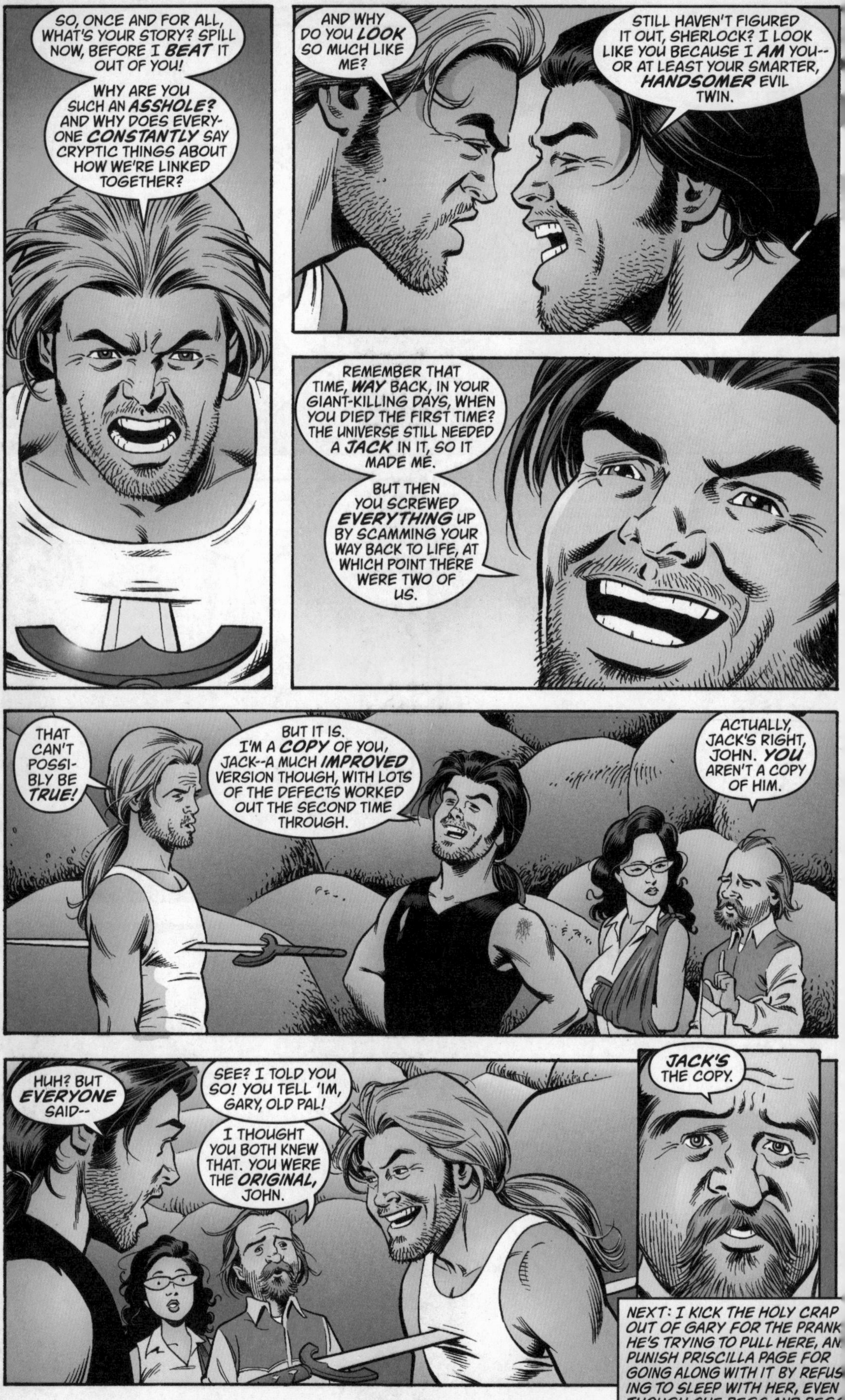
SO, ONCE AND FOR ALL, WHAT'S YOUR STORY? SPILL NOW, BEFORE I BEAT IT OUT OF YOU!
WHY ARE YOU SUCH AN ASSHOLE? AND WHY DOES EVERY-ONE CONSTANTLY SAY CRYPTIC THINGS ABOUT HOW WE'RE LINKED TOGETHER?
AND WHY DO YOU LOOK SO MUCH LIKE ME?
STILL HAVEN'T FIGURED IT OUT, SHERLOCK? I LOOK LIKE YOU BECAUSE I AM YOU--OR AT LEAST YOUR SMARTER, HANDSOMER EVIL TWIN.
REMEMBER THAT TIME, WAY BACK, IN YOUR GIANT-KILLING DAYS, WHEN YOU DIED THE FIRST TIME? THE UNIVERSE STILL NEEDED A JACK IN IT, SO IT MADE ME.
BUT THEN YOU SCREWED EVERYTHING UP BY SCAMMING YOUR WAY BACK TO LIFE, AT WHICH POINT THERE WERE TWO OF US.
THAT CAN'T POSSI-BLY BE TRUE!
BUT IT IS. I'M A COPY OF YOU, JACK--A MUCH IMPROVED VERSION THOUGH, WITH LOTS OF THE DEFECTS WORKED OUT THE SECOND TIME THROUGH.
ACTUALLY, JACK'S RIGHT, JOHN. YOU AREN'T A COPY OF HIM.
HUH? BUT EVERYONE SAID--
SEE? I TOLD YOU SO! YOU TELL 'IM, GARY, OLD PAL!
I THOUGHT YOU BOTH KNEW THAT. YOU WERE THE ORIGINAL, JOHN.
JACK'S THE COPY.
NEXT: I KICK THE HOLY CRAP OUT OF GARY FOR THE PRANK HE'S TRYING TO PULL HERE, AN PUNISH PRISCILLA PAGE FOR GOING ALONG WITH IT BY REFUS-ING TO SLEEP WITH HER, EVEN THOUGH SHE BEGS AND BEGS

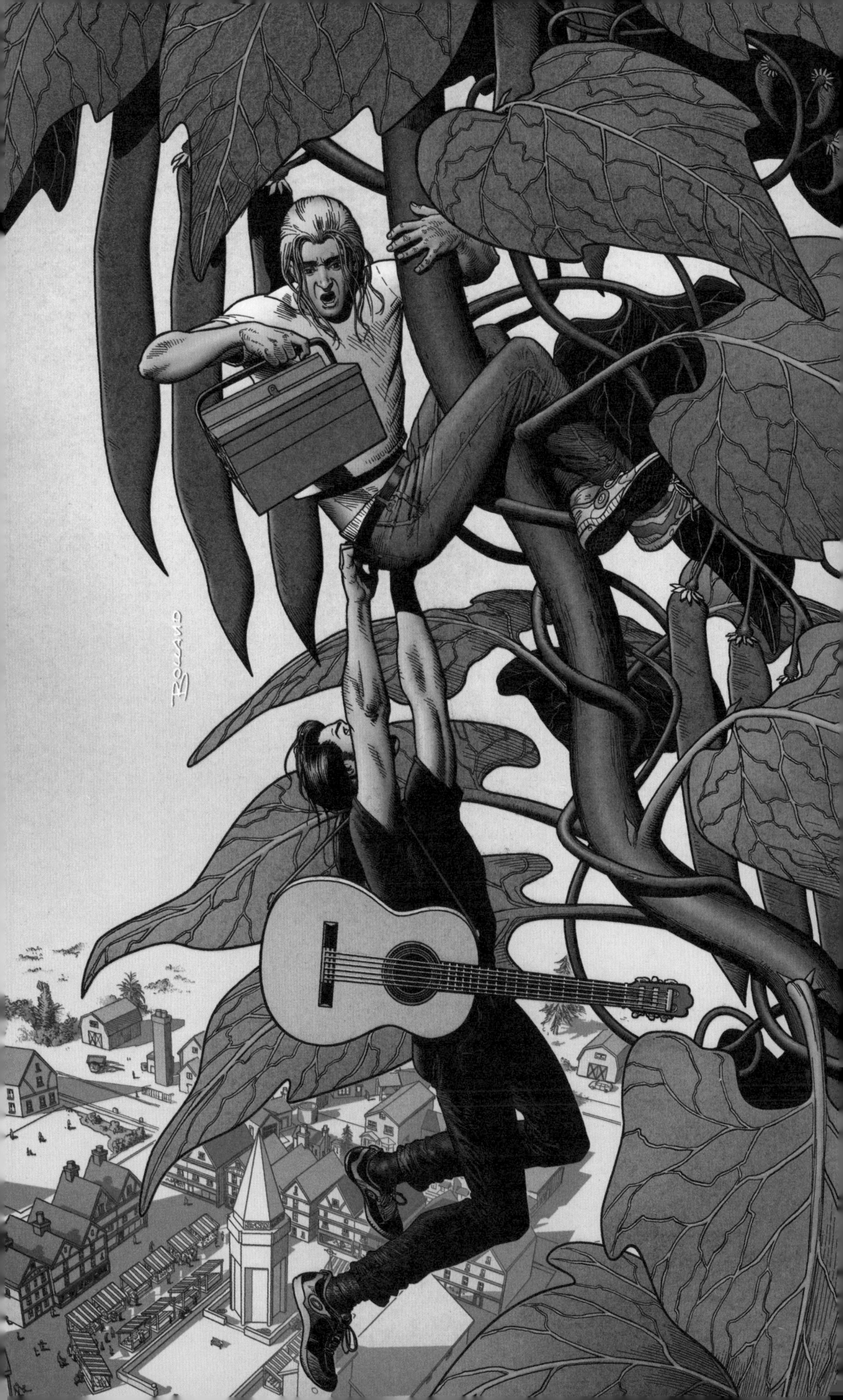
BOLLAND

"I never in my entire life
set off to explore anything.
I set off to find loot."

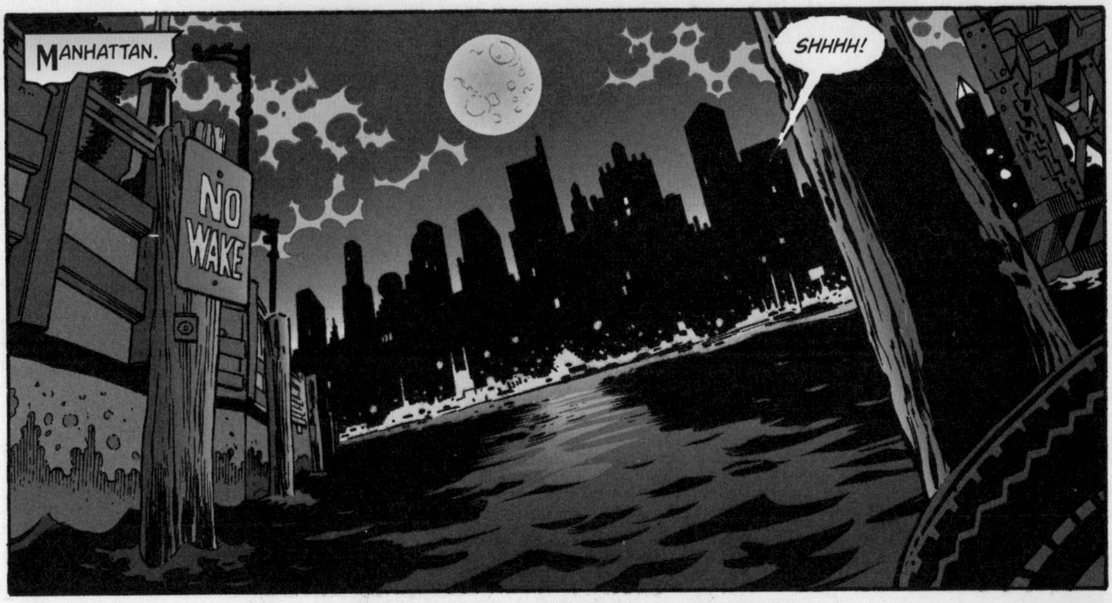
MANHATTAN.
SHHHH!
NO WAKE

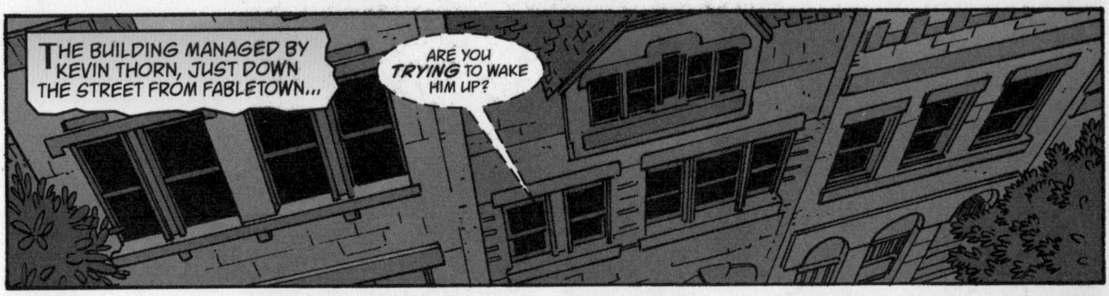
THE BUILDING MANAGED BY KEVIN THORN, JUST DOWN THE STREET FROM FABLETOWN...
ARE YOU TRYING TO WAKE HIM UP?

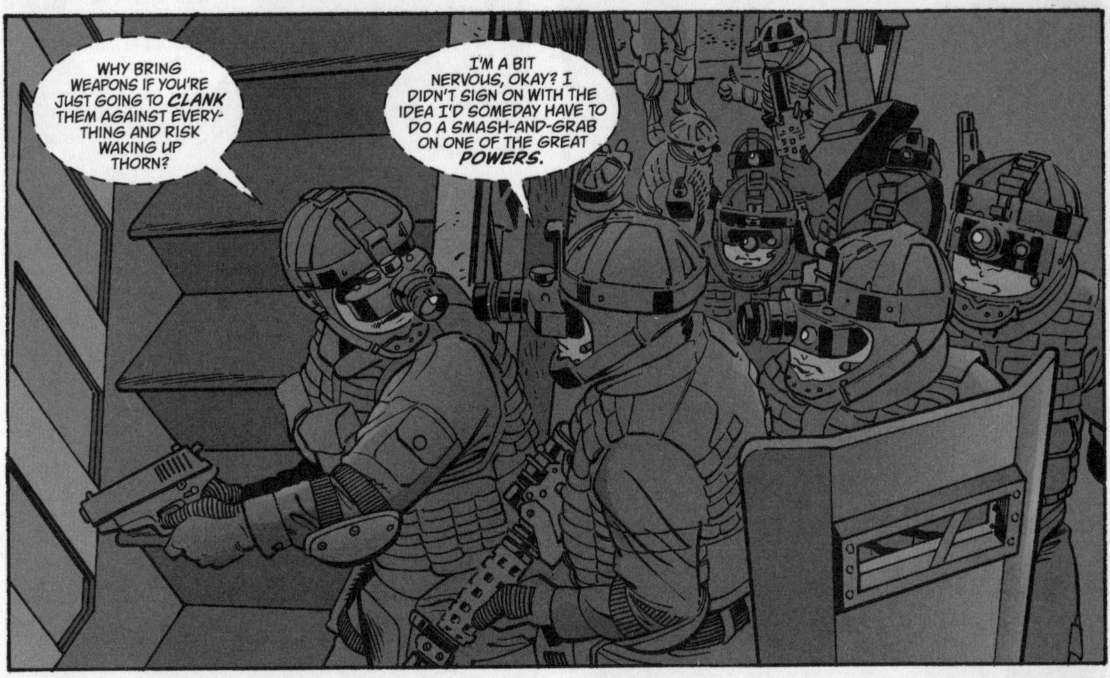
WHY BRING WEAPONS IF YOU'RE JUST GOING TO CLANK THEM AGAINST EVERYTHING AND RISK WAKING UP THORN?
I'M A BIT NERVOUS, OKAY? I DIDN'T SIGN ON WITH THE IDEA I'D SOMEDAY HAVE TO DO A SMASH-AND-GRAB ON ONE OF THE GREAT POWERS.

The Legend of Wicked John

— Part Three of THE BAD PRINCE —

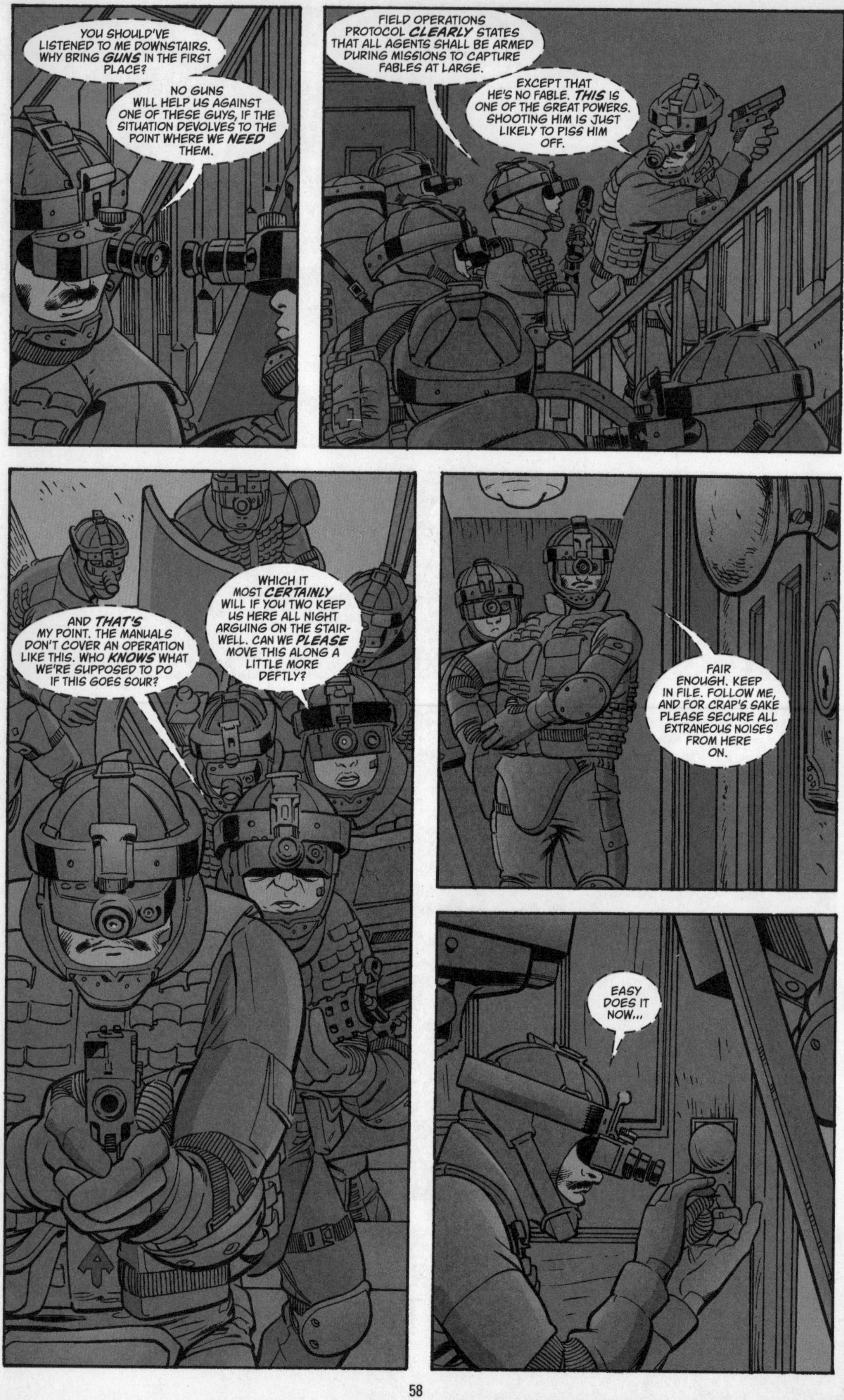
YOU SHOULD'VE LISTENED TO ME DOWNSTAIRS. WHY BRING GUNS IN THE FIRST PLACE?
NO GUNS WILL HELP US AGAINST ONE OF THESE GUYS, IF THE SITUATION DEVOLVES TO THE POINT WHERE WE NEED THEM.
FIELD OPERATIONS PROTOCOL CLEARLY STATES THAT ALL AGENTS SHALL BE ARMED DURING MISSIONS TO CAPTURE FABLES AT LARGE.
EXCEPT THAT HE'S NO FABLE. THIS IS ONE OF THE GREAT POWERS. SHOOTING HIM IS JUST LIKELY TO PISS HIM OFF.
AND THAT'S MY POINT. THE MANUALS DON'T COVER AN OPERATION LIKE THIS. WHO KNOWS WHAT WE'RE SUPPOSED TO DO IF THIS GOES SOUR?
WHICH IT MOST CERTAINLY WILL IF YOU TWO KEEP US HERE ALL NIGHT ARGUING ON THE STAIR-WELL. CAN WE PLEASE MOVE THIS ALONG A LITTLE MORE DEFTLY?
FAIR ENOUGH. KEEP IN FILE. FOLLOW ME, AND FOR CRAP'S SAKE PLEASE SECURE ALL EXTRANEOUS NOISES FROM HERE ON.
EASY DOES IT NOW...

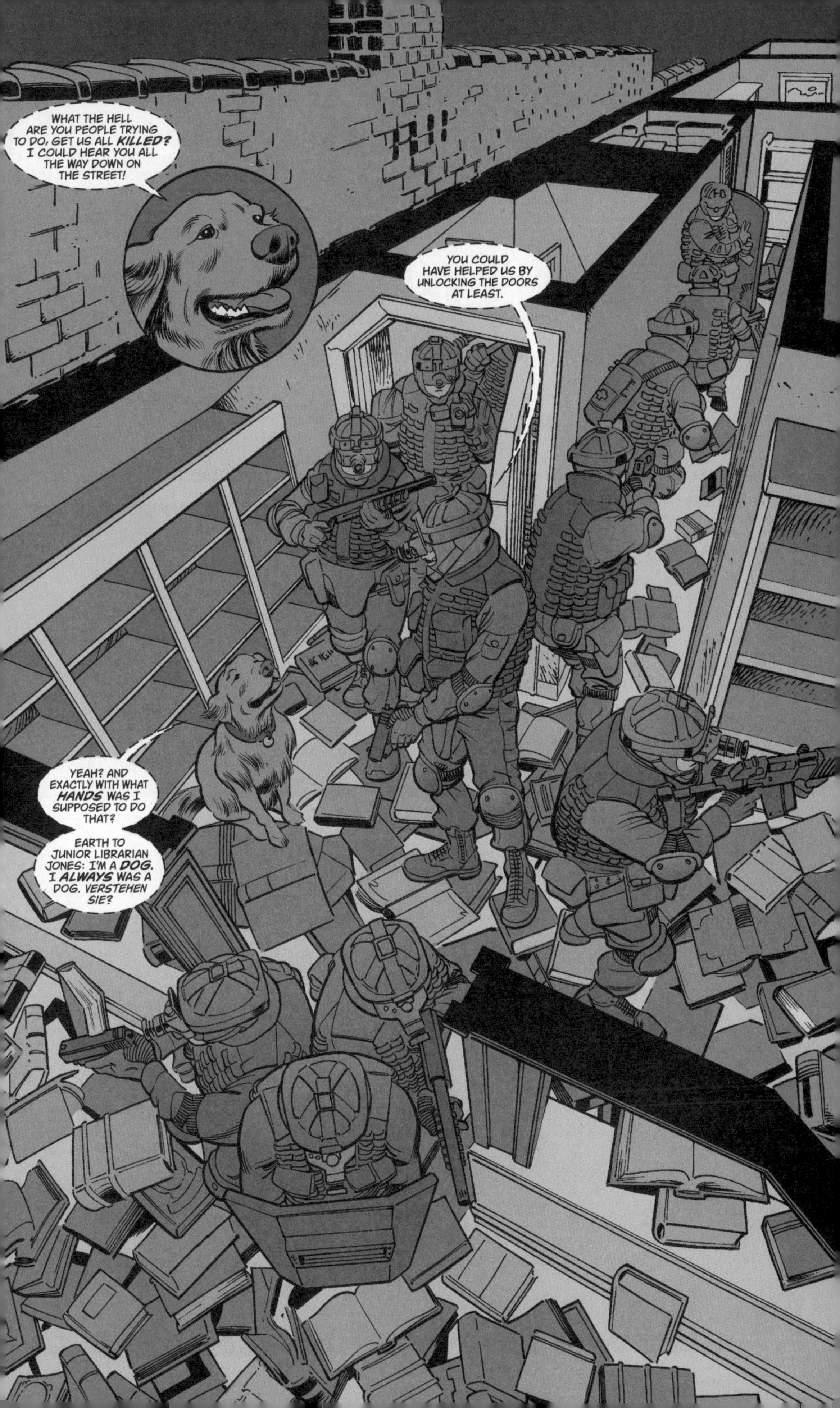
WHAT THE HELL ARE YOU PEOPLE TRYING TO DO, GET US ALL KILLED? I COULD HEAR YOU ALL THE WAY DOWN ON THE STREET!
YOU COULD HAVE HELPED US BY UNLOCKING THE DOORS AT LEAST.
YEAH? AND EXACTLY WITH WHAT HANDS WAS I SUPPOSED TO DO THAT?
EARTH TO JUNIOR LIBRARIAN JONES: I'M A DOG. I ALWAYS WAS A DOG. VERSTEHEN SIE?

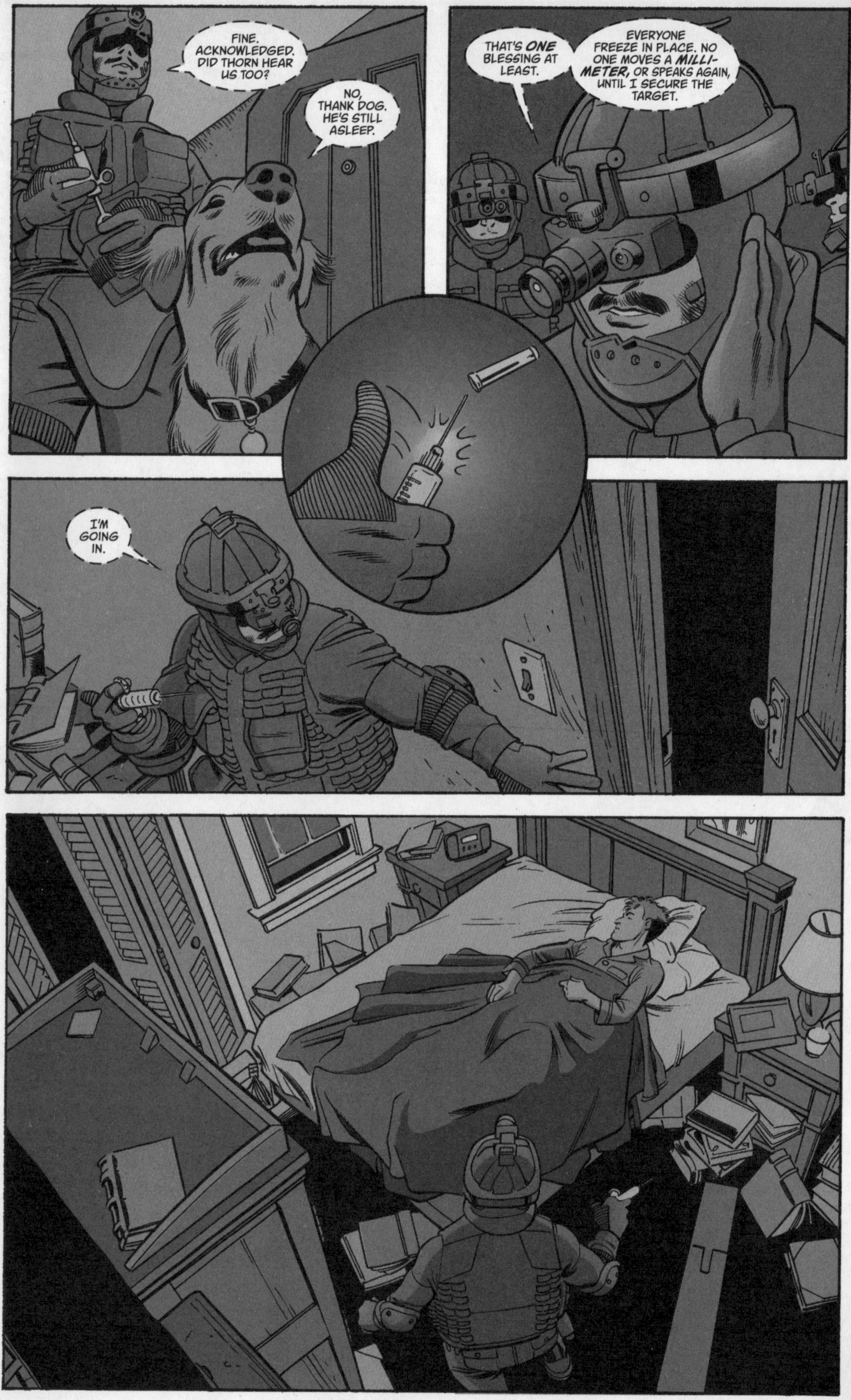
FINE. ACKNOWLEDGED. DID THORN HEAR US TOO?
NO, THANK DOG. HE'S STILL ASLEEP.
THAT'S **ONE** BLESSING AT LEAST.
EVERYONE FREEZE IN PLACE. NO ONE MOVES A ***MILLI-METER,*** OR SPEAKS AGAIN, UNTIL I SECURE THE TARGET.
I'M GOING IN.

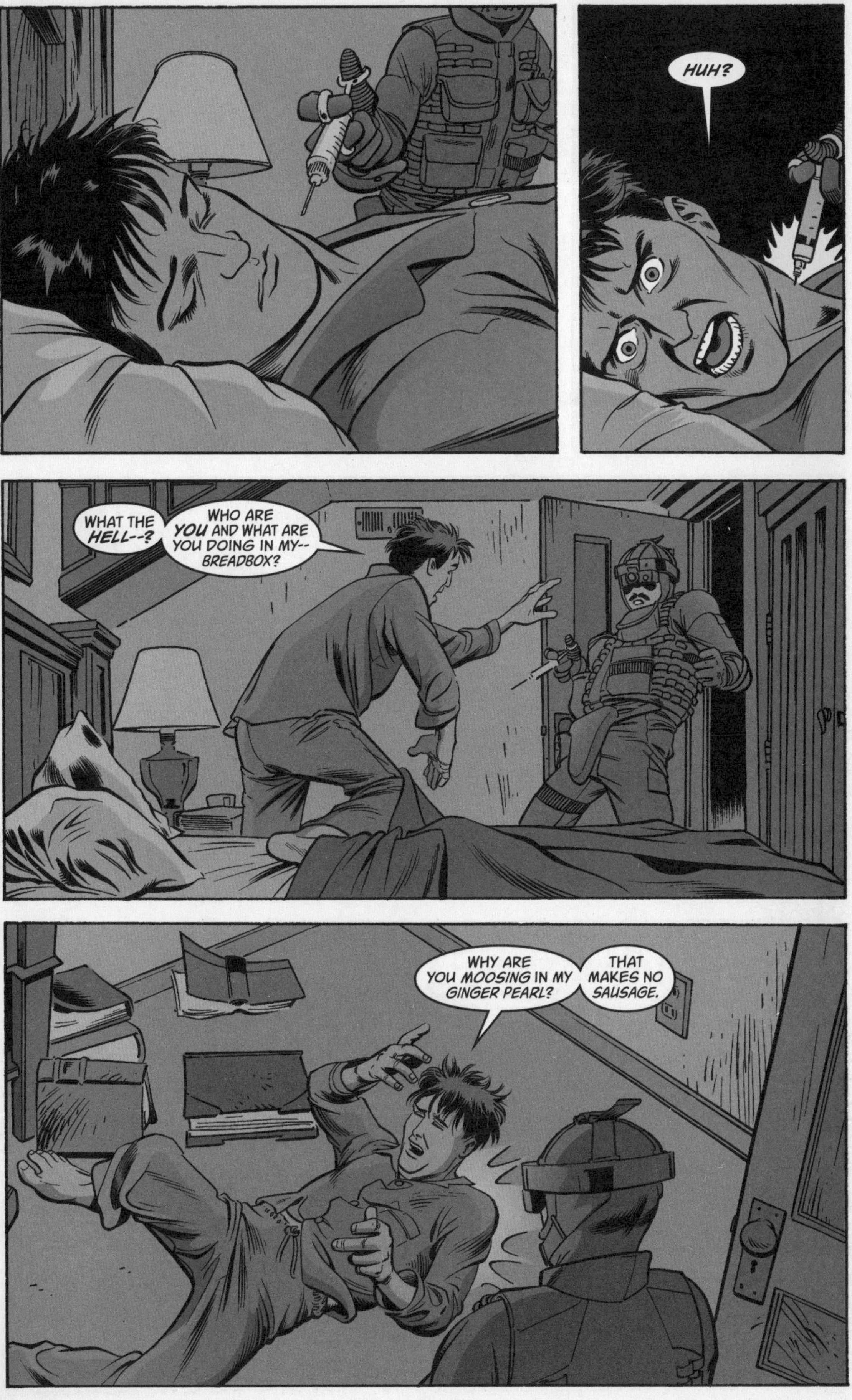
HUH?
WHAT THE HELL--?
WHO ARE YOU AND WHAT ARE YOU DOING IN MY-- BREADBOX?
WHY ARE YOU MOOSING IN MY GINGER PEARL?
THAT MAKES NO SAUSAGE.

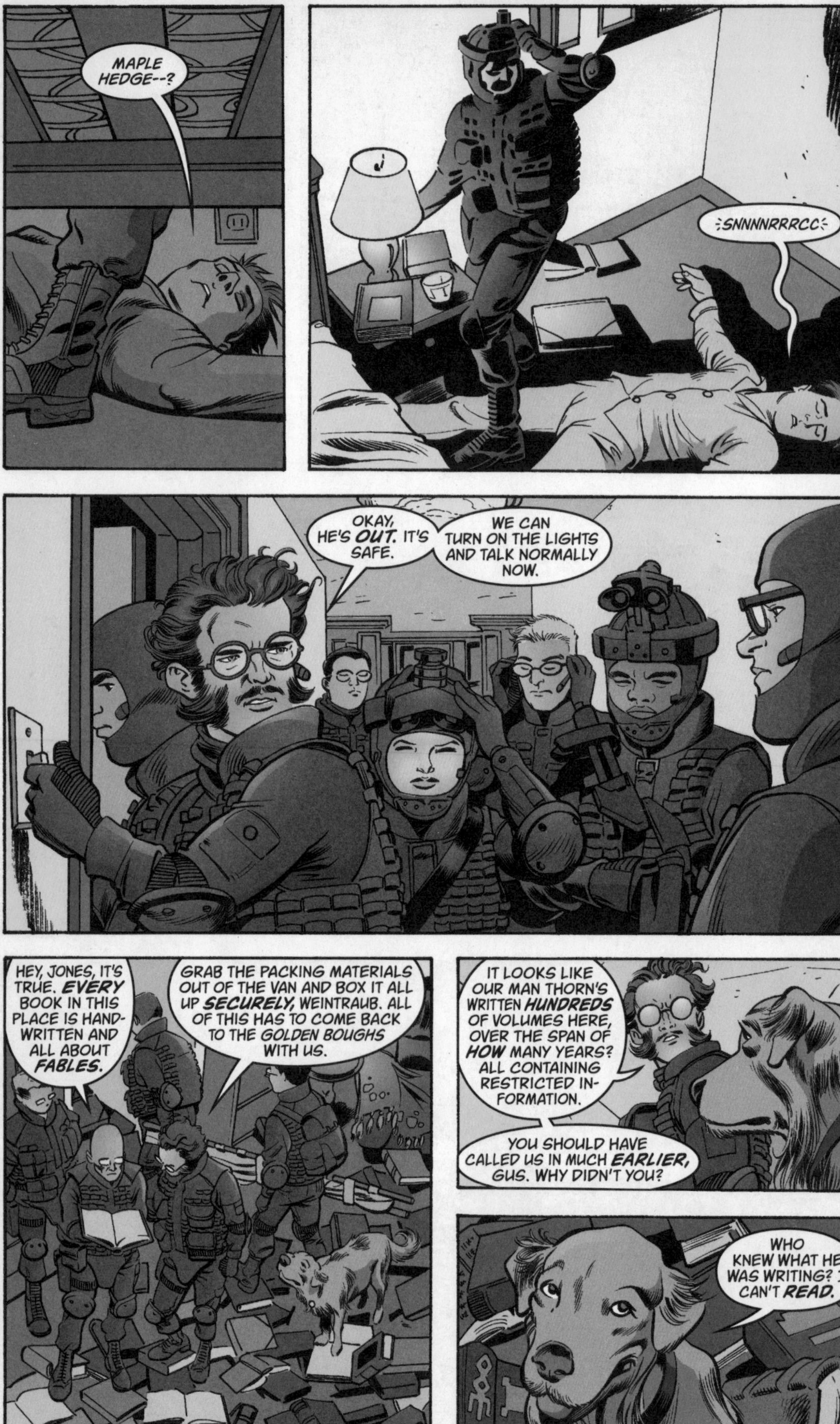
MAPLE HEDGE--?
SNNNNRRRCC
OKAY, HE'S OUT. IT'S SAFE.
WE CAN TURN ON THE LIGHTS AND TALK NORMALLY NOW.
HEY, JONES, IT'S TRUE. EVERY BOOK IN THIS PLACE IS HAND-WRITTEN AND ALL ABOUT FABLES.
GRAB THE PACKING MATERIALS OUT OF THE VAN AND BOX IT ALL UP SECURELY, WEINTRAUB. ALL OF THIS HAS TO COME BACK TO THE GOLDEN BOUGHS WITH US.
IT LOOKS LIKE OUR MAN THORN'S WRITTEN HUNDREDS OF VOLUMES HERE, OVER THE SPAN OF HOW MANY YEARS? ALL CONTAINING RESTRICTED IN-FORMATION.
YOU SHOULD HAVE CALLED US IN MUCH EARLIER, GUS. WHY DIDN'T YOU?
WHO KNEW WHAT HE WAS WRITING? I CAN'T READ.

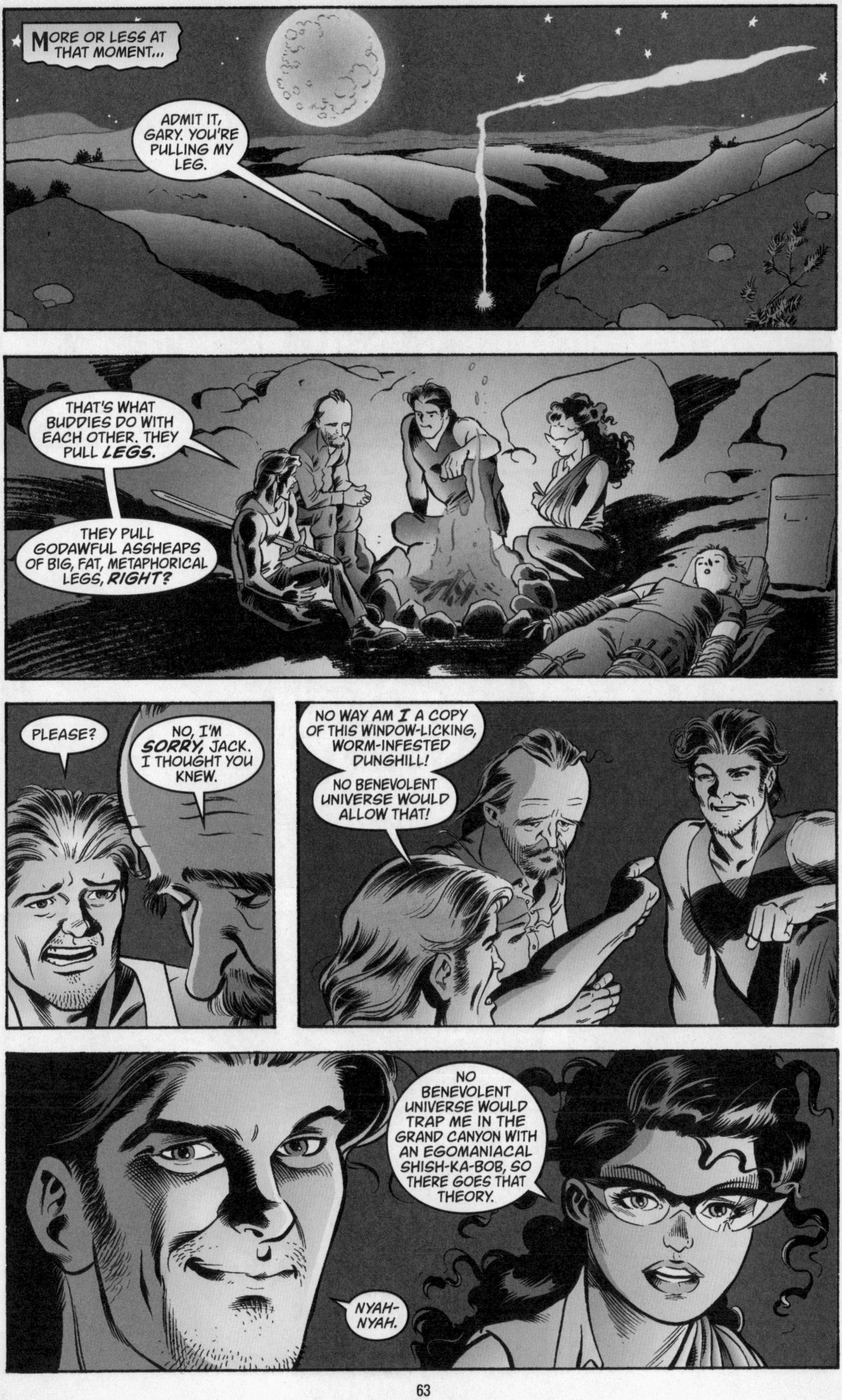
MORE OR LESS AT THAT MOMENT...
ADMIT IT, GARY. YOU'RE PULLING MY LEG.
THAT'S WHAT BUDDIES DO WITH EACH OTHER. THEY PULL LEGS.
THEY PULL GODAWFUL ASSHEAPS OF BIG, FAT, METAPHORICAL LEGS, RIGHT?
PLEASE?
NO, I'M SORRY, JACK. I THOUGHT YOU KNEW.
NO WAY AM I A COPY OF THIS WINDOW-LICKING, WORM-INFESTED DUNGHILL!
NO BENEVOLENT UNIVERSE WOULD ALLOW THAT!
NO BENEVOLENT UNIVERSE WOULD TRAP ME IN THE GRAND CANYON WITH AN EGOMANIACAL SHISH-KA-BOB, SO THERE GOES THAT THEORY.
NYAH-NYAH.

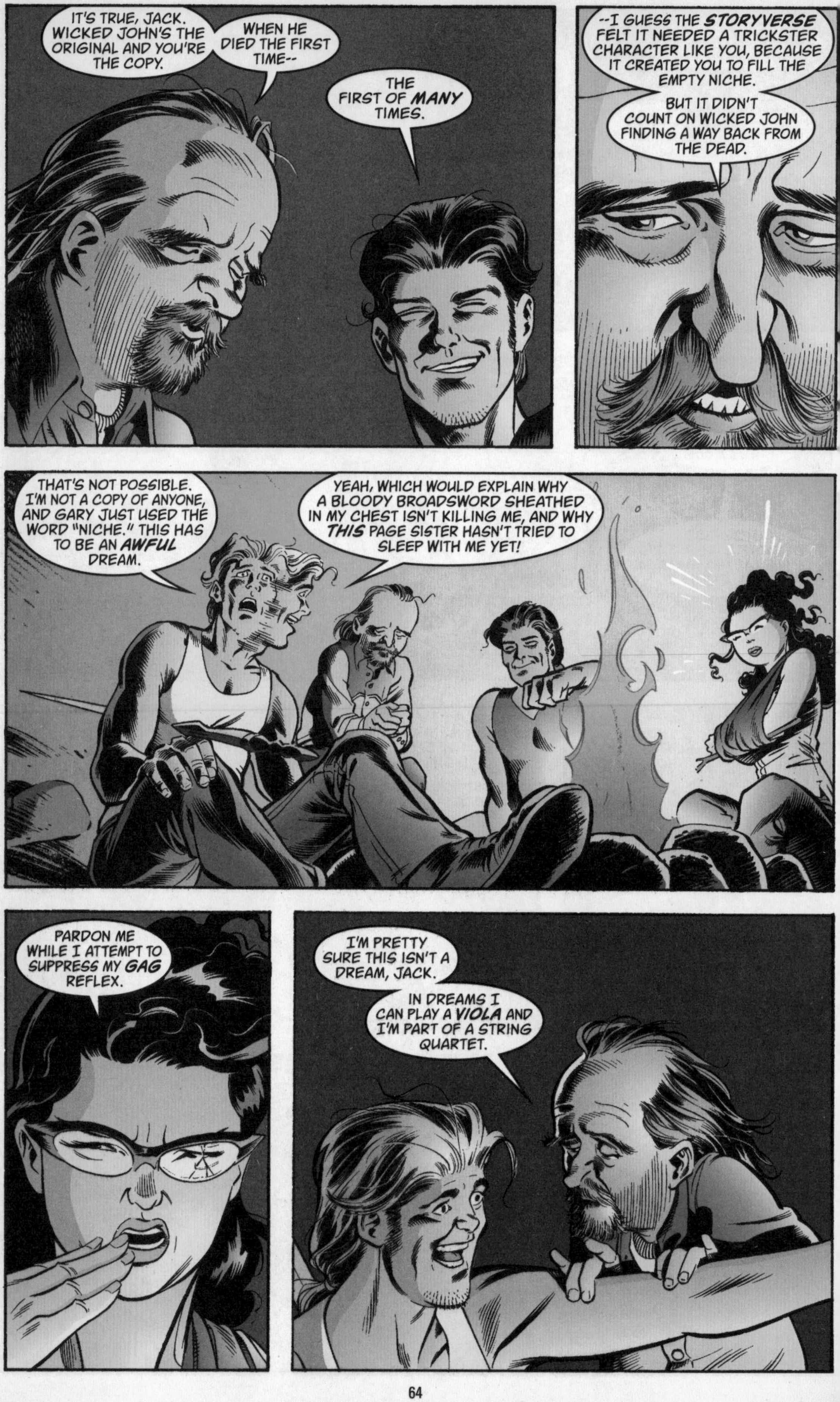
IT'S TRUE, JACK. WICKED JOHN'S THE ORIGINAL AND YOU'RE THE COPY.
WHEN HE DIED THE FIRST TIME--
THE FIRST OF MANY TIMES.
--I GUESS THE STORYVERSE FELT IT NEEDED A TRICKSTER CHARACTER LIKE YOU, BECAUSE IT CREATED YOU TO FILL THE EMPTY NICHE.
BUT IT DIDN'T COUNT ON WICKED JOHN FINDING A WAY BACK FROM THE DEAD.
THAT'S NOT POSSIBLE. I'M NOT A COPY OF ANYONE, AND GARY JUST USED THE WORD "NICHE." THIS HAS TO BE AN AWFUL DREAM.
YEAH, WHICH WOULD EXPLAIN WHY A BLOODY BROADSWORD SHEATHED IN MY CHEST ISN'T KILLING ME, AND WHY THIS PAGE SISTER HASN'T TRIED TO SLEEP WITH ME YET!
PARDON ME WHILE I ATTEMPT TO SUPPRESS MY GAG REFLEX.
I'M PRETTY SURE THIS ISN'T A DREAM, JACK.
IN DREAMS I CAN PLAY A VIOLA AND I'M PART OF A STRING QUARTET.

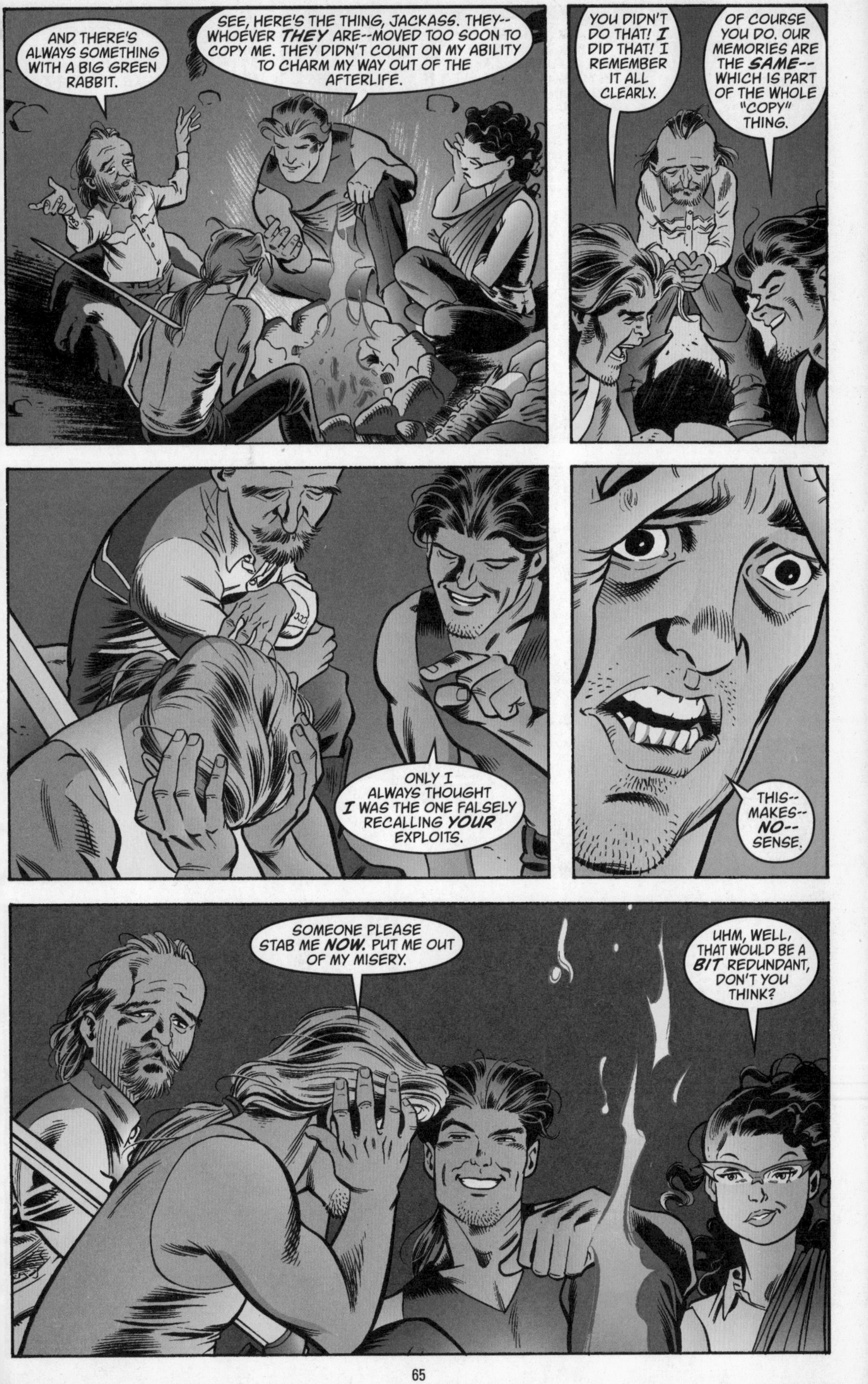
AND THERE'S ALWAYS SOMETHING WITH A BIG GREEN RABBIT.
SEE, HERE'S THE THING, JACKASS. THEY-- WHOEVER THEY ARE--MOVED TOO SOON TO COPY ME. THEY DIDN'T COUNT ON MY ABILITY TO CHARM MY WAY OUT OF THE AFTERLIFE.
YOU DIDN'T DO THAT! I DID THAT! I REMEMBER IT ALL CLEARLY.
OF COURSE YOU DO. OUR MEMORIES ARE THE SAME-- WHICH IS PART OF THE WHOLE "COPY" THING.
ONLY I ALWAYS THOUGHT I WAS THE ONE FALSELY RECALLING YOUR EXPLOITS.
THIS-- MAKES-- NO-- SENSE.
SOMEONE PLEASE STAB ME NOW. PUT ME OUT OF MY MISERY.
UHM, WELL, THAT WOULD BE A BIT REDUNDANT, DON'T YOU THINK?

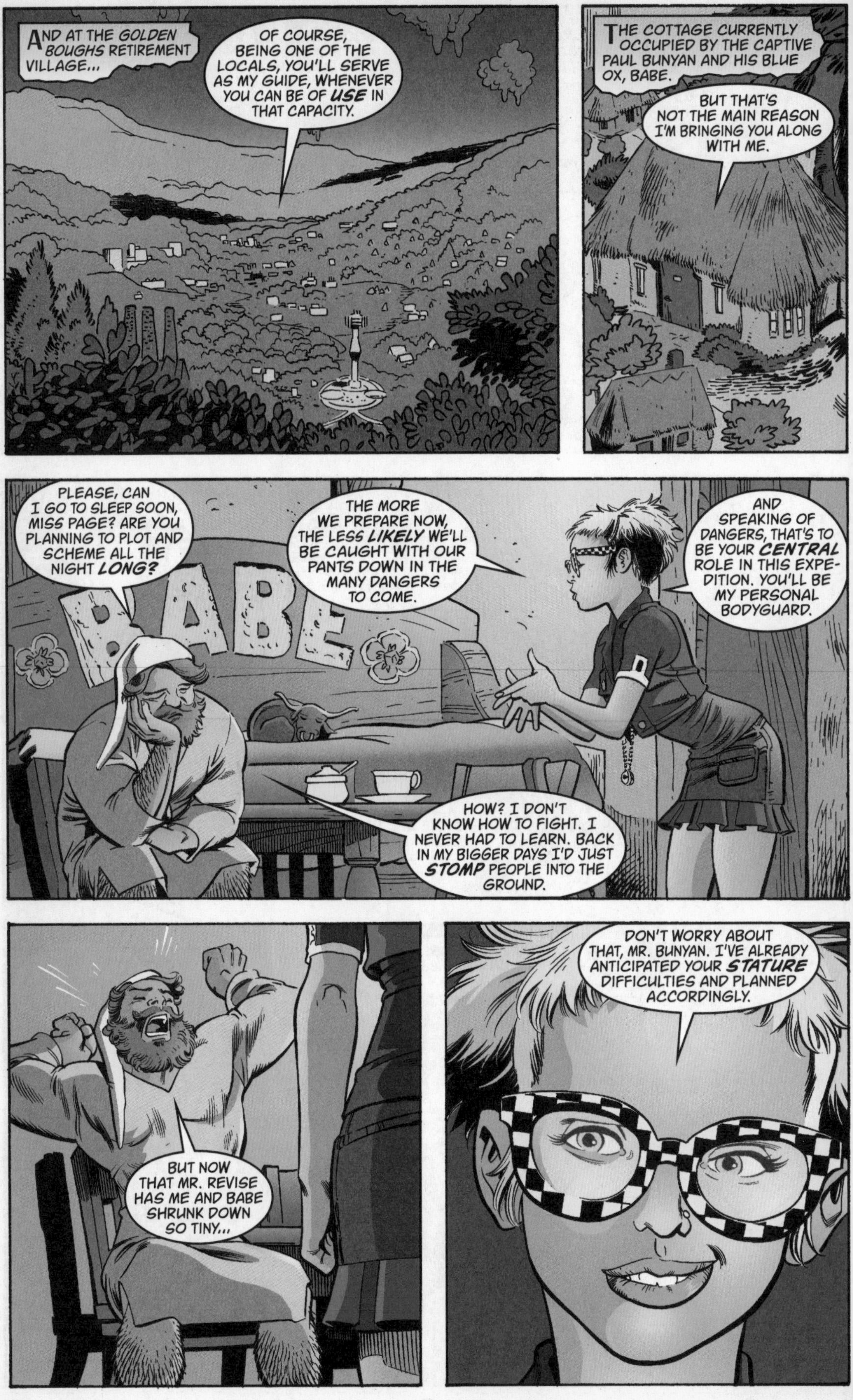
AND AT THE GOLDEN BOUGHS RETIREMENT VILLAGE...
OF COURSE, BEING ONE OF THE LOCALS, YOU'LL SERVE AS MY GUIDE, WHENEVER YOU CAN BE OF USE IN THAT CAPACITY.
THE COTTAGE CURRENTLY OCCUPIED BY THE CAPTIVE PAUL BUNYAN AND HIS BLUE OX, BABE.
BUT THAT'S NOT THE MAIN REASON I'M BRINGING YOU ALONG WITH ME.
PLEASE, CAN I GO TO SLEEP SOON, MISS PAGE? ARE YOU PLANNING TO PLOT AND SCHEME ALL THE NIGHT LONG?
THE MORE WE PREPARE NOW, THE LESS LIKELY WE'LL BE CAUGHT WITH OUR PANTS DOWN IN THE MANY DANGERS TO COME.
AND SPEAKING OF DANGERS, THAT'S TO BE YOUR CENTRAL ROLE IN THIS EXPEDITION. YOU'LL BE MY PERSONAL BODYGUARD.
BABE
HOW? I DON'T KNOW HOW TO FIGHT. I NEVER HAD TO LEARN. BACK IN MY BIGGER DAYS I'D JUST STOMP PEOPLE INTO THE GROUND.
BUT NOW THAT MR. REVISE HAS ME AND BABE SHRUNK DOWN SO TINY...
DON'T WORRY ABOUT THAT, MR. BUNYAN. I'VE ALREADY ANTICIPATED YOUR STATURE DIFFICULTIES AND PLANNED ACCORDINGLY.

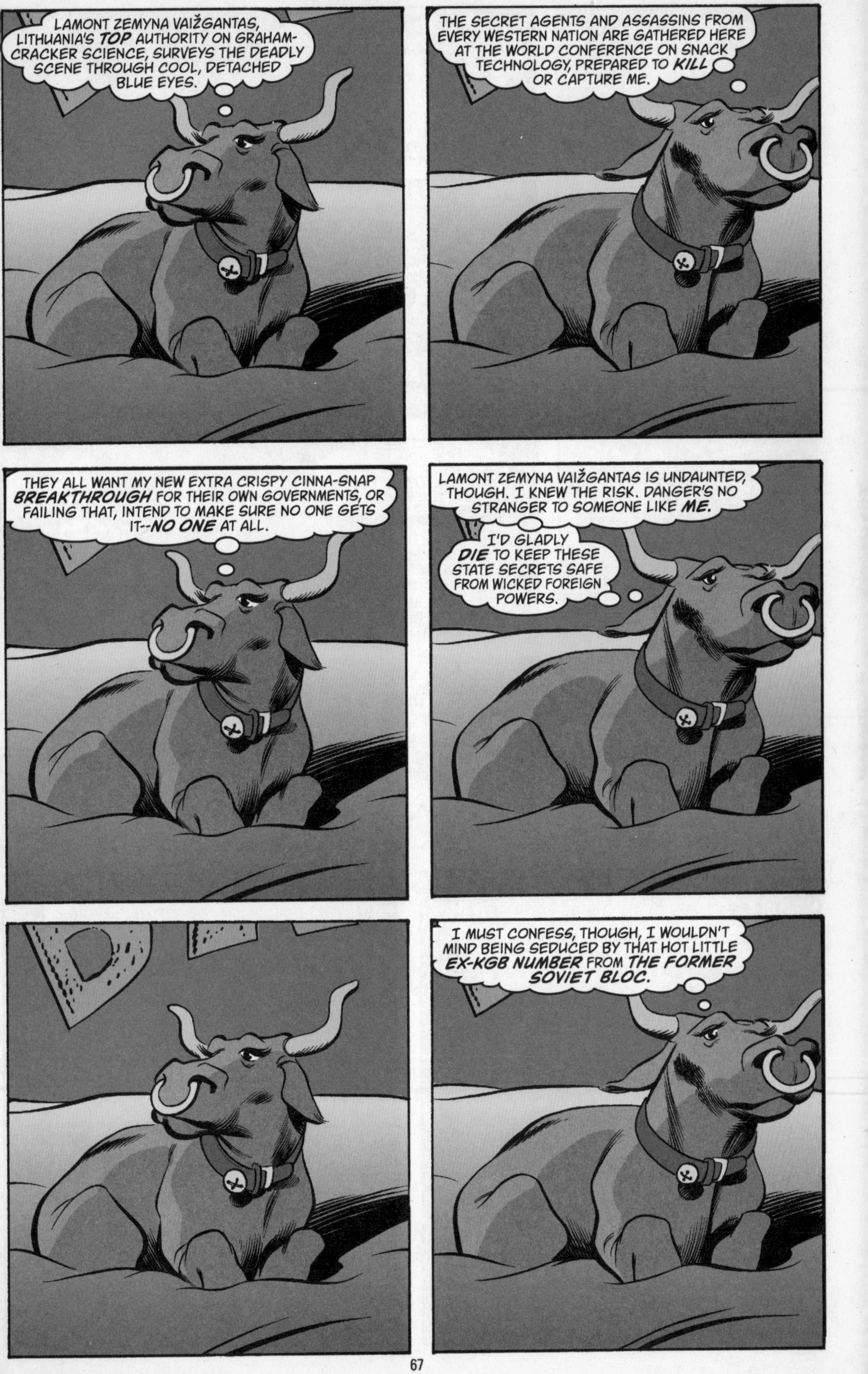
LAMONT ZEMYNA VAIŽGANTAS, LITHUANIA'S TOP AUTHORITY ON GRAHAM-CRACKER SCIENCE, SURVEYS THE DEADLY SCENE THROUGH COOL, DETACHED BLUE EYES.
THE SECRET AGENTS AND ASSASSINS FROM EVERY WESTERN NATION ARE GATHERED HERE AT THE WORLD CONFERENCE ON SNACK TECHNOLOGY, PREPARED TO KILL OR CAPTURE ME.
THEY ALL WANT MY NEW EXTRA CRISPY CINNA-SNAP BREAKTHROUGH FOR THEIR OWN GOVERNMENTS, OR FAILING THAT, INTEND TO MAKE SURE NO ONE GETS IT--NO ONE AT ALL.
LAMONT ZEMYNA VAIŽGANTAS IS UNDAUNTED, THOUGH. I KNEW THE RISK. DANGER'S NO STRANGER TO SOMEONE LIKE ME.
I'D GLADLY DIE TO KEEP THESE STATE SECRETS SAFE FROM WICKED FOREIGN POWERS.
I MUST CONFESS, THOUGH, I WOULDN'T MIND BEING SEDUCED BY THAT HOT LITTLE EX-KGB NUMBER FROM THE FORMER SOVIET BLOC.

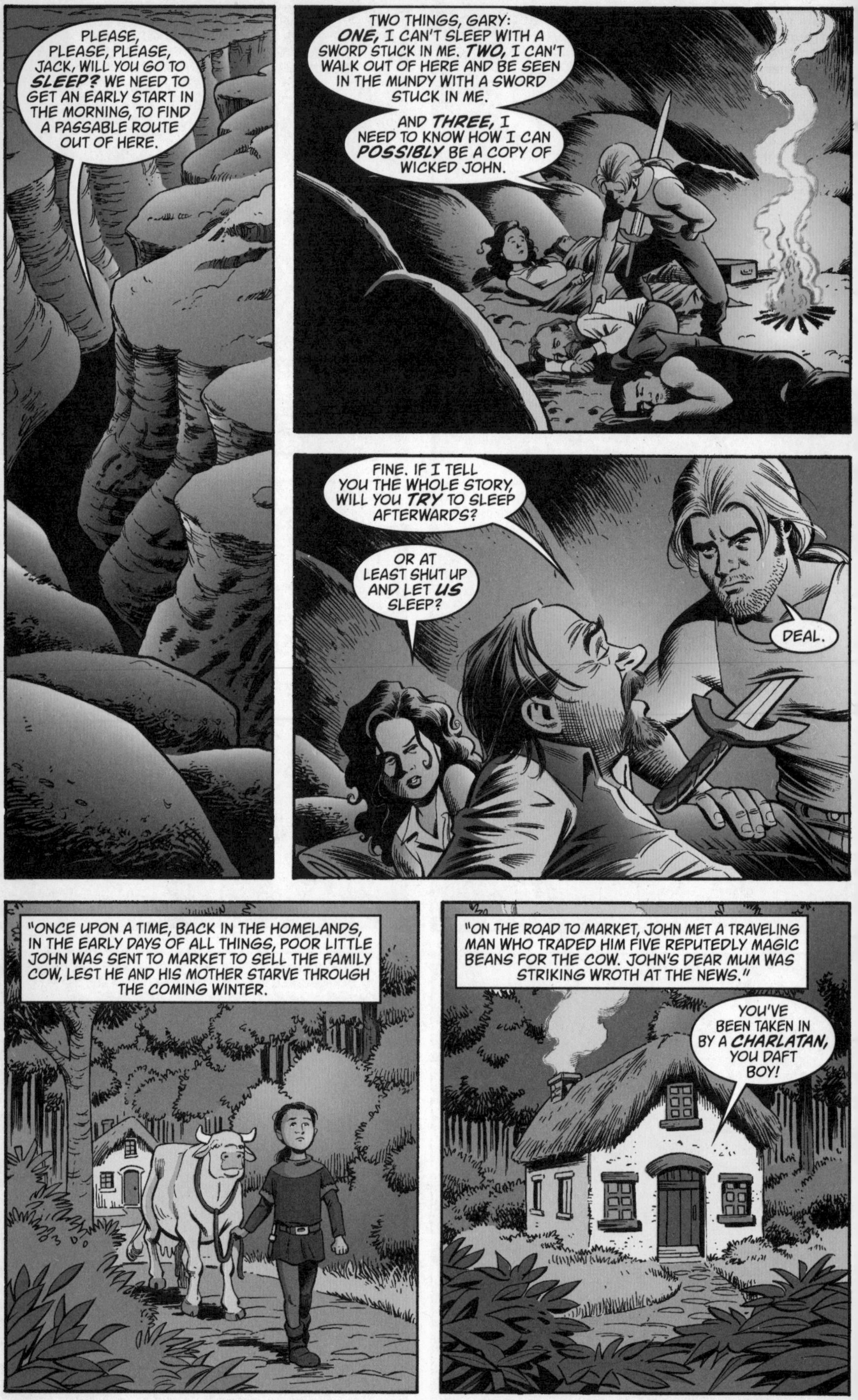
PLEASE, PLEASE, PLEASE, JACK, WILL YOU GO TO SLEEP? WE NEED TO GET AN EARLY START IN THE MORNING, TO FIND A PASSABLE ROUTE OUT OF HERE.
TWO THINGS, GARY: ONE, I CAN'T SLEEP WITH A SWORD STUCK IN ME. TWO, I CAN'T WALK OUT OF HERE AND BE SEEN IN THE MUNDY WITH A SWORD STUCK IN ME.
AND THREE, I NEED TO KNOW HOW I CAN POSSIBLY BE A COPY OF WICKED JOHN.
FINE. IF I TELL YOU THE WHOLE STORY, WILL YOU TRY TO SLEEP AFTERWARDS?
OR AT LEAST SHUT UP AND LET US SLEEP?
DEAL.
"ONCE UPON A TIME, BACK IN THE HOMELANDS, IN THE EARLY DAYS OF ALL THINGS, POOR LITTLE JOHN WAS SENT TO MARKET TO SELL THE FAMILY COW, LEST HE AND HIS MOTHER STARVE THROUGH THE COMING WINTER.
"ON THE ROAD TO MARKET, JOHN MET A TRAVELING MAN WHO TRADED HIM FIVE REPUTEDLY MAGIC BEANS FOR THE COW. JOHN'S DEAR MUM WAS STRIKING WROTH AT THE NEWS."
YOU'VE BEEN TAKEN IN BY A CHARLATAN, YOU DAFT BOY!

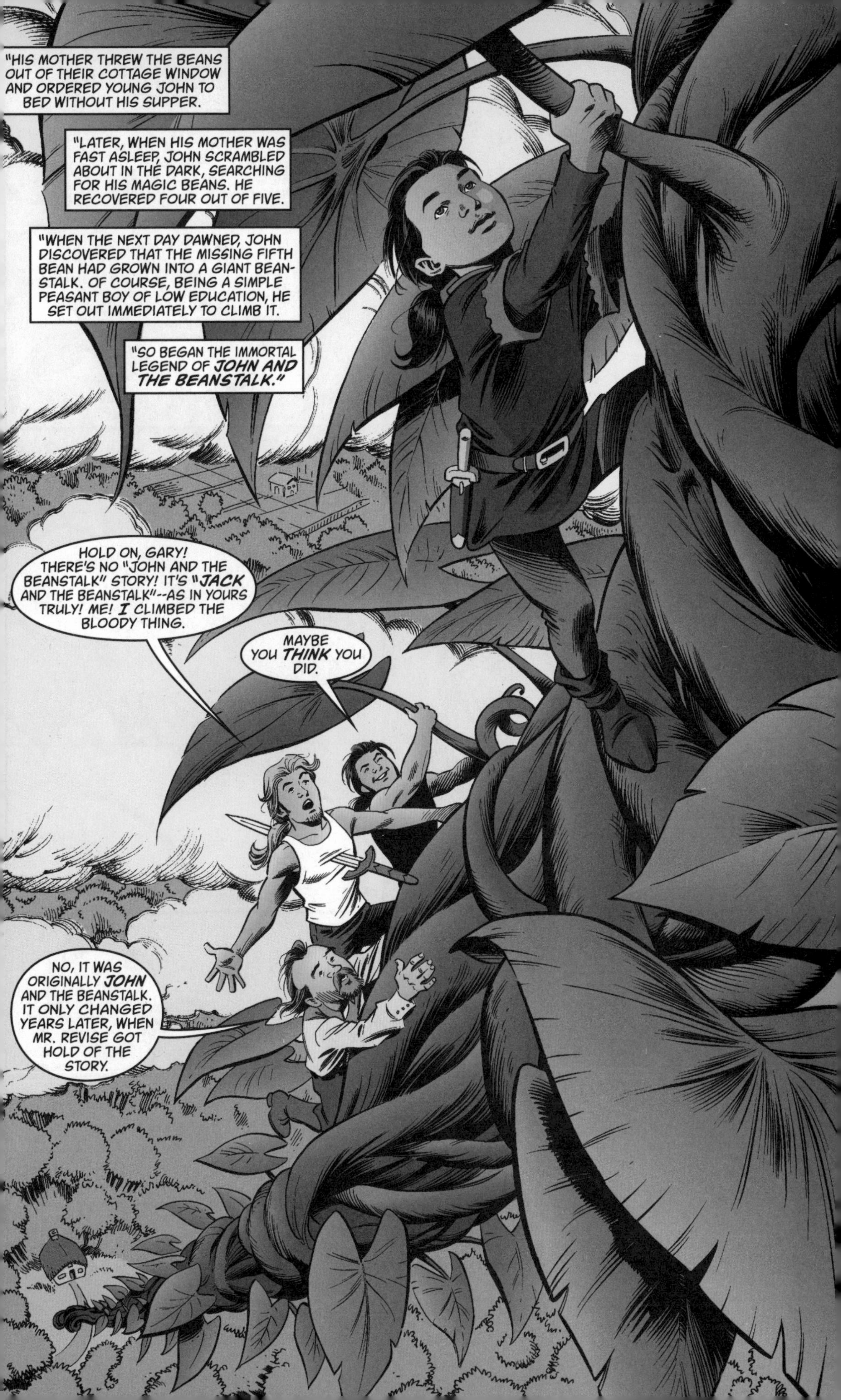
"HIS MOTHER THREW THE BEANS OUT OF THEIR COTTAGE WINDOW AND ORDERED YOUNG JOHN TO BED WITHOUT HIS SUPPER.
"LATER, WHEN HIS MOTHER WAS FAST ASLEEP, JOHN SCRAMBLED ABOUT IN THE DARK, SEARCHING FOR HIS MAGIC BEANS. HE RECOVERED FOUR OUT OF FIVE.
"WHEN THE NEXT DAY DAWNED, JOHN DISCOVERED THAT THE MISSING FIFTH BEAN HAD GROWN INTO A GIANT BEAN-STALK. OF COURSE, BEING A SIMPLE PEASANT BOY OF LOW EDUCATION, HE SET OUT IMMEDIATELY TO CLIMB IT.
"SO BEGAN THE IMMORTAL LEGEND OF ***JOHN AND THE BEANSTALK.***"
HOLD ON, GARY! THERE'S NO "JOHN AND THE BEANSTALK" STORY! IT'S "***JACK*** AND THE BEANSTALK"--AS IN YOURS TRULY! ME! ***I*** CLIMBED THE BLOODY THING.
MAYBE YOU ***THINK*** YOU DID.
NO, IT WAS ORIGINALLY ***JOHN*** AND THE BEANSTALK. IT ONLY CHANGED YEARS LATER, WHEN MR. REVISE GOT HOLD OF THE STORY.

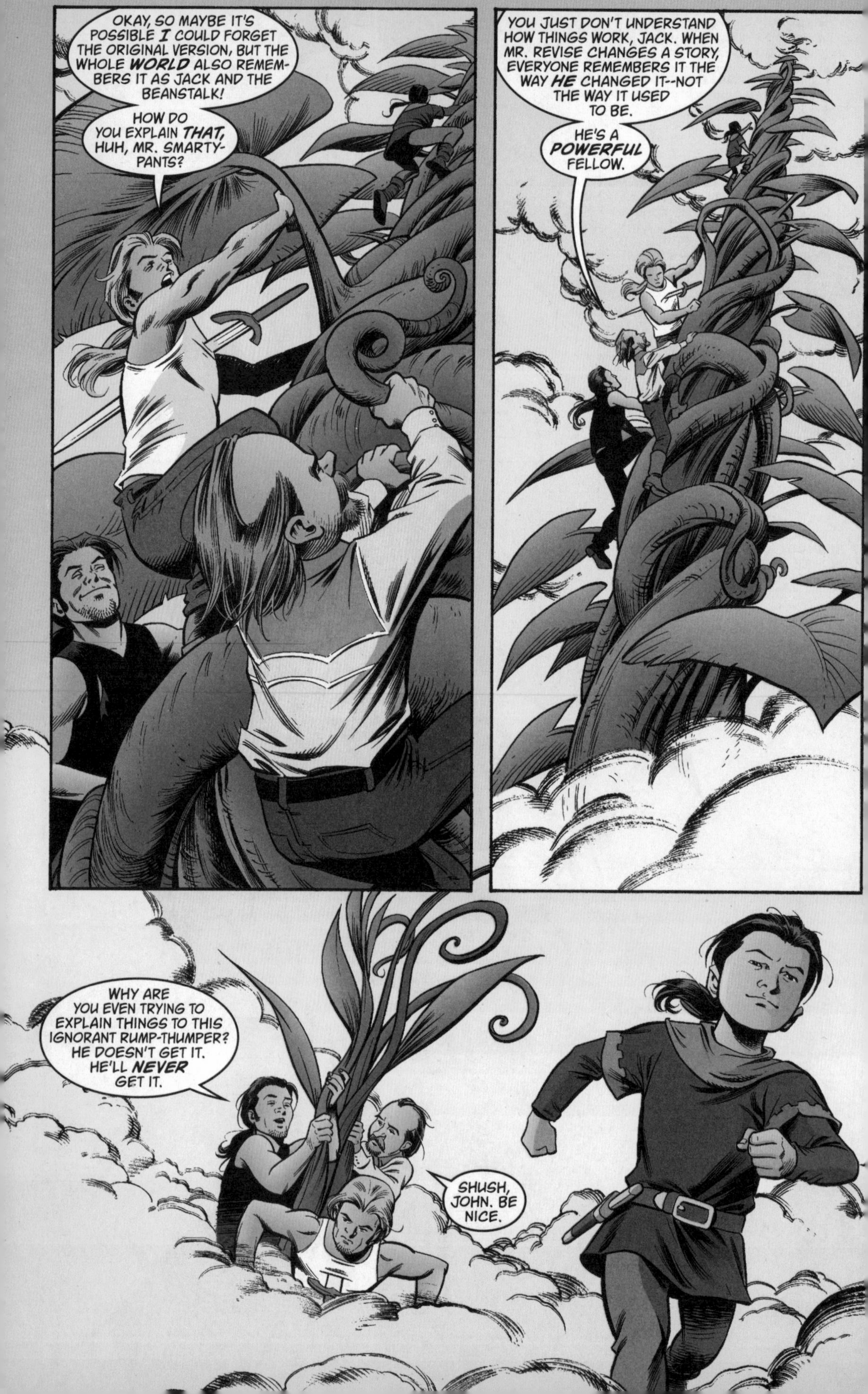
OKAY, SO MAYBE IT'S POSSIBLE *I* COULD FORGET THE ORIGINAL VERSION, BUT THE WHOLE *WORLD* ALSO REMEMBERS IT AS JACK AND THE BEANSTALK!
HOW DO YOU EXPLAIN *THAT,* HUH, MR. SMARTY-PANTS?
YOU JUST DON'T UNDERSTAND HOW THINGS WORK, JACK. WHEN MR. REVISE CHANGES A STORY, EVERYONE REMEMBERS IT THE WAY *HE* CHANGED IT--NOT THE WAY IT USED TO BE.
HE'S A *POWERFUL* FELLOW.
WHY ARE YOU EVEN TRYING TO EXPLAIN THINGS TO THIS IGNORANT RUMP-THUMPER? HE DOESN'T GET IT. HE'LL *NEVER* GET IT.
SHUSH, JOHN. BE NICE.

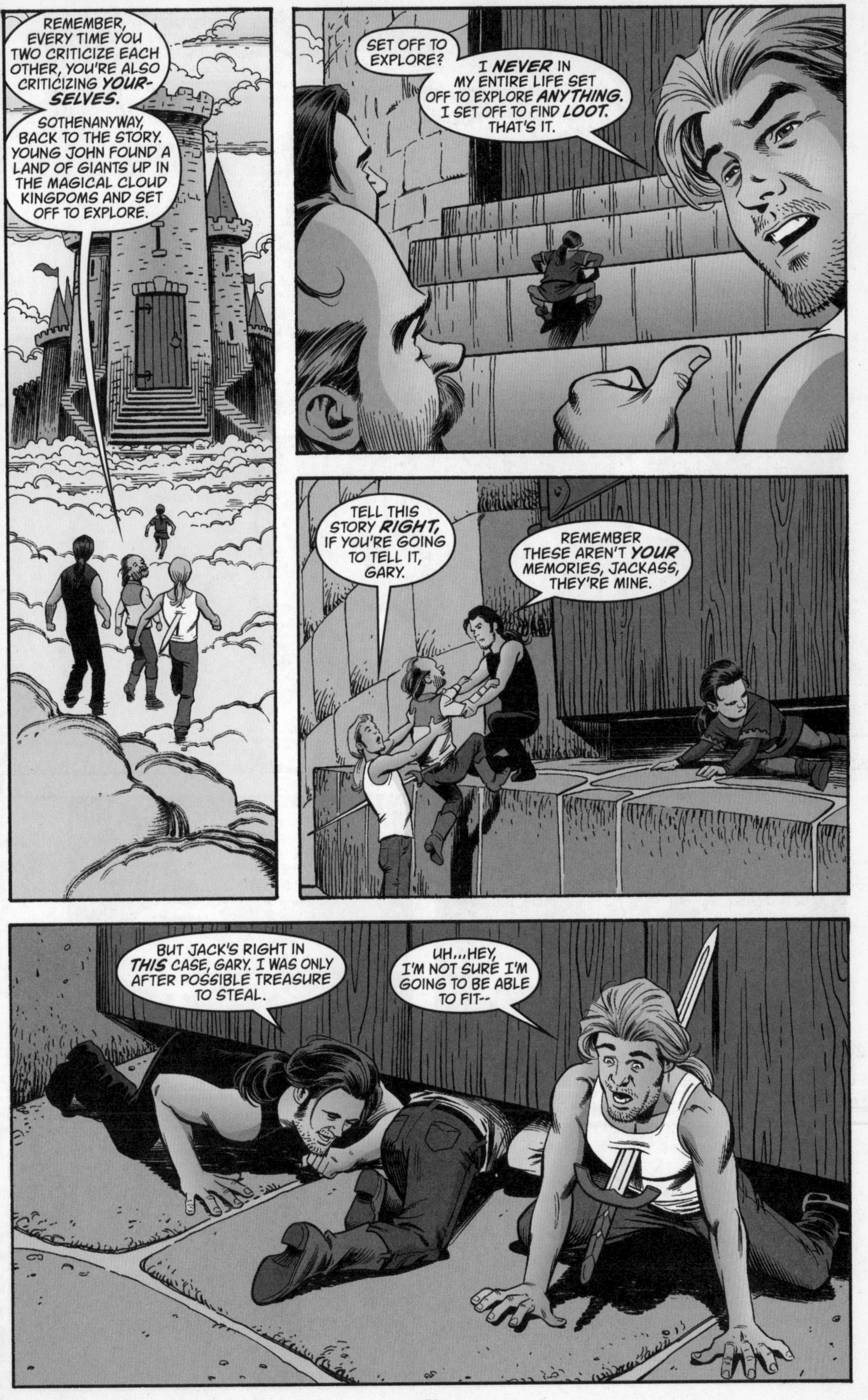
REMEMBER, EVERY TIME YOU TWO CRITICIZE EACH OTHER, YOU'RE ALSO CRITICIZING YOURSELVES.
SOTHENANYWAY, BACK TO THE STORY. YOUNG JOHN FOUND A LAND OF GIANTS UP IN THE MAGICAL CLOUD KINGDOMS AND SET OFF TO EXPLORE.
SET OFF TO EXPLORE?
I NEVER IN MY ENTIRE LIFE SET OFF TO EXPLORE ANYTHING. I SET OFF TO FIND LOOT. THAT'S IT.
TELL THIS STORY RIGHT, IF YOU'RE GOING TO TELL IT, GARY.
REMEMBER THESE AREN'T YOUR MEMORIES, JACKASS, THEY'RE MINE.
BUT JACK'S RIGHT IN THIS CASE, GARY. I WAS ONLY AFTER POSSIBLE TREASURE TO STEAL.
UH...HEY, I'M NOT SURE I'M GOING TO BE ABLE TO FIT--

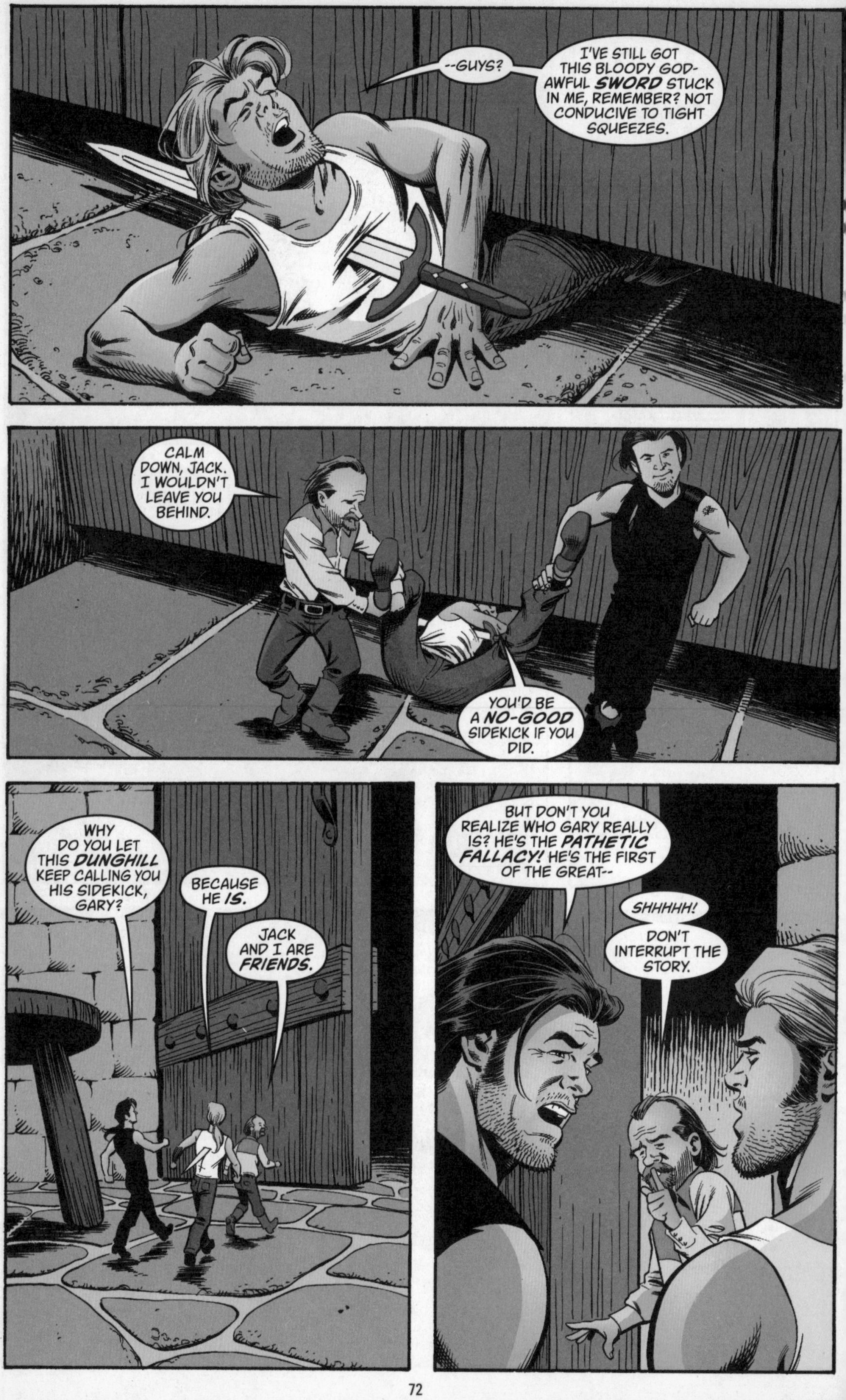
--GUYS?
I'VE STILL GOT THIS BLOODY GOD-AWFUL SWORD STUCK IN ME, REMEMBER? NOT CONDUCIVE TO TIGHT SQUEEZES.
CALM DOWN, JACK. I WOULDN'T LEAVE YOU BEHIND.
YOU'D BE A NO-GOOD SIDEKICK IF YOU DID.
WHY DO YOU LET THIS DUNGHILL KEEP CALLING YOU HIS SIDEKICK, GARY?
BECAUSE HE IS.
JACK AND I ARE FRIENDS.
BUT DON'T YOU REALIZE WHO GARY REALLY IS? HE'S THE PATHETIC FALLACY! HE'S THE FIRST OF THE GREAT--
SHHHHH!
DON'T INTERRUPT THE STORY.

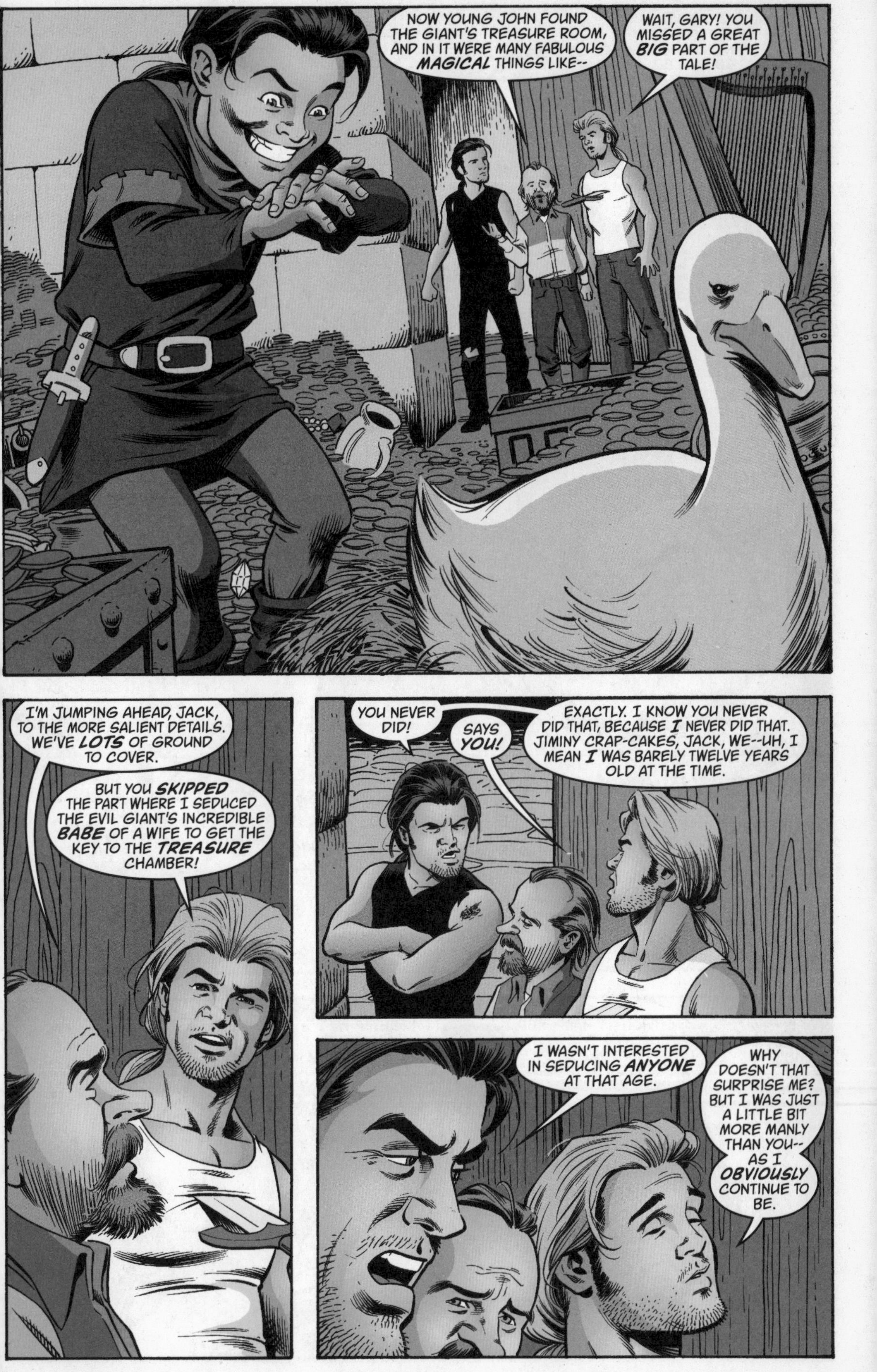
NOW YOUNG JOHN FOUND THE GIANT'S TREASURE ROOM, AND IN IT WERE MANY FABULOUS MAGICAL THINGS LIKE--
WAIT, GARY! YOU MISSED A GREAT BIG PART OF THE TALE!
I'M JUMPING AHEAD, JACK, TO THE MORE SALIENT DETAILS. WE'VE LOTS OF GROUND TO COVER.
BUT YOU SKIPPED THE PART WHERE I SEDUCED THE EVIL GIANT'S INCREDIBLE BABE OF A WIFE TO GET THE KEY TO THE TREASURE CHAMBER!
YOU NEVER DID!
SAYS YOU!
EXACTLY. I KNOW YOU NEVER DID THAT, BECAUSE I NEVER DID THAT. JIMINY CRAP-CAKES, JACK, WE--UH, I MEAN I WAS BARELY TWELVE YEARS OLD AT THE TIME.
I WASN'T INTERESTED IN SEDUCING ANYONE AT THAT AGE.
WHY DOESN'T THAT SURPRISE ME? BUT I WAS JUST A LITTLE BIT MORE MANLY THAN YOU-- AS I OBVIOUSLY CONTINUE TO BE.

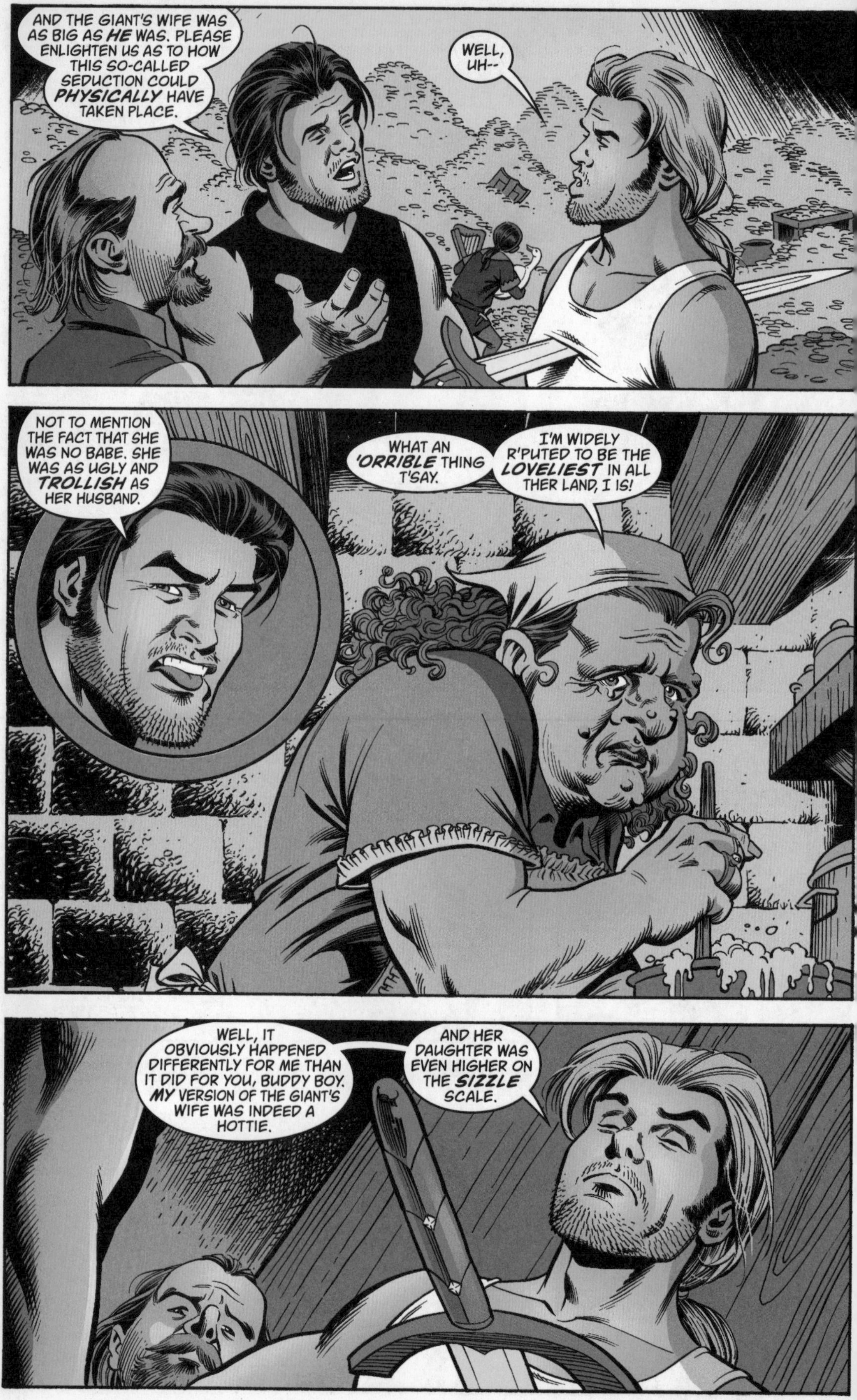
AND THE GIANT'S WIFE WAS AS BIG AS HE WAS. PLEASE ENLIGHTEN US AS TO HOW THIS SO-CALLED SEDUCTION COULD PHYSICALLY HAVE TAKEN PLACE.
WELL, UH--
NOT TO MENTION THE FACT THAT SHE WAS NO BABE. SHE WAS AS UGLY AND TROLLISH AS HER HUSBAND.
WHAT AN 'ORRIBLE THING T'SAY.
I'M WIDELY R'PUTED TO BE THE LOVELIEST IN ALL THEIR LAND, I IS!
WELL, IT OBVIOUSLY HAPPENED DIFFERENTLY FOR ME THAN IT DID FOR YOU, BUDDY BOY. MY VERSION OF THE GIANT'S WIFE WAS INDEED A HOTTIE.
AND HER DAUGHTER WAS EVEN HIGHER ON THE SIZZLE SCALE.

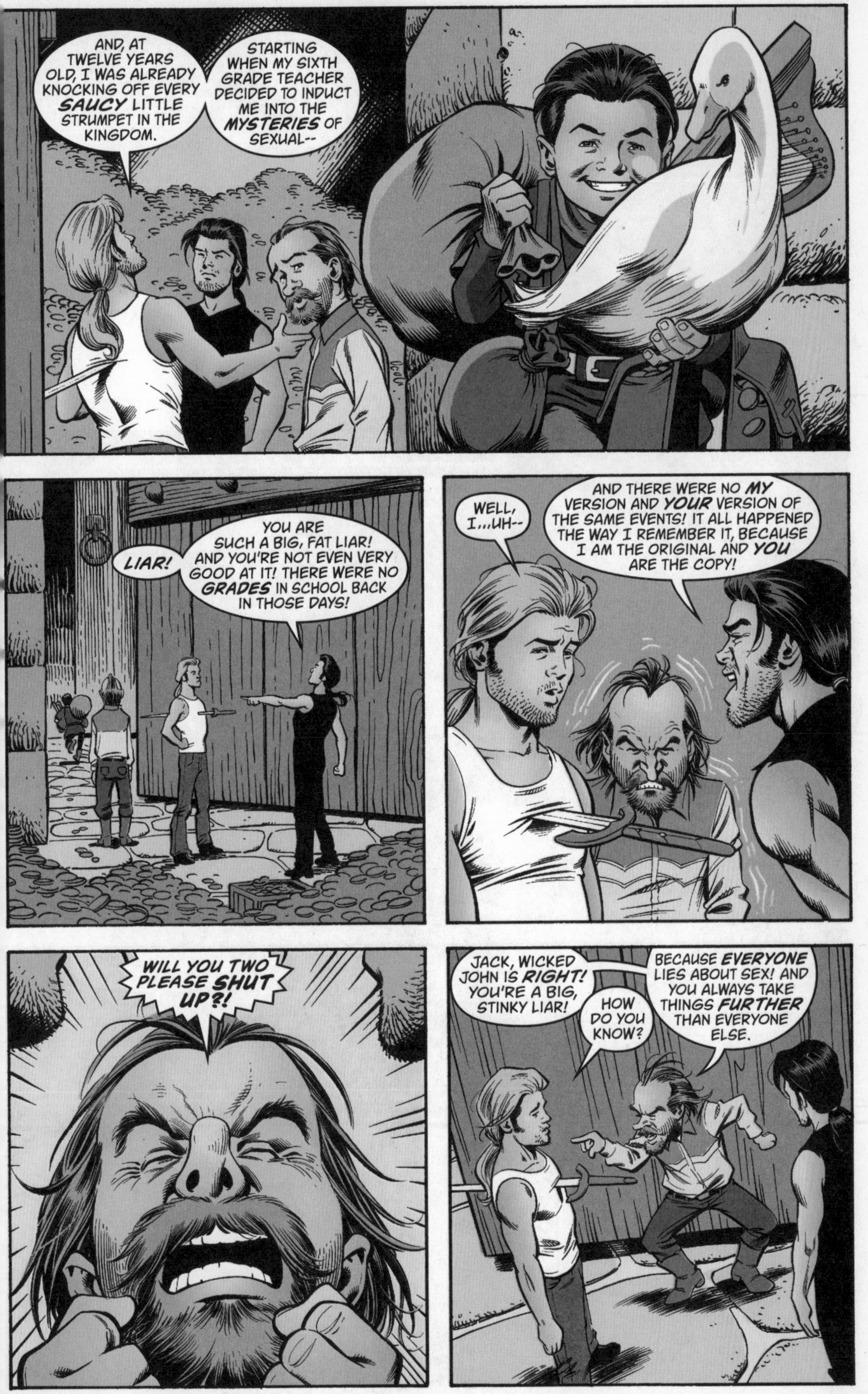
AND, AT TWELVE YEARS OLD, I WAS ALREADY KNOCKING OFF EVERY SAUCY LITTLE STRUMPET IN THE KINGDOM.
STARTING WHEN MY SIXTH GRADE TEACHER DECIDED TO INDUCT ME INTO THE MYSTERIES OF SEXUAL--
LIAR!
YOU ARE SUCH A BIG, FAT LIAR! AND YOU'RE NOT EVEN VERY GOOD AT IT! THERE WERE NO GRADES IN SCHOOL BACK IN THOSE DAYS!
WELL, I...UH--
AND THERE WERE NO MY VERSION AND YOUR VERSION OF THE SAME EVENTS! IT ALL HAPPENED THE WAY I REMEMBER IT, BECAUSE I AM THE ORIGINAL AND YOU ARE THE COPY!
WILL YOU TWO PLEASE SHUT UP?!
JACK, WICKED JOHN IS RIGHT! YOU'RE A BIG, STINKY LIAR!
HOW DO YOU KNOW?
BECAUSE EVERYONE LIES ABOUT SEX! AND YOU ALWAYS TAKE THINGS FURTHER THAN EVERYONE ELSE.

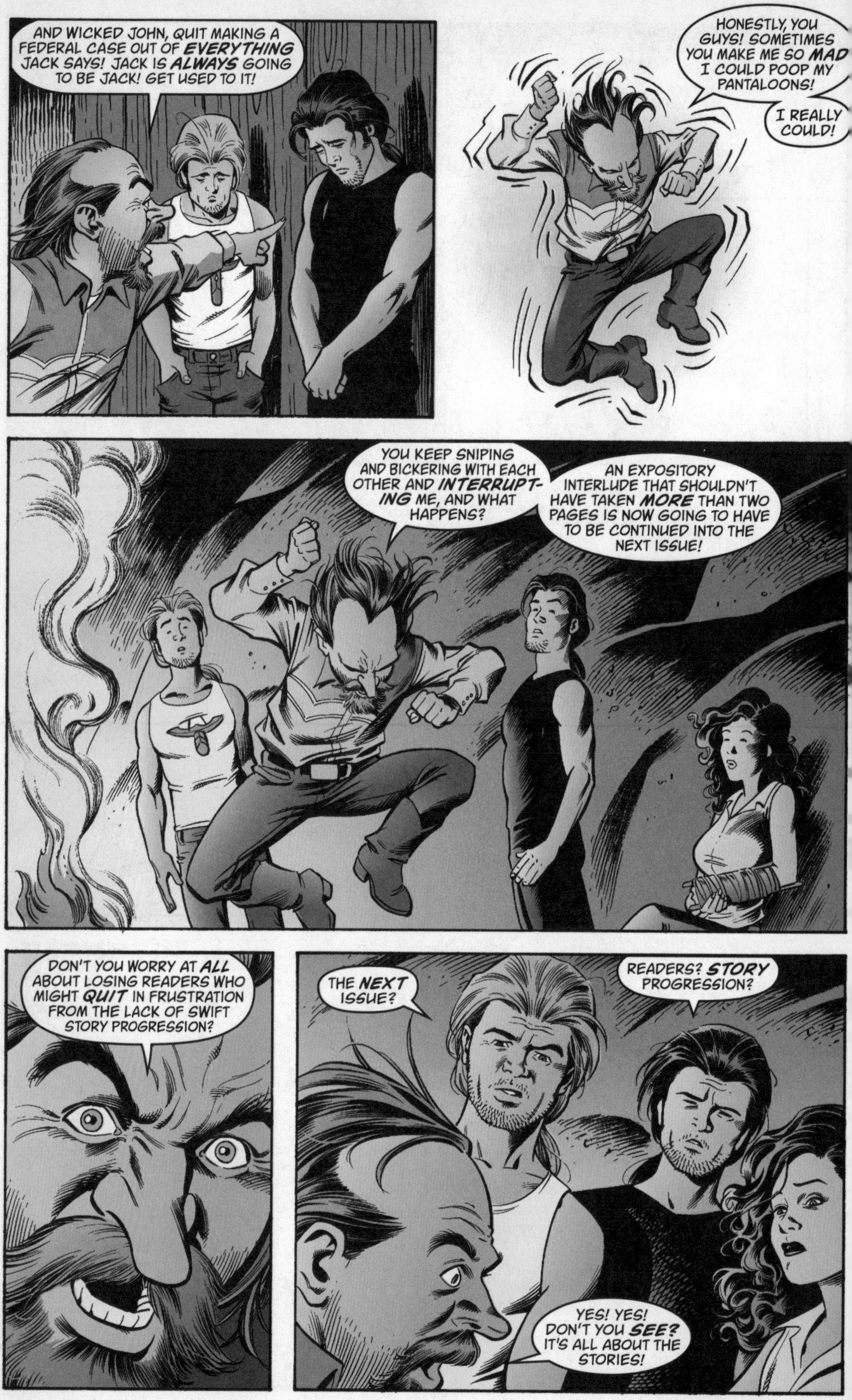
AND WICKED JOHN, QUIT MAKING A FEDERAL CASE OUT OF EVERYTHING JACK SAYS! JACK IS ALWAYS GOING TO BE JACK! GET USED TO IT!
HONESTLY, YOU GUYS! SOMETIMES YOU MAKE ME SO MAD I COULD POOP MY PANTALOONS!
I REALLY COULD!
YOU KEEP SNIPING AND BICKERING WITH EACH OTHER AND INTERRUPT-ING ME, AND WHAT HAPPENS?
AN EXPOSITORY INTERLUDE THAT SHOULDN'T HAVE TAKEN MORE THAN TWO PAGES IS NOW GOING TO HAVE TO BE CONTINUED INTO THE NEXT ISSUE!
DON'T YOU WORRY AT ALL ABOUT LOSING READERS WHO MIGHT QUIT IN FRUSTRATION FROM THE LACK OF SWIFT STORY PROGRESSION?
THE NEXT ISSUE?
READERS? STORY PROGRESSION?
YES! YES! DON'T YOU SEE? IT'S ALL ABOUT THE STORIES!

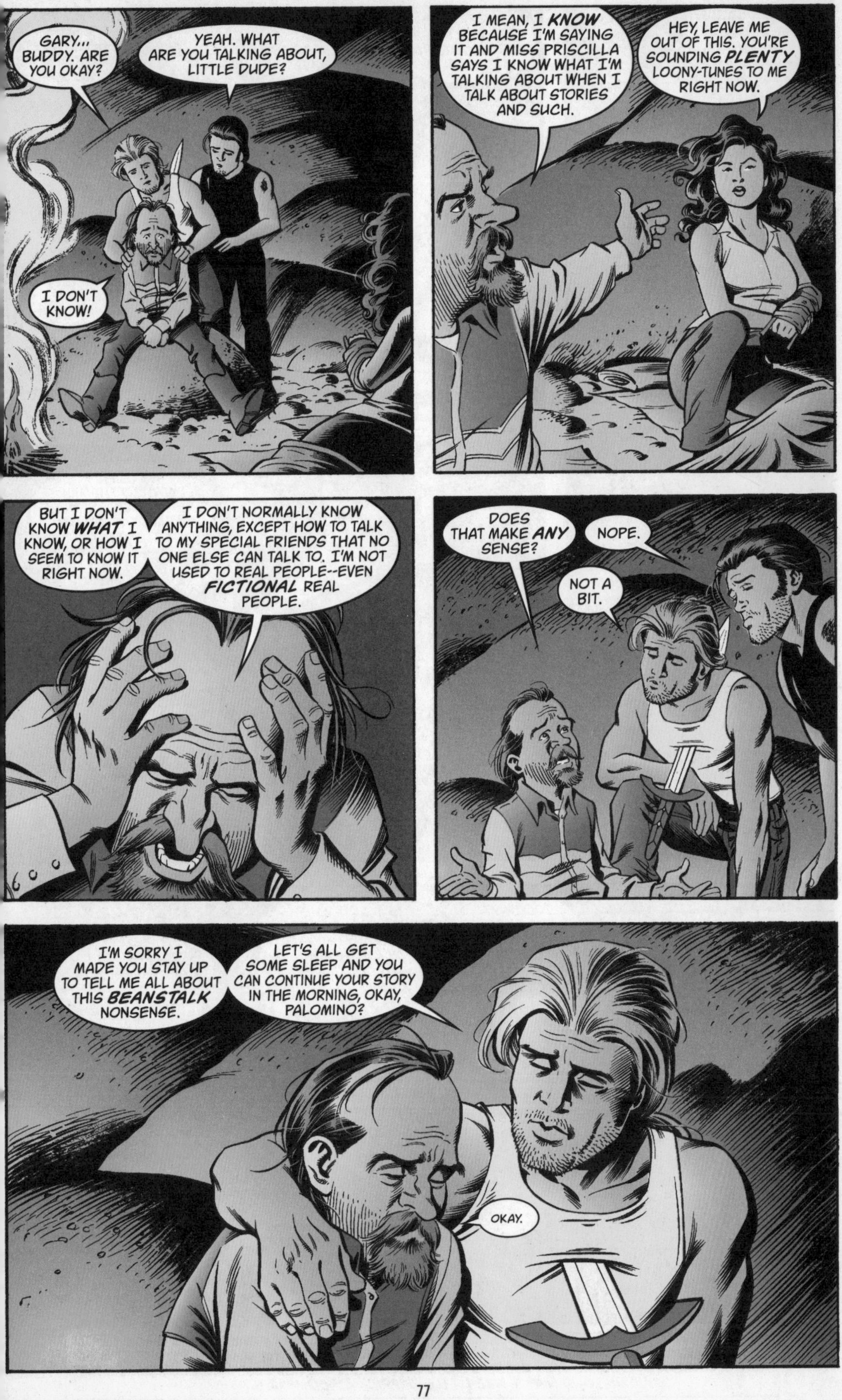
GARY... BUDDY. ARE YOU OKAY?
YEAH. WHAT ARE YOU TALKING ABOUT, LITTLE DUDE?
I DON'T KNOW!
I MEAN, I KNOW BECAUSE I'M SAYING IT AND MISS PRISCILLA SAYS I KNOW WHAT I'M TALKING ABOUT WHEN I TALK ABOUT STORIES AND SUCH.
HEY, LEAVE ME OUT OF THIS. YOU'RE SOUNDING PLENTY LOONY-TUNES TO ME RIGHT NOW.
BUT I DON'T KNOW WHAT I KNOW, OR HOW I SEEM TO KNOW IT RIGHT NOW.
I DON'T NORMALLY KNOW ANYTHING, EXCEPT HOW TO TALK TO MY SPECIAL FRIENDS THAT NO ONE ELSE CAN TALK TO. I'M NOT USED TO REAL PEOPLE--EVEN FICTIONAL REAL PEOPLE.
DOES THAT MAKE ANY SENSE?
NOPE.
NOT A BIT.
I'M SORRY I MADE YOU STAY UP TO TELL ME ALL ABOUT THIS BEANSTALK NONSENSE.
LET'S ALL GET SOME SLEEP AND YOU CAN CONTINUE YOUR STORY IN THE MORNING, OKAY, PALOMINO?
OKAY.

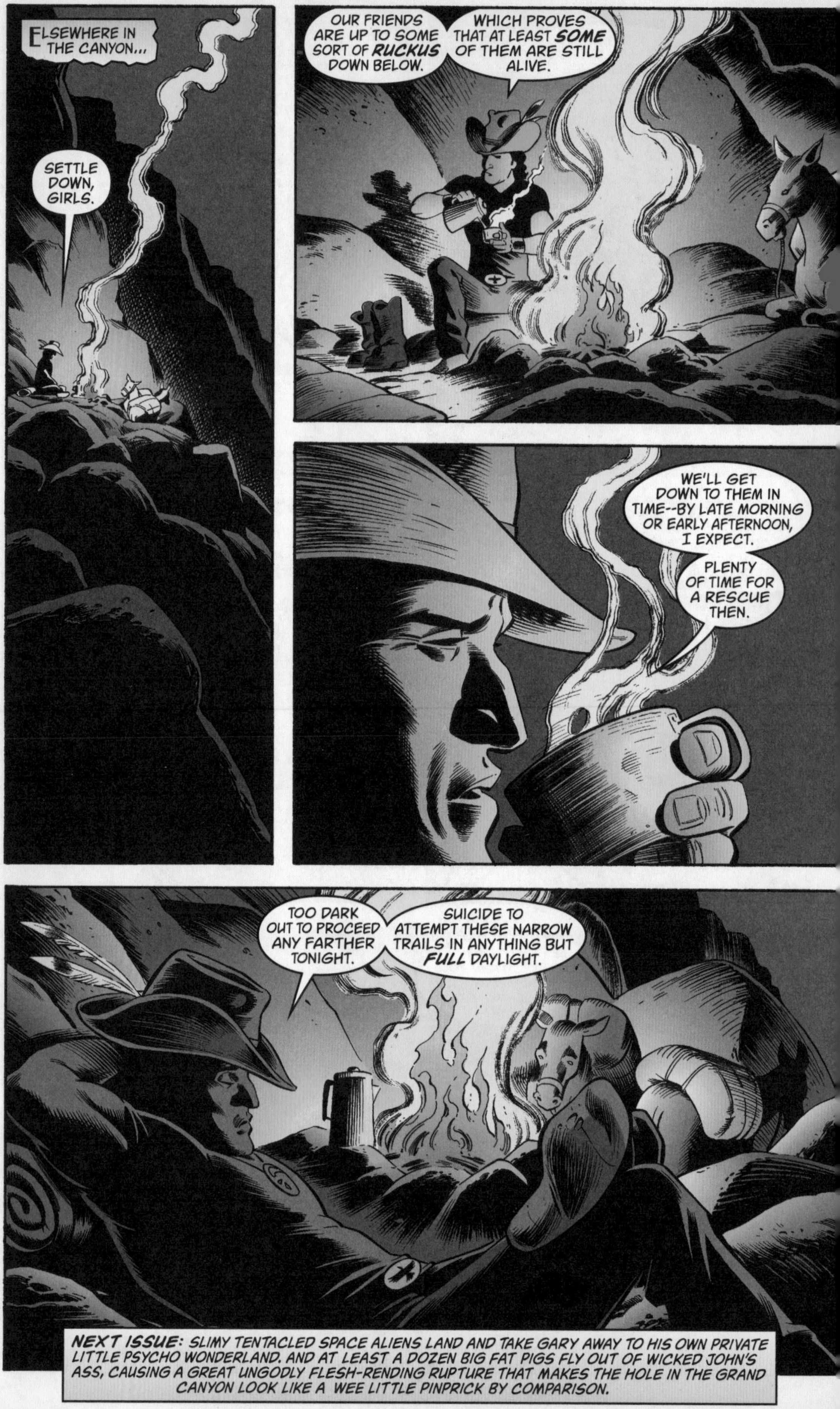

ELSEWHERE IN THE CANYON...
SETTLE DOWN, GIRLS.
OUR FRIENDS ARE UP TO SOME SORT OF RUCKUS DOWN BELOW.
WHICH PROVES THAT AT LEAST SOME OF THEM ARE STILL ALIVE.
WE'LL GET DOWN TO THEM IN TIME--BY LATE MORNING OR EARLY AFTERNOON, I EXPECT.
PLENTY OF TIME FOR A RESCUE THEN.
TOO DARK OUT TO PROCEED ANY FARTHER TONIGHT.
SUICIDE TO ATTEMPT THESE NARROW TRAILS IN ANYTHING BUT FULL DAYLIGHT.
NEXT ISSUE: SLIMY TENTACLED SPACE ALIENS LAND AND TAKE GARY AWAY TO HIS OWN PRIVATE LITTLE PSYCHO WONDERLAND. AND AT LEAST A DOZEN BIG FAT PIGS FLY OUT OF WICKED JOHN'S ASS, CAUSING A GREAT UNGODLY FLESH-RENDING RUPTURE THAT MAKES THE HOLE IN THE GRAND CANYON LOOK LIKE A WEE LITTLE PINPRICK BY COMPARISON.

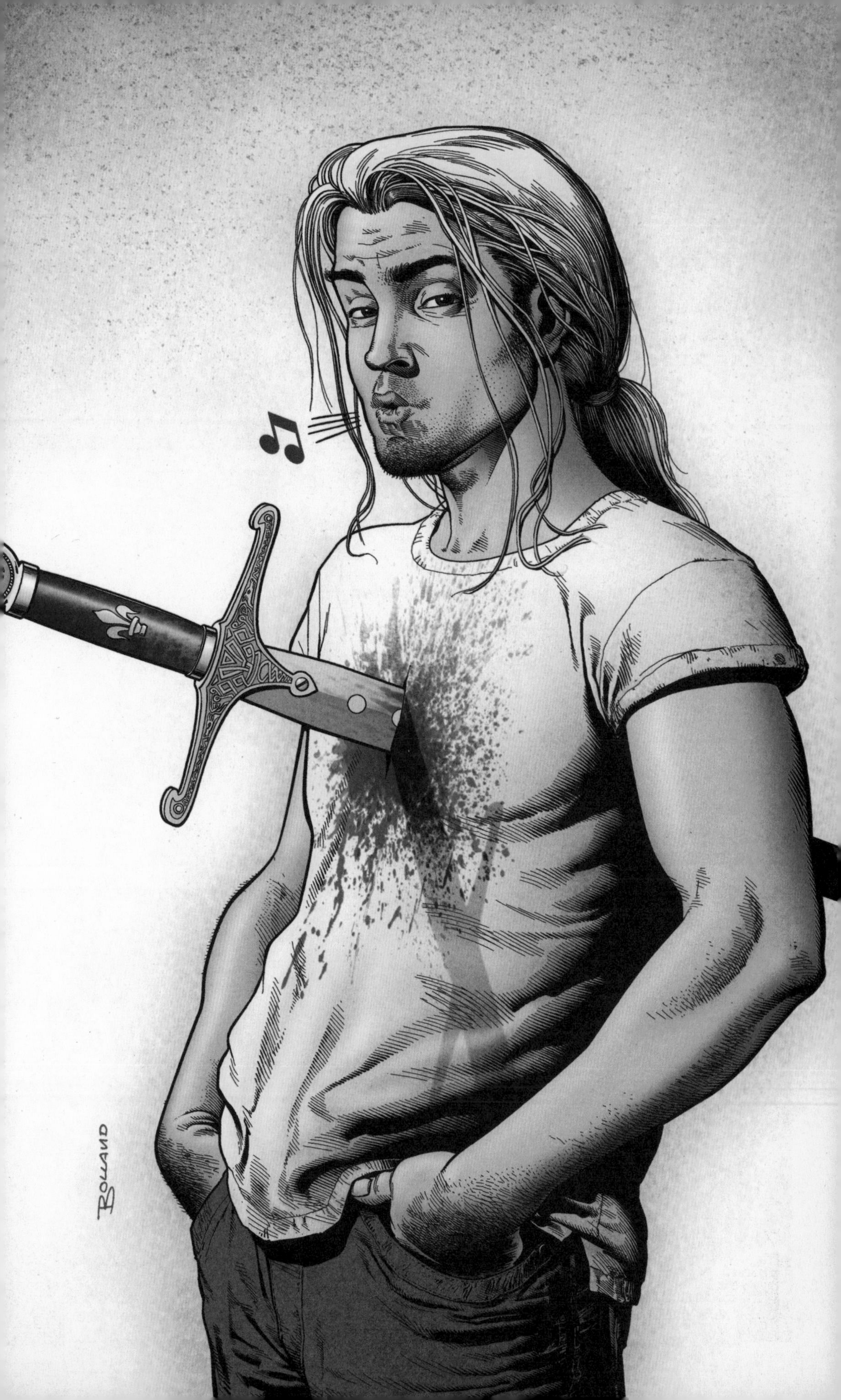
BOLLAND

"*I can't just*
gun down a woman who's
madly in love with me."

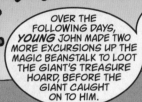

OVER THE FOLLOWING DAYS, *YOUNG* JOHN MADE TWO MORE EXCURSIONS UP THE MAGIC BEANSTALK TO LOOT THE GIANT'S TREASURE HOARD, BEFORE THE GIANT CAUGHT ON TO HIM.

THE GIANT FOLLOWED JOHN DOWN THE BEANSTALK, DESCENDING *CLOSE* BEHIND HIM.

Y'KNOW, SOME OF YOU IGNORANT PEASANTS *MIGHT* GET YOUR OWN AXES AND HELP ME!

IT'S NOT AS IF THIS *MONSTER'S* LIKELY TO LEAVE YOU ALL IN PEACE AFTER HE *CRUSHES* ME INTO A SMALL WET PUDDLE!

THUNK

KRRRKKK

THERE WE GO!

AND HERE COMES THE *GIANT!*

I'D CONSIDER MOVING OUT OF HIS WAY, IF *I* WERE SOME OF YOU!

(Enchanted) Blade Runner
Part Four of THE BAD PRINCE

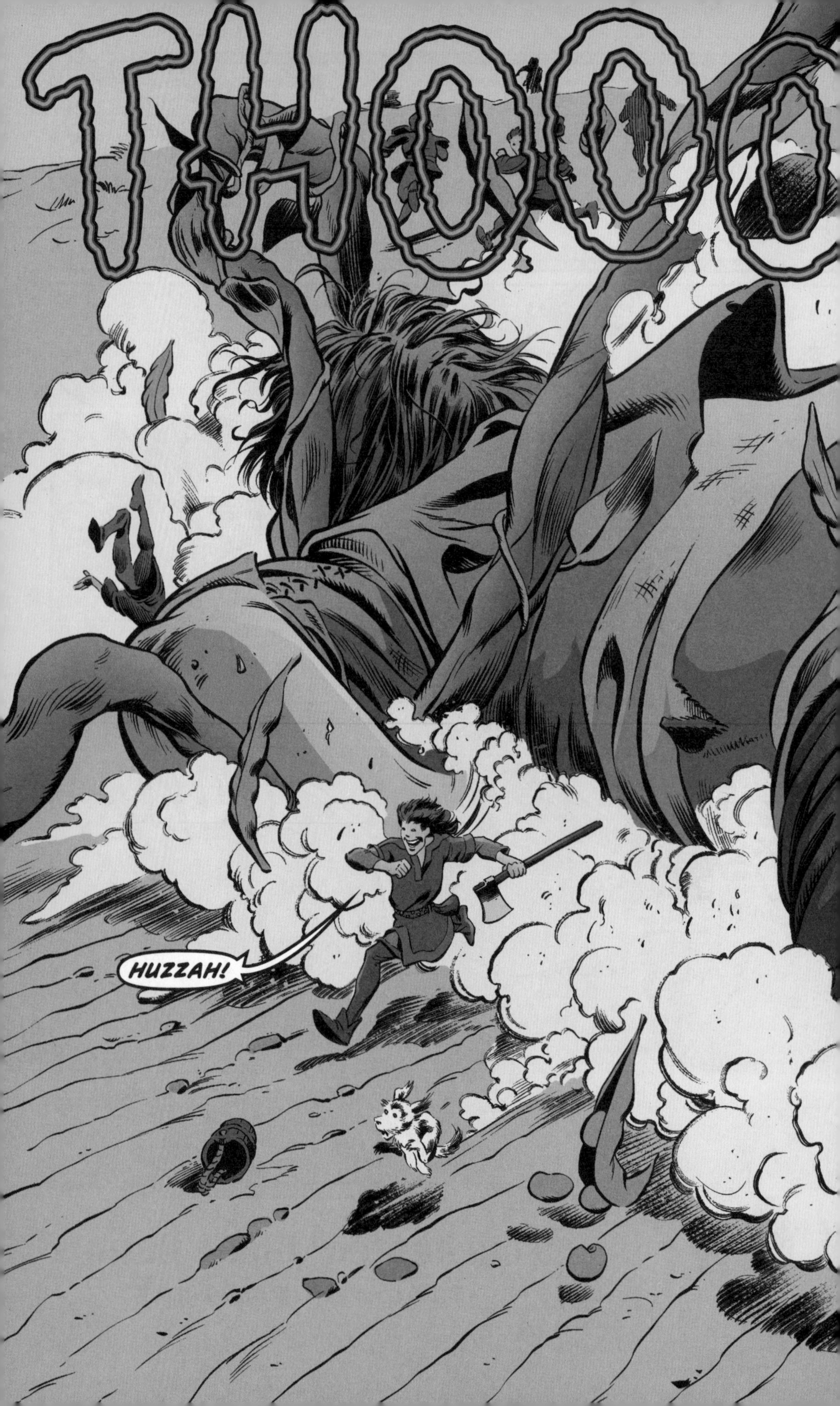
THOOOO
HUZZAH!

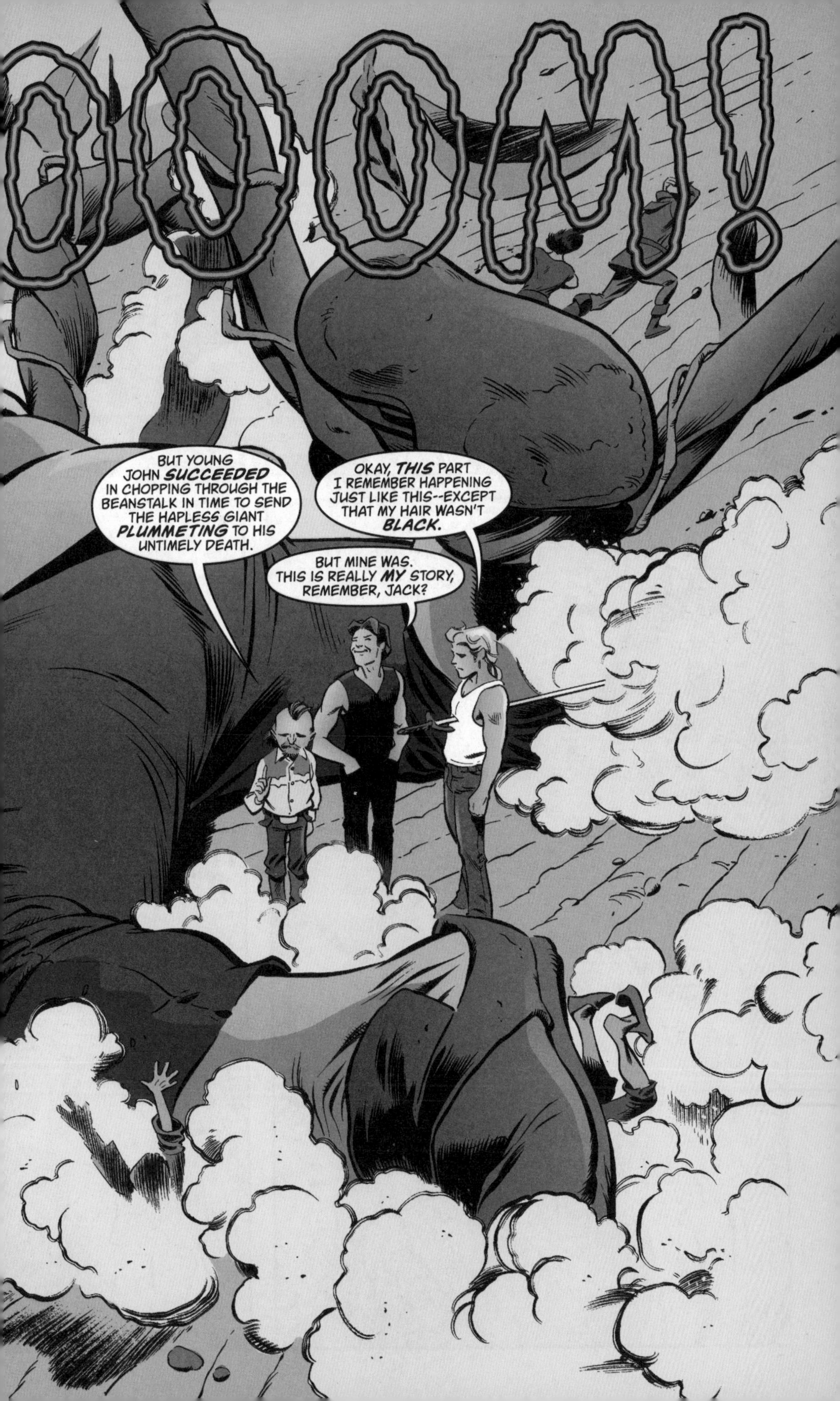
OOOOM!
BUT YOUNG JOHN SUCCEEDED IN CHOPPING THROUGH THE BEANSTALK IN TIME TO SEND THE HAPLESS GIANT PLUMMETING TO HIS UNTIMELY DEATH.
OKAY, THIS PART I REMEMBER HAPPENING JUST LIKE THIS--EXCEPT THAT MY HAIR WASN'T BLACK.
BUT MINE WAS. THIS IS REALLY MY STORY, REMEMBER, JACK?

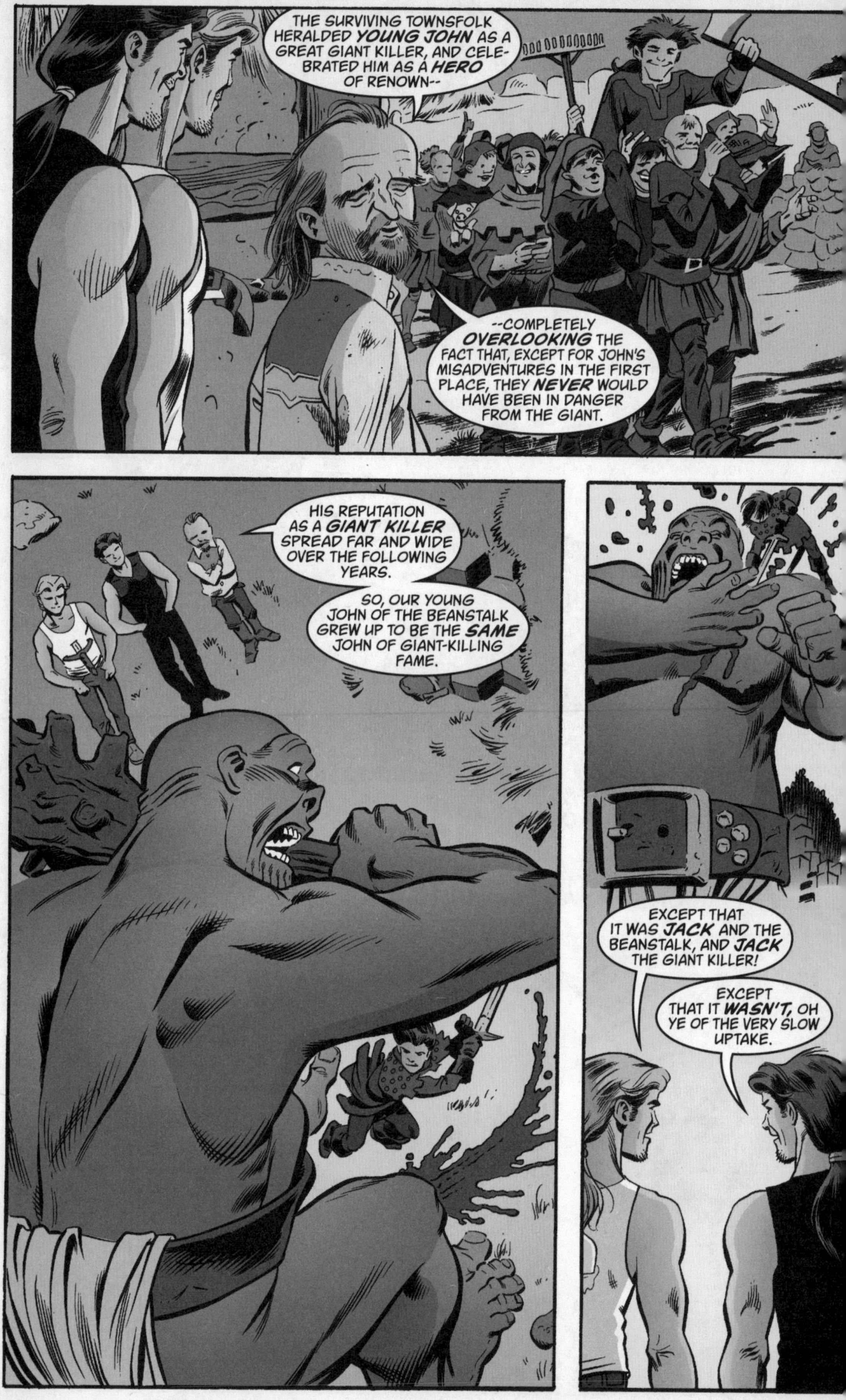
THE SURVIVING TOWNSFOLK HERALDED YOUNG JOHN AS A GREAT GIANT KILLER, AND CELEBRATED HIM AS A HERO OF RENOWN--
--COMPLETELY OVERLOOKING THE FACT THAT, EXCEPT FOR JOHN'S MISADVENTURES IN THE FIRST PLACE, THEY NEVER WOULD HAVE BEEN IN DANGER FROM THE GIANT.
HIS REPUTATION AS A GIANT KILLER SPREAD FAR AND WIDE OVER THE FOLLOWING YEARS.
SO, OUR YOUNG JOHN OF THE BEANSTALK GREW UP TO BE THE SAME JOHN OF GIANT-KILLING FAME.
EXCEPT THAT IT WAS JACK AND THE BEANSTALK, AND JACK THE GIANT KILLER!
EXCEPT THAT IT WASN'T, OH YE OF THE VERY SLOW UPTAKE.

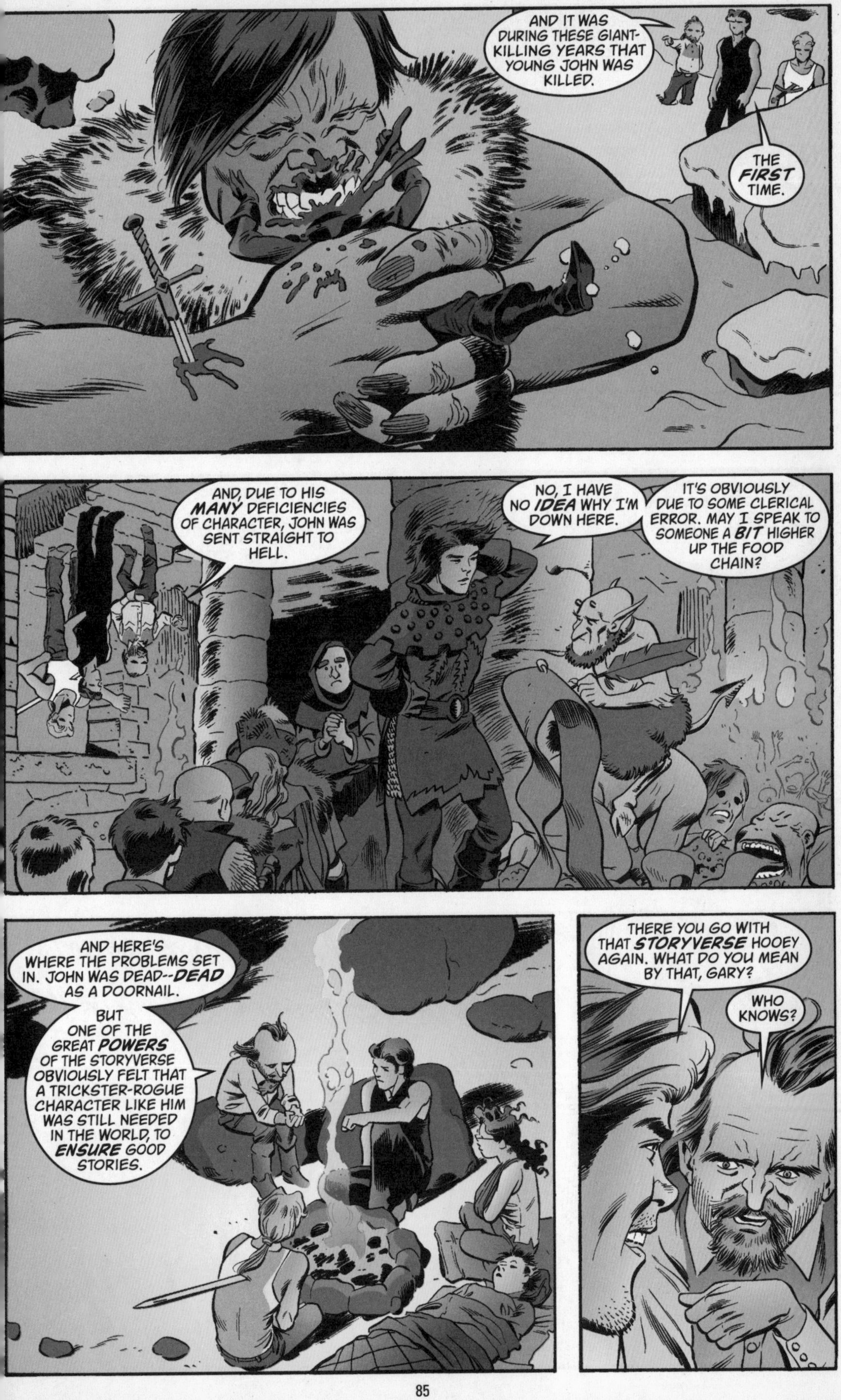

AND IT WAS DURING THESE GIANT-KILLING YEARS THAT YOUNG JOHN WAS KILLED.
THE *FIRST* TIME.
AND, DUE TO HIS *MANY* DEFICIENCIES OF CHARACTER, JOHN WAS SENT STRAIGHT TO HELL.
NO, I HAVE NO *IDEA* WHY I'M DOWN HERE.
IT'S OBVIOUSLY DUE TO SOME CLERICAL ERROR. MAY I SPEAK TO SOMEONE A *BIT* HIGHER UP THE FOOD CHAIN?
AND HERE'S WHERE THE PROBLEMS SET IN. JOHN WAS DEAD--*DEAD* AS A DOORNAIL.
BUT ONE OF THE GREAT *POWERS* OF THE STORYVERSE OBVIOUSLY FELT THAT A TRICKSTER-ROGUE CHARACTER LIKE HIM WAS STILL NEEDED IN THE WORLD, TO *ENSURE* GOOD STORIES.
THERE YOU GO WITH THAT *STORYVERSE* HOOEY AGAIN. WHAT DO YOU MEAN BY THAT, GARY?
WHO KNOWS?

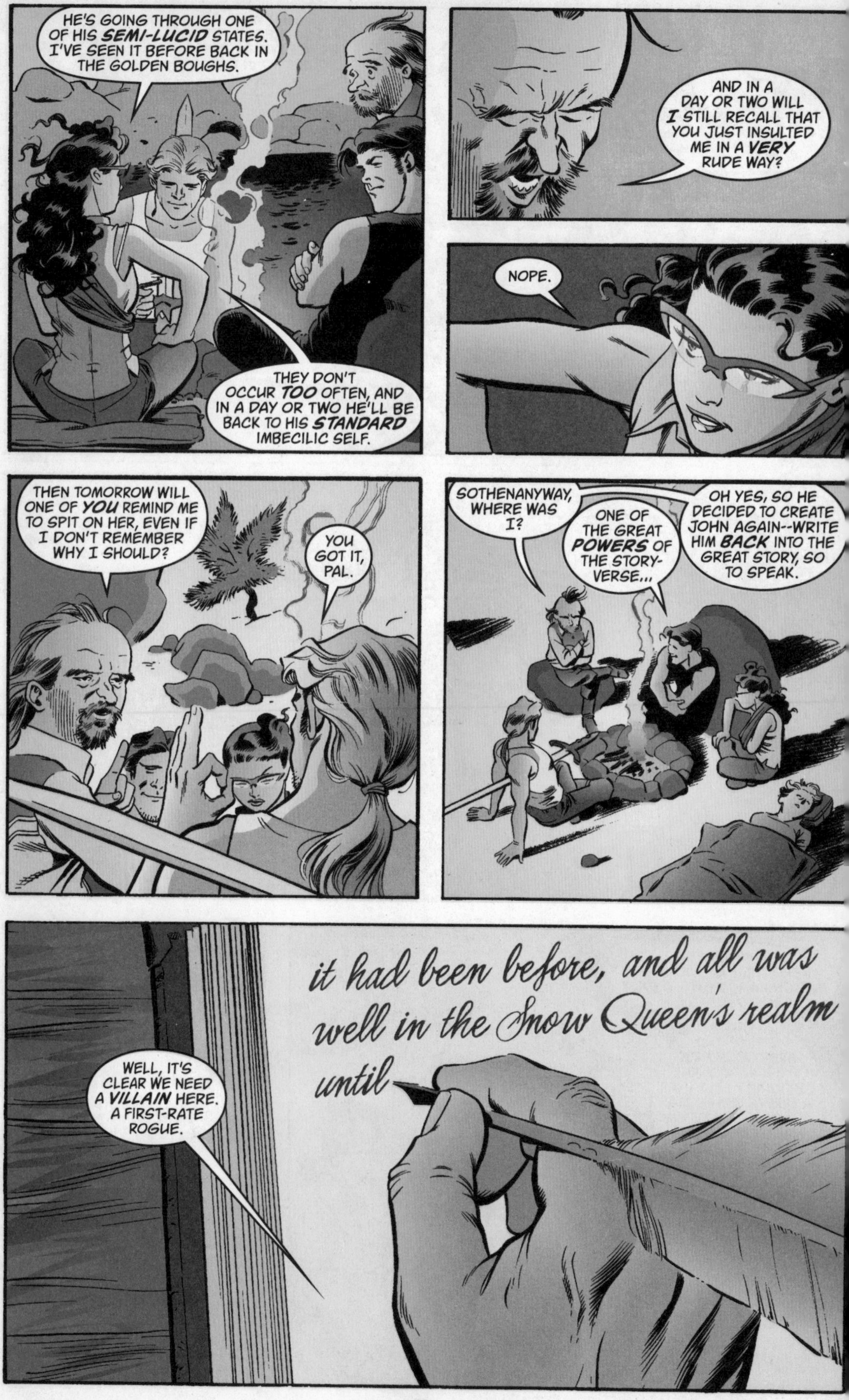
HE'S GOING THROUGH ONE OF HIS SEMI-LUCID STATES. I'VE SEEN IT BEFORE BACK IN THE GOLDEN BOUGHS.
THEY DON'T OCCUR TOO OFTEN, AND IN A DAY OR TWO HE'LL BE BACK TO HIS STANDARD IMBECILIC SELF.
AND IN A DAY OR TWO WILL I STILL RECALL THAT YOU JUST INSULTED ME IN A VERY RUDE WAY?
NOPE.
THEN TOMORROW WILL ONE OF YOU REMIND ME TO SPIT ON HER, EVEN IF I DON'T REMEMBER WHY I SHOULD?
YOU GOT IT, PAL.
SOTHENANYWAY, WHERE WAS I?
ONE OF THE GREAT POWERS OF THE STORY-VERSE...
OH YES, SO HE DECIDED TO CREATE JOHN AGAIN--WRITE HIM BACK INTO THE GREAT STORY, SO TO SPEAK.
it had been before, and all was well in the Snow Queen's realm until
WELL, IT'S CLEAR WE NEED A VILLAIN HERE. A FIRST-RATE ROGUE.

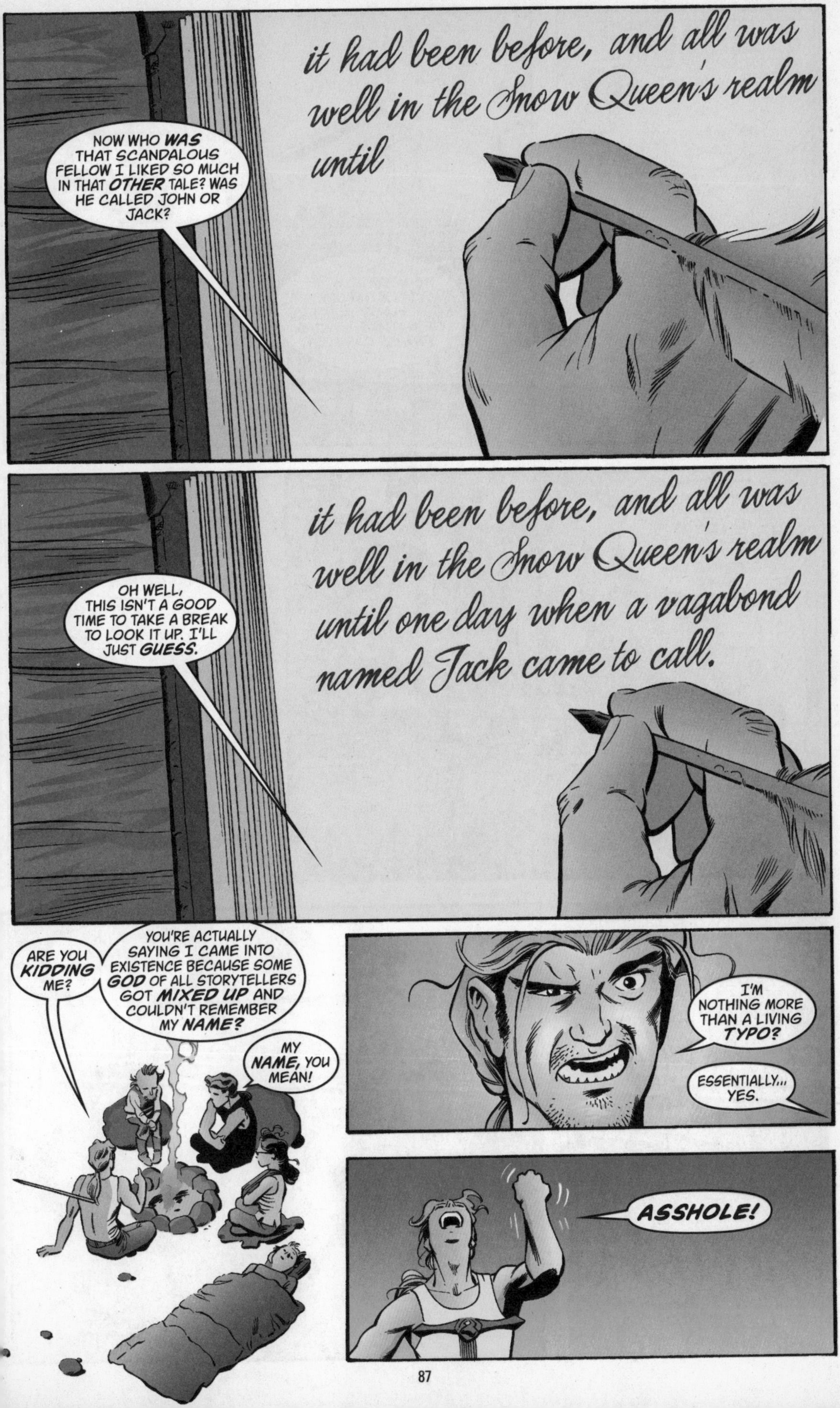

it had been before, and all was well in the Snow Queen's realm until
NOW WHO WAS THAT SCANDALOUS FELLOW I LIKED SO MUCH IN THAT OTHER TALE? WAS HE CALLED JOHN OR JACK?
it had been before, and all was well in the Snow Queen's realm until one day when a vagabond named Jack came to call.
OH WELL, THIS ISN'T A GOOD TIME TO TAKE A BREAK TO LOOK IT UP. I'LL JUST GUESS.
ARE YOU KIDDING ME?
YOU'RE ACTUALLY SAYING I CAME INTO EXISTENCE BECAUSE SOME GOD OF ALL STORYTELLERS GOT MIXED UP AND COULDN'T REMEMBER MY NAME?
MY NAME, YOU MEAN!
I'M NOTHING MORE THAN A LIVING TYPO?
ESSENTIALLY... YES.
ASSHOLE!

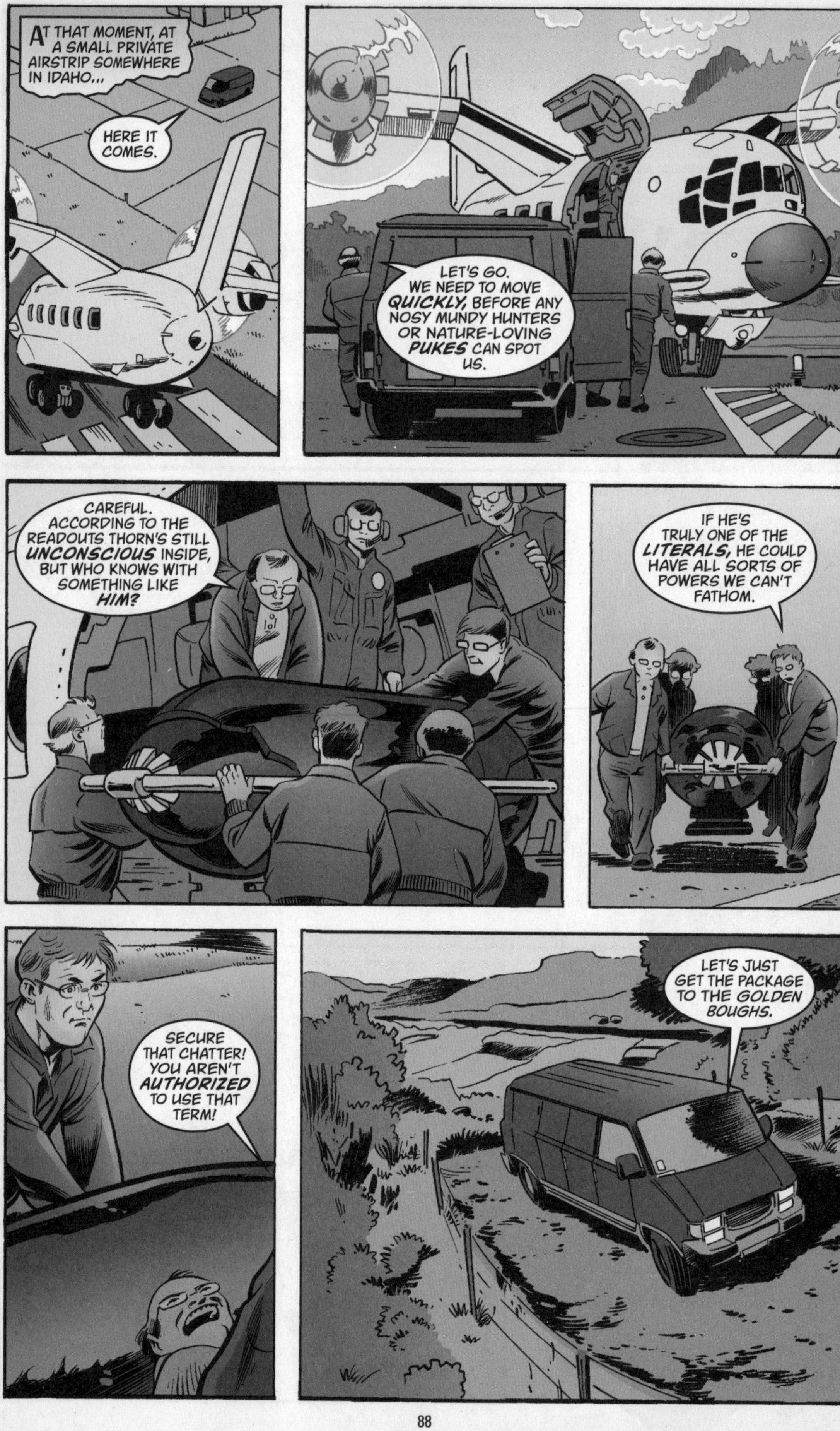

AT THAT MOMENT, AT A SMALL PRIVATE AIRSTRIP SOMEWHERE IN IDAHO...
HERE IT COMES.
LET'S GO. WE NEED TO MOVE QUICKLY, BEFORE ANY NOSY MUNDY HUNTERS OR NATURE-LOVING PUKES CAN SPOT US.
CAREFUL. ACCORDING TO THE READOUTS THORN'S STILL UNCONSCIOUS INSIDE, BUT WHO KNOWS WITH SOMETHING LIKE HIM?
IF HE'S TRULY ONE OF THE LITERALS, HE COULD HAVE ALL SORTS OF POWERS WE CAN'T FATHOM.
SECURE THAT CHATTER! YOU AREN'T AUTHORIZED TO USE THAT TERM!
LET'S JUST GET THE PACKAGE TO THE GOLDEN BOUGHS.

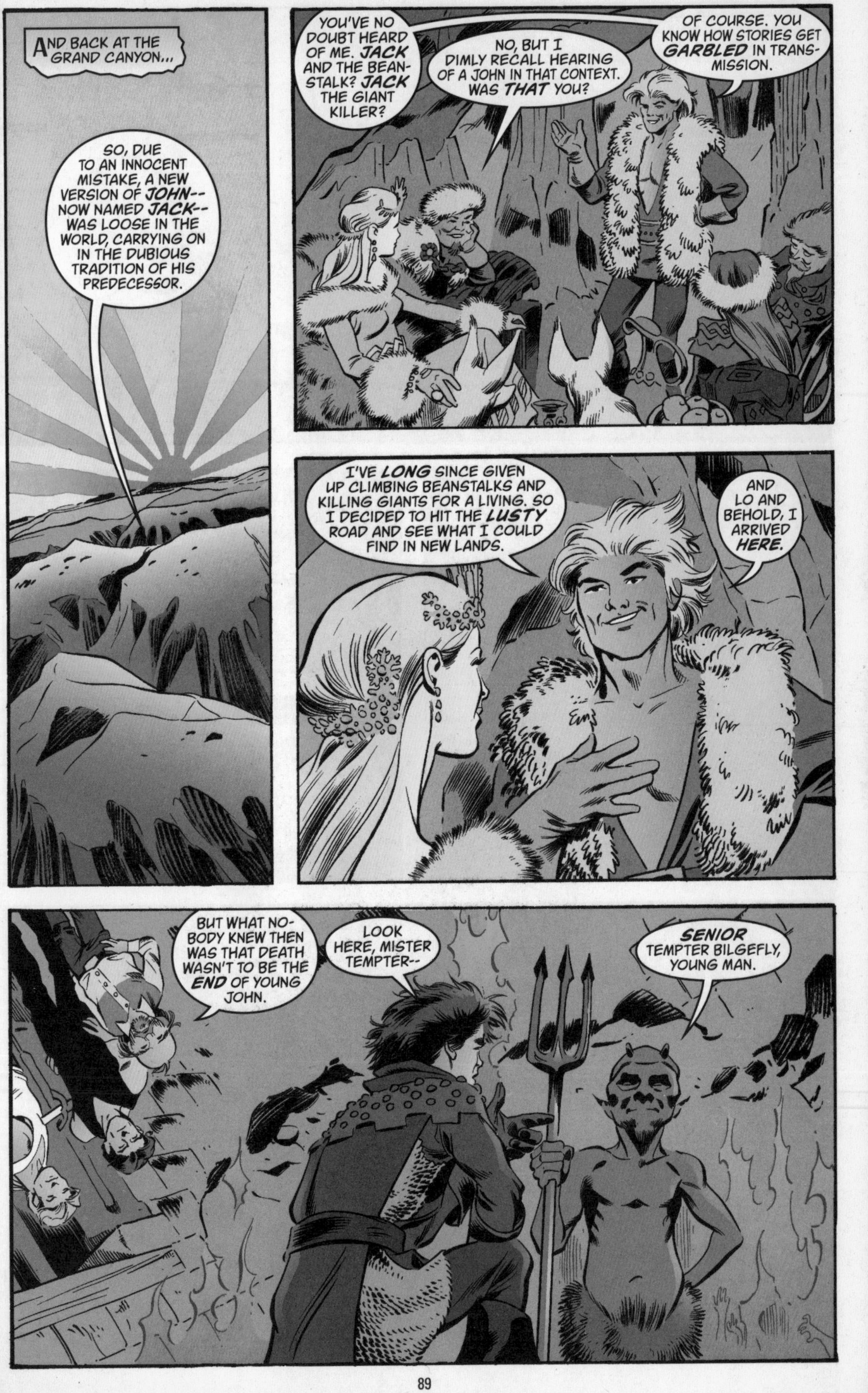
AND BACK AT THE GRAND CANYON...
SO, DUE TO AN INNOCENT MISTAKE, A NEW VERSION OF JOHN-- NOW NAMED JACK-- WAS LOOSE IN THE WORLD, CARRYING ON IN THE DUBIOUS TRADITION OF HIS PREDECESSOR.
YOU'VE NO DOUBT HEARD OF ME. JACK AND THE BEANSTALK? JACK THE GIANT KILLER?
NO, BUT I DIMLY RECALL HEARING OF A JOHN IN THAT CONTEXT. WAS THAT YOU?
OF COURSE. YOU KNOW HOW STORIES GET GARBLED IN TRANSMISSION.
I'VE LONG SINCE GIVEN UP CLIMBING BEANSTALKS AND KILLING GIANTS FOR A LIVING. SO I DECIDED TO HIT THE LUSTY ROAD AND SEE WHAT I COULD FIND IN NEW LANDS.
AND LO AND BEHOLD, I ARRIVED HERE.
BUT WHAT NOBODY KNEW THEN WAS THAT DEATH WASN'T TO BE THE END OF YOUNG JOHN.
LOOK HERE, MISTER TEMPTER--
SENIOR TEMPTER BILGEFLY, YOUNG MAN.

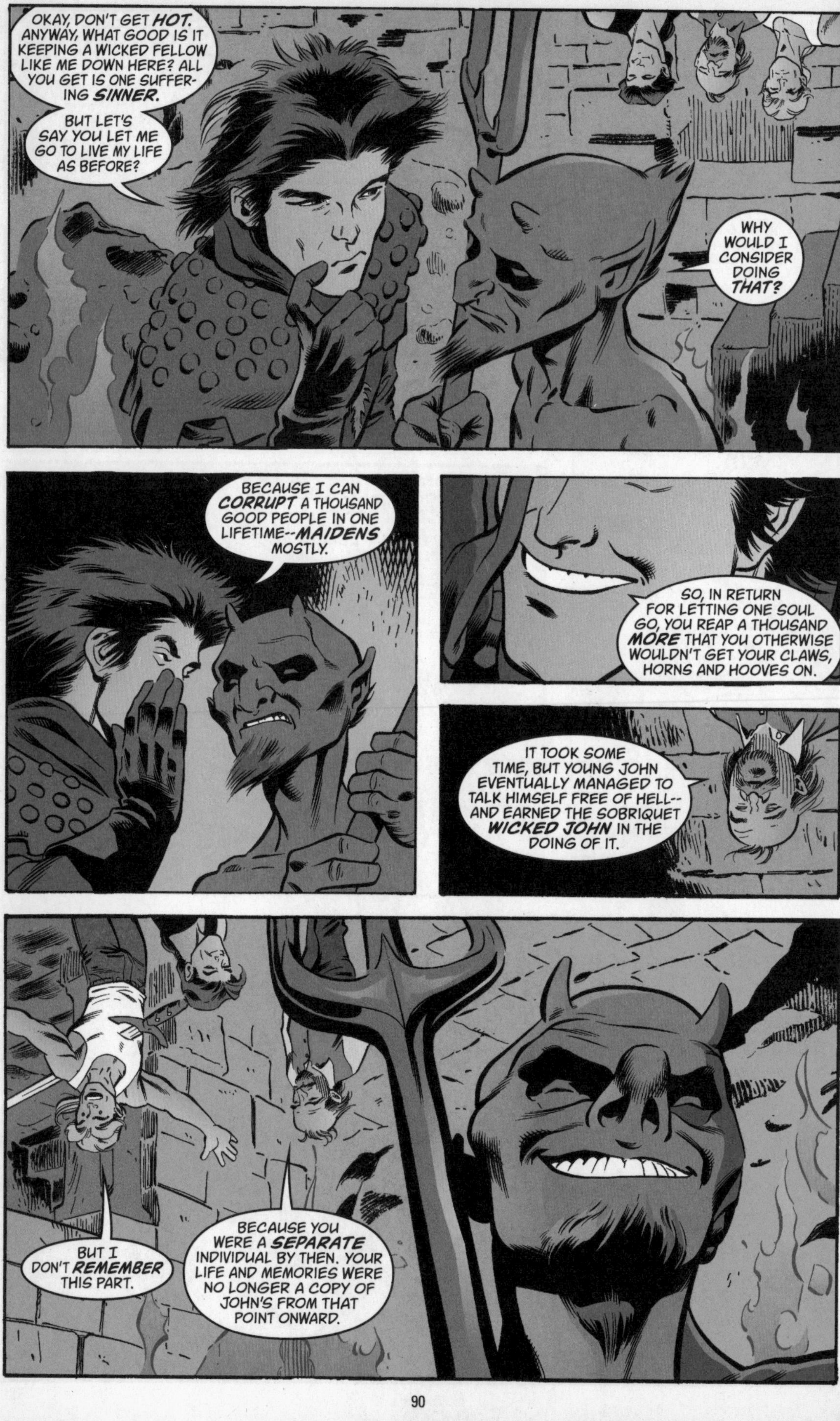

OKAY, DON'T GET HOT. ANYWAY, WHAT GOOD IS IT KEEPING A WICKED FELLOW LIKE ME DOWN HERE? ALL YOU GET IS ONE SUFFERING SINNER.
BUT LET'S SAY YOU LET ME GO TO LIVE MY LIFE AS BEFORE?
WHY WOULD I CONSIDER DOING THAT?
BECAUSE I CAN CORRUPT A THOUSAND GOOD PEOPLE IN ONE LIFETIME--MAIDENS MOSTLY.
SO, IN RETURN FOR LETTING ONE SOUL GO, YOU REAP A THOUSAND MORE THAT YOU OTHERWISE WOULDN'T GET YOUR CLAWS, HORNS AND HOOVES ON.
IT TOOK SOME TIME, BUT YOUNG JOHN EVENTUALLY MANAGED TO TALK HIMSELF FREE OF HELL--AND EARNED THE SOBRIQUET WICKED JOHN IN THE DOING OF IT.
BUT I DON'T REMEMBER THIS PART.
BECAUSE YOU WERE A SEPARATE INDIVIDUAL BY THEN. YOUR LIFE AND MEMORIES WERE NO LONGER A COPY OF JOHN'S FROM THAT POINT ONWARD.

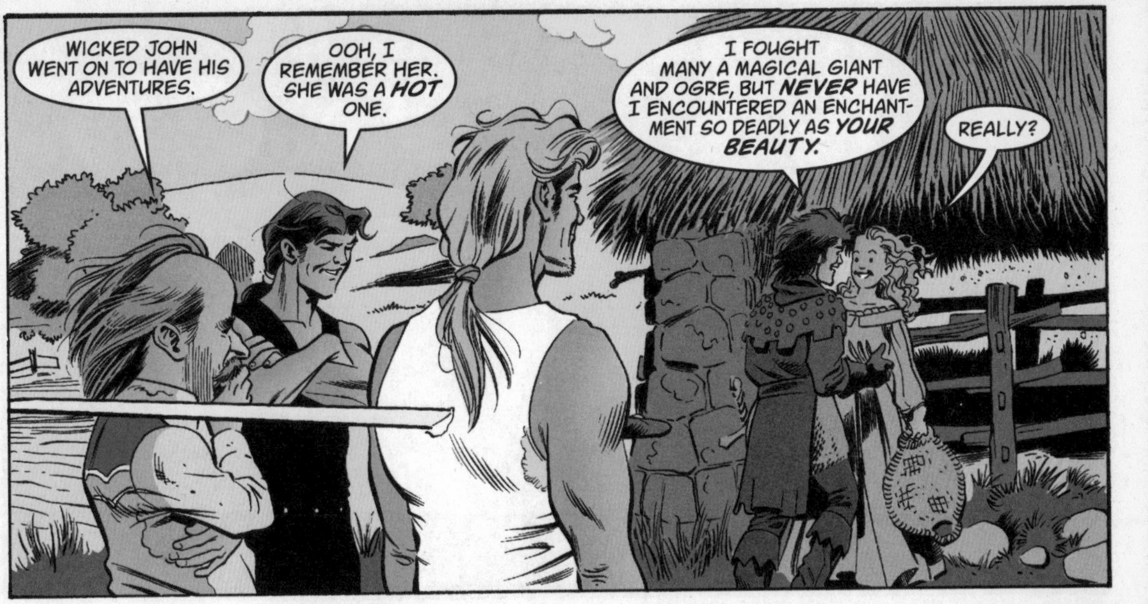
WICKED JOHN WENT ON TO HAVE HIS ADVENTURES.
OOH, I REMEMBER HER. SHE WAS A **HOT** ONE.
I FOUGHT MANY A MAGICAL GIANT AND OGRE, BUT **NEVER** HAVE I ENCOUNTERED AN ENCHANT-MENT SO DEADLY AS **YOUR BEAUTY.**
REALLY?

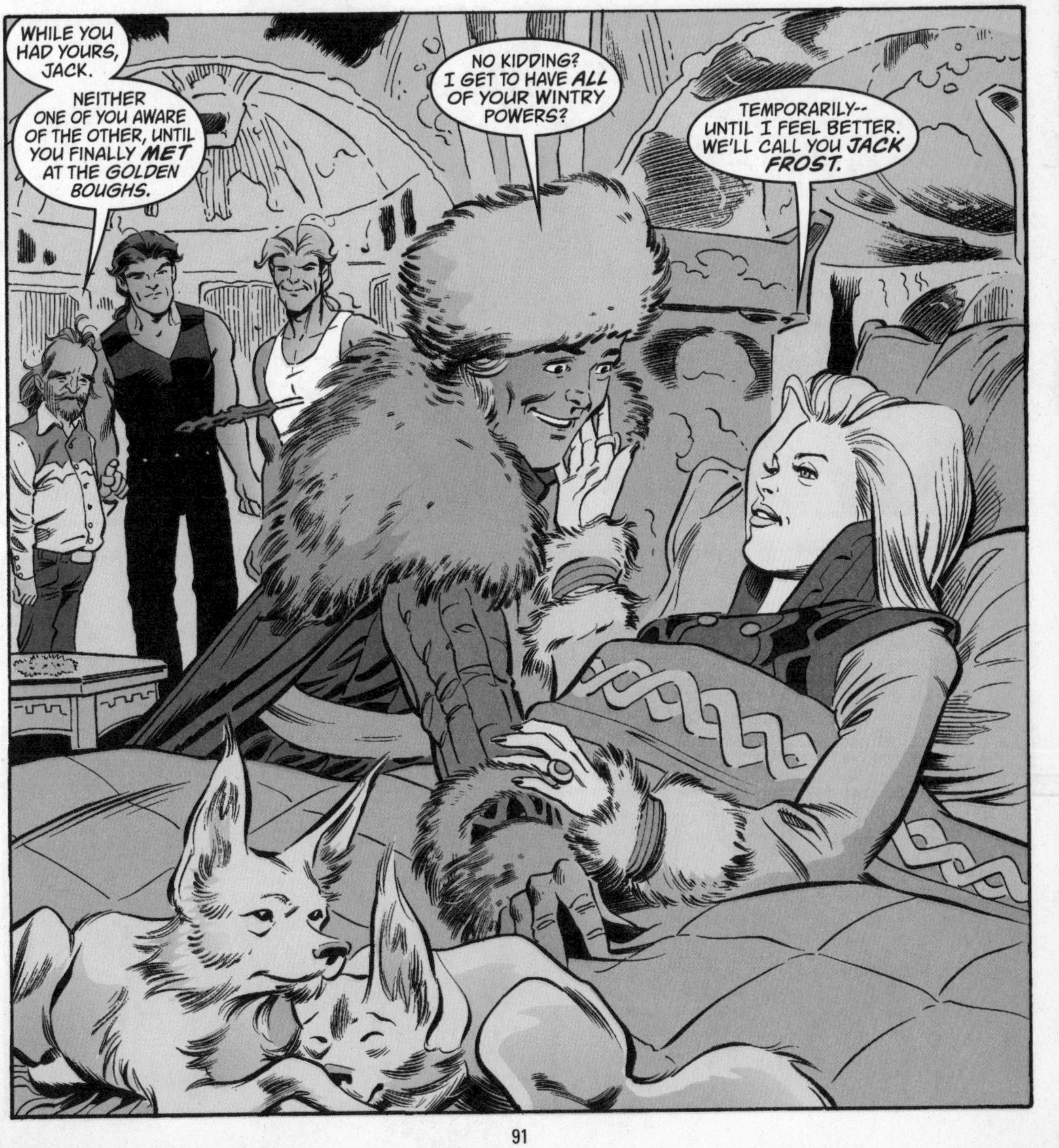
WHILE YOU HAD YOURS, JACK.
NEITHER ONE OF YOU AWARE OF THE OTHER, UNTIL YOU FINALLY **MET** AT THE *GOLDEN BOUGHS.*
NO KIDDING? I GET TO HAVE **ALL** OF YOUR WINTRY POWERS?
TEMPORARILY-- UNTIL I FEEL BETTER. WE'LL CALL YOU **JACK FROST.**

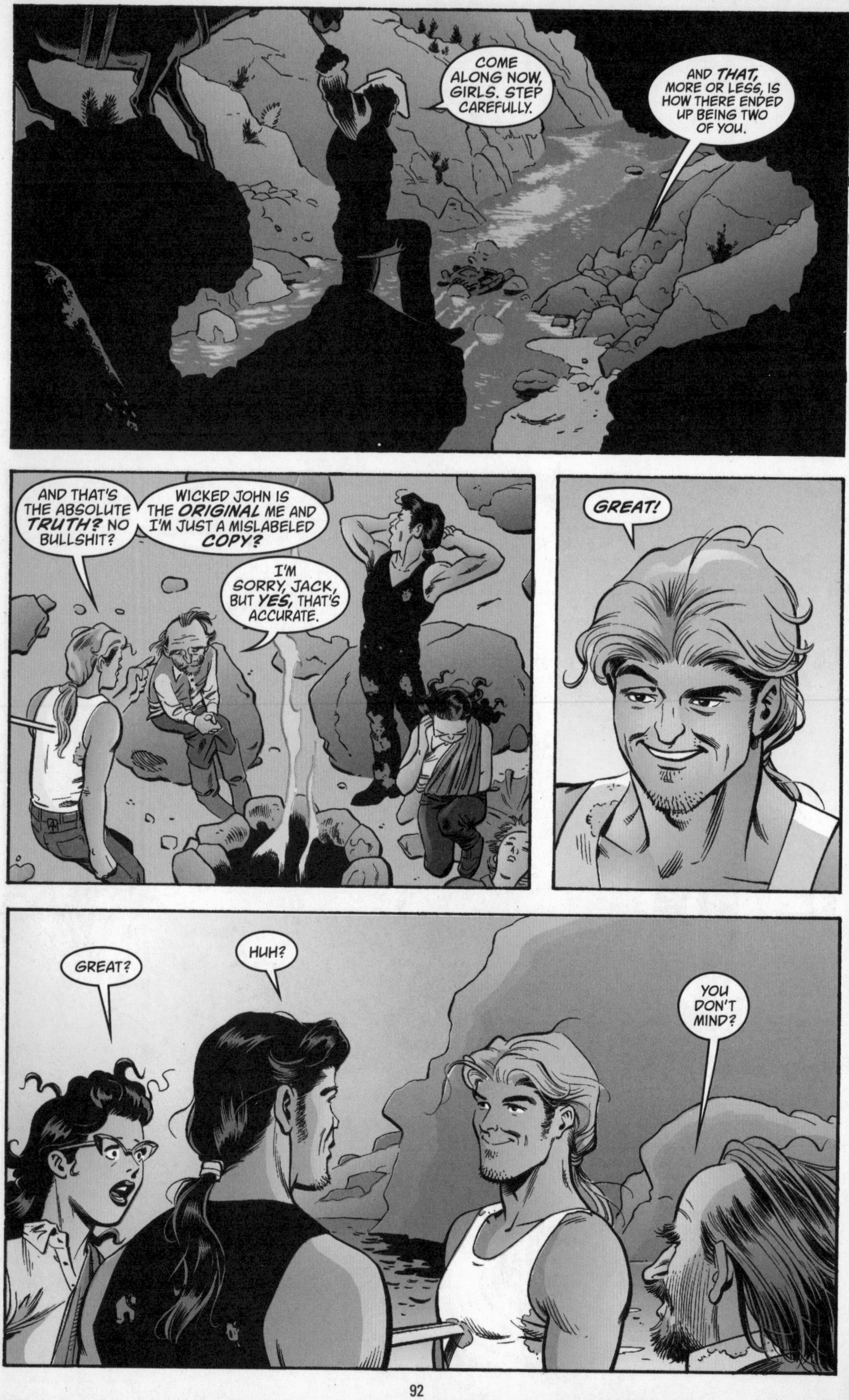
COME ALONG NOW, GIRLS. STEP CAREFULLY.
AND *THAT,* MORE OR LESS, IS HOW THERE ENDED UP BEING TWO OF YOU.
AND THAT'S THE ABSOLUTE ***TRUTH?*** NO BULLSHIT?
WICKED JOHN IS THE ***ORIGINAL*** ME AND I'M JUST A MISLABELED ***COPY?***
I'M SORRY, JACK, BUT ***YES,*** THAT'S ACCURATE.
GREAT!
GREAT?
HUH?
YOU DON'T MIND?

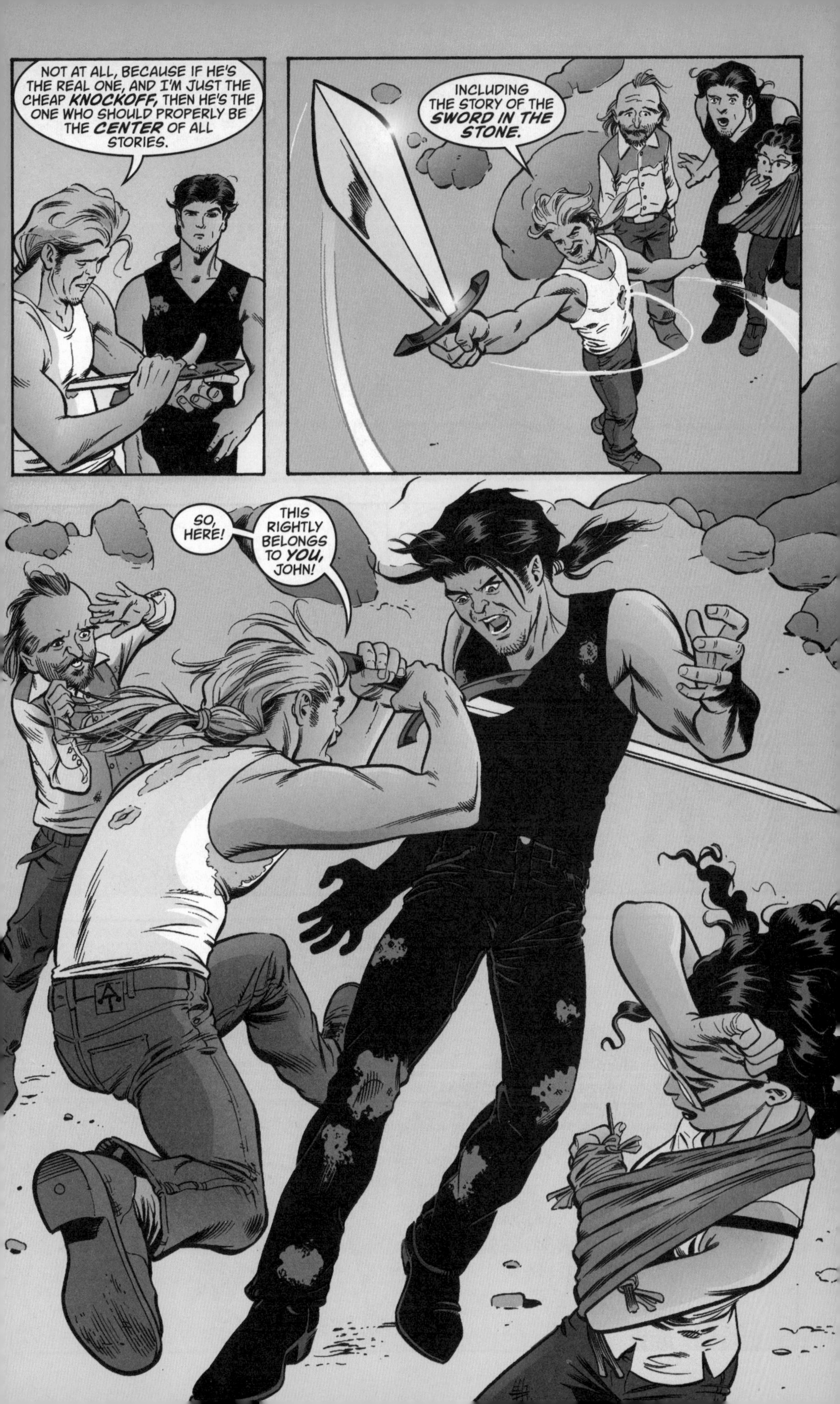
NOT AT ALL, BECAUSE IF HE'S THE REAL ONE, AND I'M JUST THE CHEAP KNOCKOFF, THEN HE'S THE ONE WHO SHOULD PROPERLY BE THE CENTER OF ALL STORIES.
INCLUDING THE STORY OF THE SWORD IN THE STONE.
SO, HERE!
THIS RIGHTLY BELONGS TO YOU, JOHN!

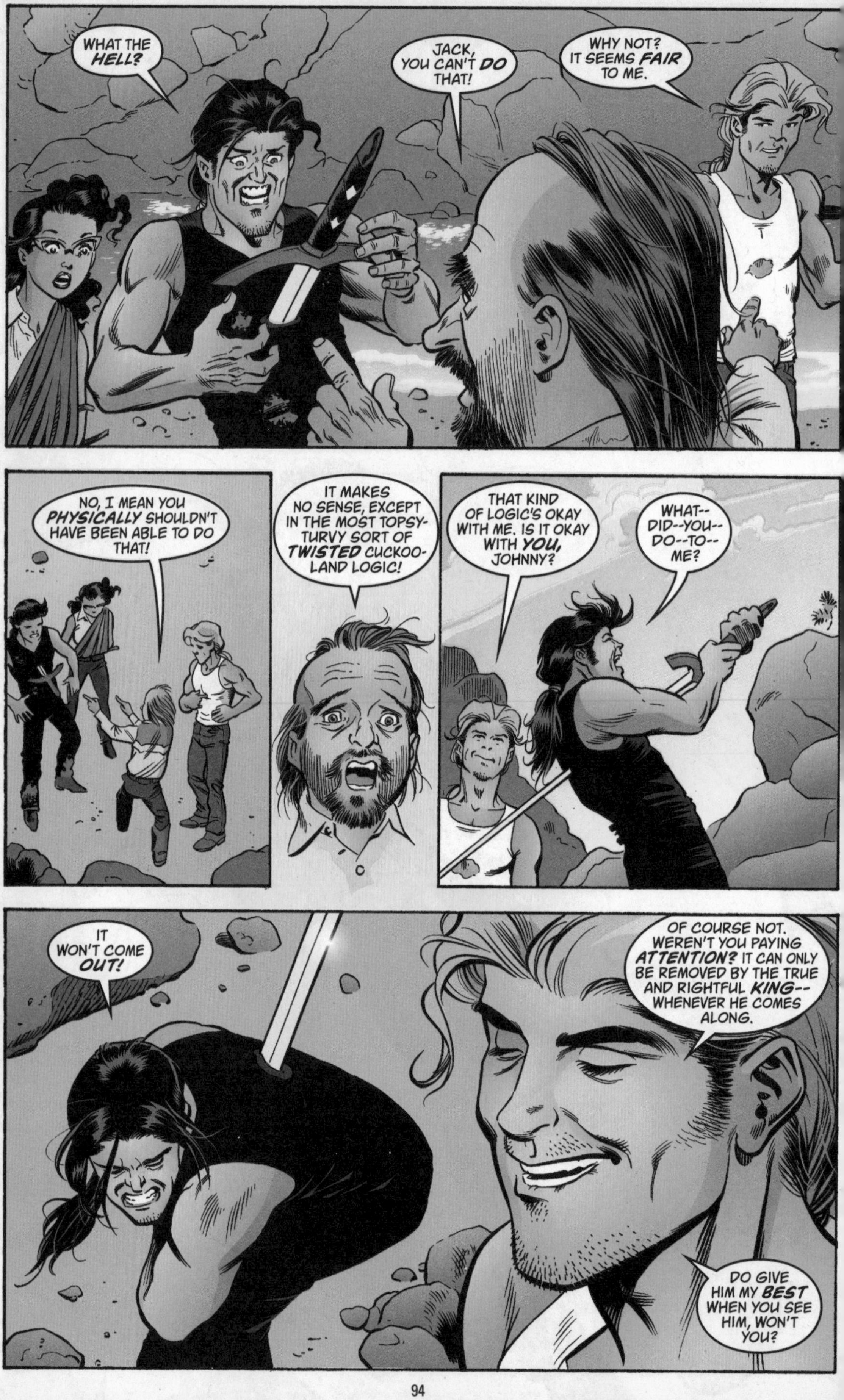

WHAT THE HELL?
JACK, YOU CAN'T DO THAT!
WHY NOT? IT SEEMS FAIR TO ME.
NO, I MEAN YOU PHYSICALLY SHOULDN'T HAVE BEEN ABLE TO DO THAT!
IT MAKES NO SENSE, EXCEPT IN THE MOST TOPSY-TURVY SORT OF TWISTED CUCKOO-LAND LOGIC!
THAT KIND OF LOGIC'S OKAY WITH ME. IS IT OKAY WITH YOU, JOHNNY?
WHAT--DID--YOU--DO--TO--ME?
IT WON'T COME OUT!
OF COURSE NOT. WEREN'T YOU PAYING ATTENTION? IT CAN ONLY BE REMOVED BY THE TRUE AND RIGHTFUL KING--WHENEVER HE COMES ALONG.
DO GIVE HIM MY BEST WHEN YOU SEE HIM, WON'T YOU?

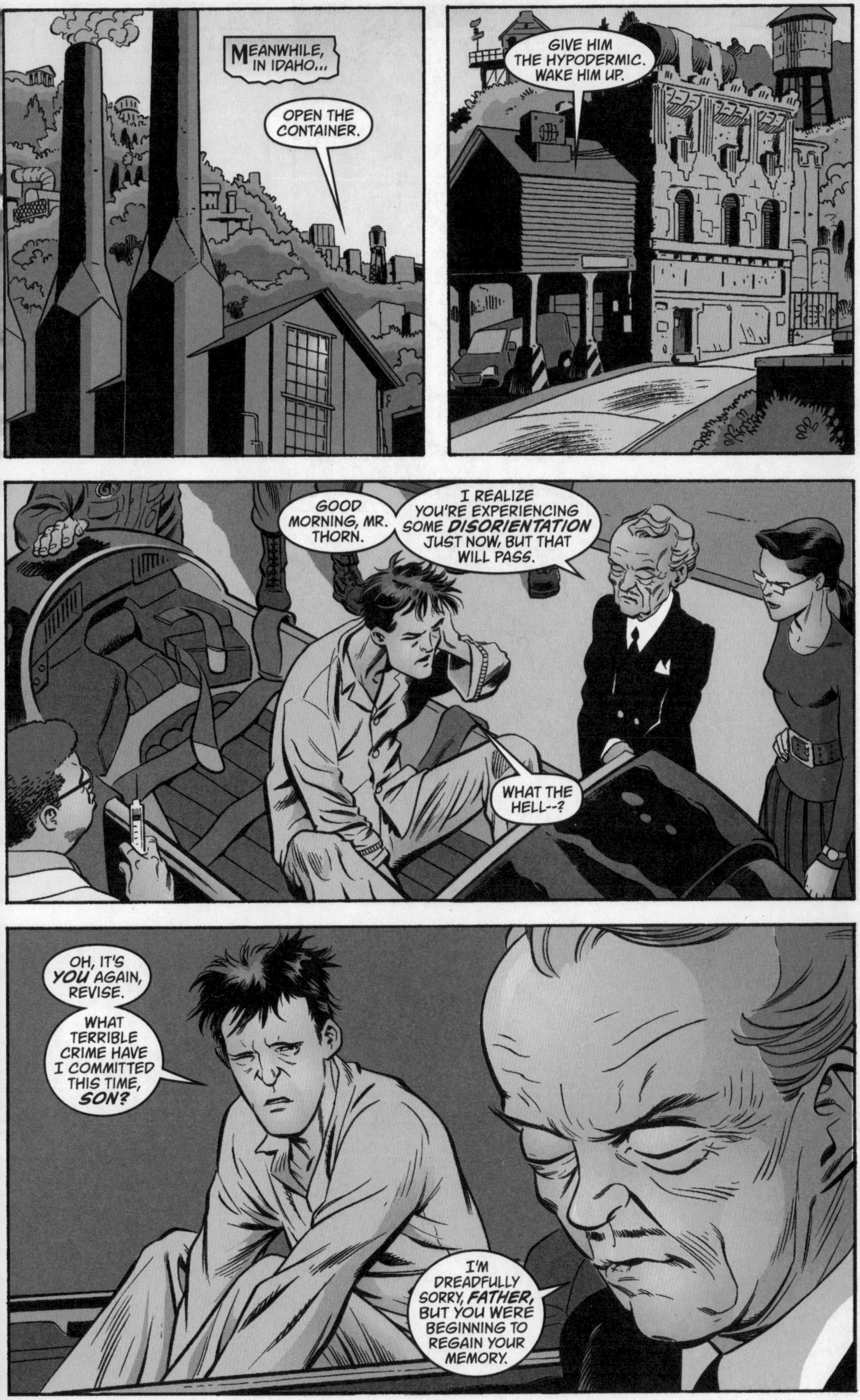
MEANWHILE, IN IDAHO...
OPEN THE CONTAINER.
GIVE HIM THE HYPODERMIC. WAKE HIM UP.
GOOD MORNING, MR. THORN.
I REALIZE YOU'RE EXPERIENCING SOME DISORIENTATION JUST NOW, BUT THAT WILL PASS.
WHAT THE HELL--?
OH, IT'S YOU AGAIN, REVISE.
WHAT TERRIBLE CRIME HAVE I COMMITTED THIS TIME, SON?
I'M DREADFULLY SORRY, FATHER, BUT YOU WERE BEGINNING TO REGAIN YOUR MEMORY.

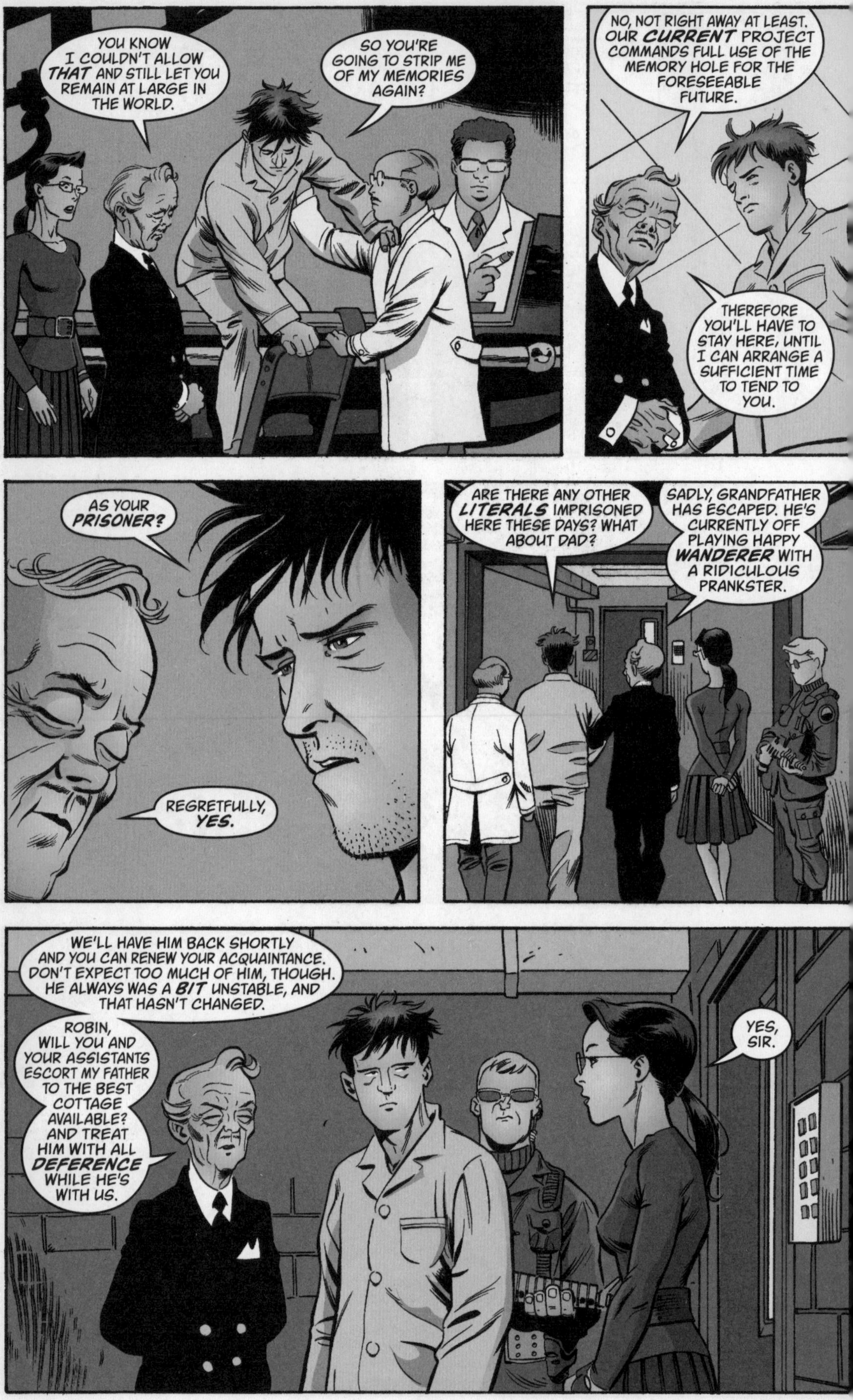
YOU KNOW I COULDN'T ALLOW THAT AND STILL LET YOU REMAIN AT LARGE IN THE WORLD.
SO YOU'RE GOING TO STRIP ME OF MY MEMORIES AGAIN?
NO, NOT RIGHT AWAY AT LEAST. OUR CURRENT PROJECT COMMANDS FULL USE OF THE MEMORY HOLE FOR THE FORESEEABLE FUTURE.
THEREFORE YOU'LL HAVE TO STAY HERE, UNTIL I CAN ARRANGE A SUFFICIENT TIME TO TEND TO YOU.
AS YOUR PRISONER?
REGRETFULLY, YES.
ARE THERE ANY OTHER LITERALS IMPRISONED HERE THESE DAYS? WHAT ABOUT DAD?
SADLY, GRANDFATHER HAS ESCAPED. HE'S CURRENTLY OFF PLAYING HAPPY WANDERER WITH A RIDICULOUS PRANKSTER.
WE'LL HAVE HIM BACK SHORTLY AND YOU CAN RENEW YOUR ACQUAINTANCE. DON'T EXPECT TOO MUCH OF HIM, THOUGH. HE ALWAYS WAS A BIT UNSTABLE, AND THAT HASN'T CHANGED.
ROBIN, WILL YOU AND YOUR ASSISTANTS ESCORT MY FATHER TO THE BEST COTTAGE AVAILABLE? AND TREAT HIM WITH ALL DEFERENCE WHILE HE'S WITH US.
YES, SIR.

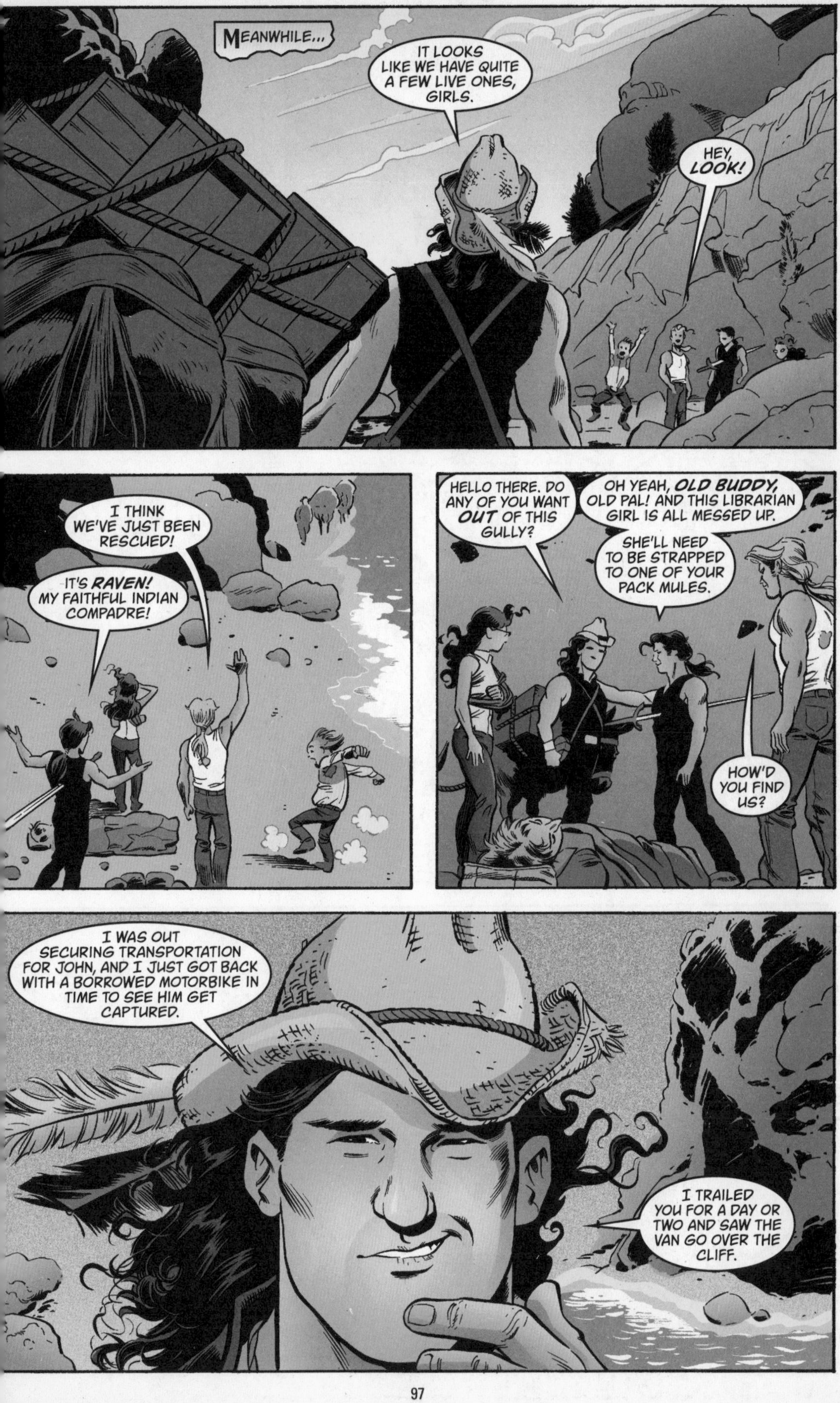
MEANWHILE...
IT LOOKS LIKE WE HAVE QUITE A FEW LIVE ONES, GIRLS.
HEY, LOOK!
I THINK WE'VE JUST BEEN RESCUED!
IT'S RAVEN! MY FAITHFUL INDIAN COMPADRE!
HELLO THERE. DO ANY OF YOU WANT OUT OF THIS GULLY?
OH YEAH, OLD BUDDY, OLD PAL! AND THIS LIBRARIAN GIRL IS ALL MESSED UP.
SHE'LL NEED TO BE STRAPPED TO ONE OF YOUR PACK MULES.
HOW'D YOU FIND US?
I WAS OUT SECURING TRANSPORTATION FOR JOHN, AND I JUST GOT BACK WITH A BORROWED MOTORBIKE IN TIME TO SEE HIM GET CAPTURED.
I TRAILED YOU FOR A DAY OR TWO AND SAW THE VAN GO OVER THE CLIFF.

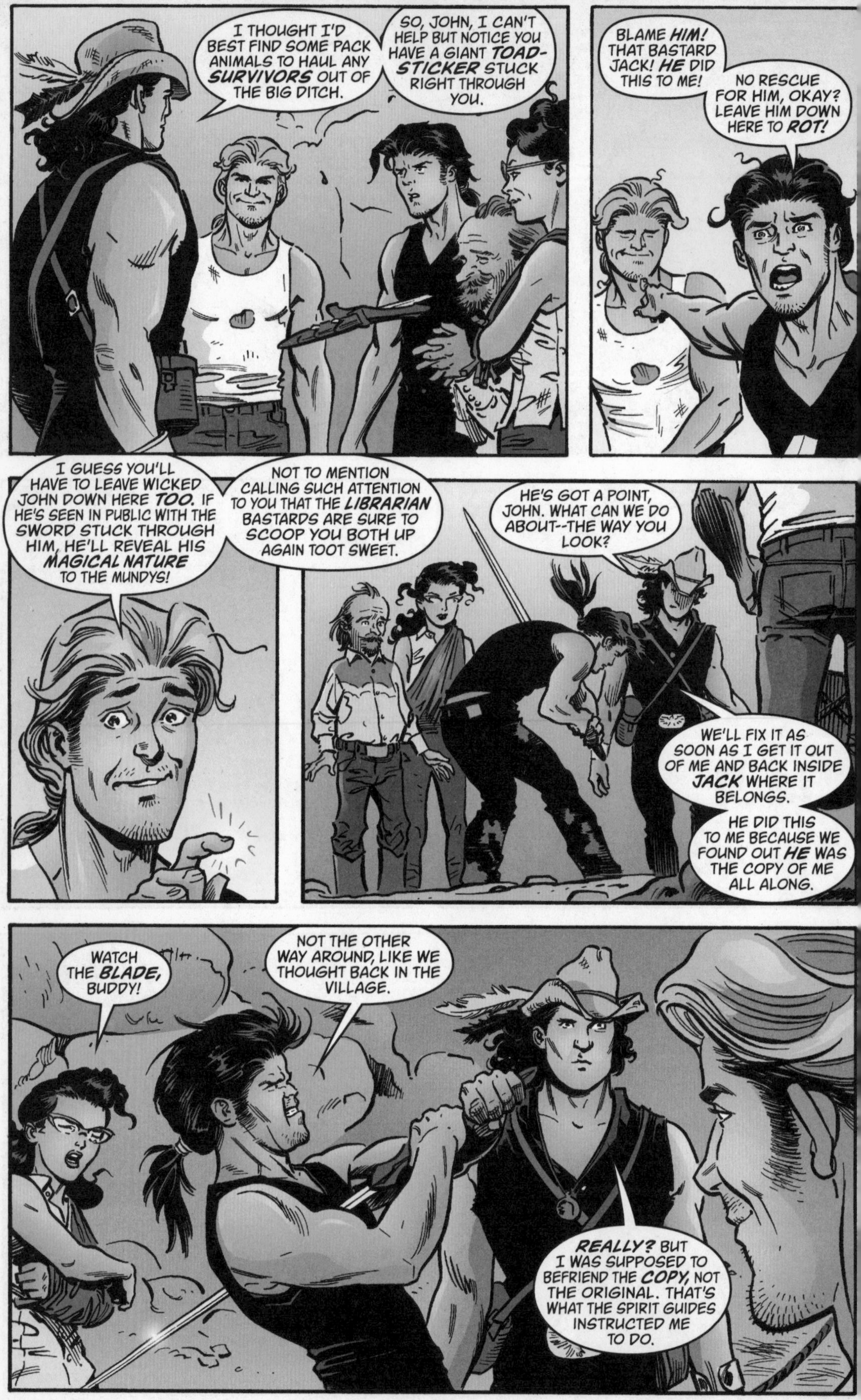
I THOUGHT I'D BEST FIND SOME PACK ANIMALS TO HAUL ANY SURVIVORS OUT OF THE BIG DITCH.
SO, JOHN, I CAN'T HELP BUT NOTICE YOU HAVE A GIANT TOAD-STICKER STUCK RIGHT THROUGH YOU.
BLAME HIM! THAT BASTARD JACK! HE DID THIS TO ME!
NO RESCUE FOR HIM, OKAY? LEAVE HIM DOWN HERE TO ROT!
I GUESS YOU'LL HAVE TO LEAVE WICKED JOHN DOWN HERE TOO. IF HE'S SEEN IN PUBLIC WITH THE SWORD STUCK THROUGH HIM, HE'LL REVEAL HIS MAGICAL NATURE TO THE MUNDYS!
NOT TO MENTION CALLING SUCH ATTENTION TO YOU THAT THE LIBRARIAN BASTARDS ARE SURE TO SCOOP YOU BOTH UP AGAIN TOOT SWEET.
HE'S GOT A POINT, JOHN. WHAT CAN WE DO ABOUT--THE WAY YOU LOOK?
WE'LL FIX IT AS SOON AS I GET IT OUT OF ME AND BACK INSIDE JACK WHERE IT BELONGS.
HE DID THIS TO ME BECAUSE WE FOUND OUT HE WAS THE COPY OF ME ALL ALONG.
WATCH THE BLADE, BUDDY!
NOT THE OTHER WAY AROUND, LIKE WE THOUGHT BACK IN THE VILLAGE.
REALLY? BUT I WAS SUPPOSED TO BEFRIEND THE COPY, NOT THE ORIGINAL. THAT'S WHAT THE SPIRIT GUIDES INSTRUCTED ME TO DO.

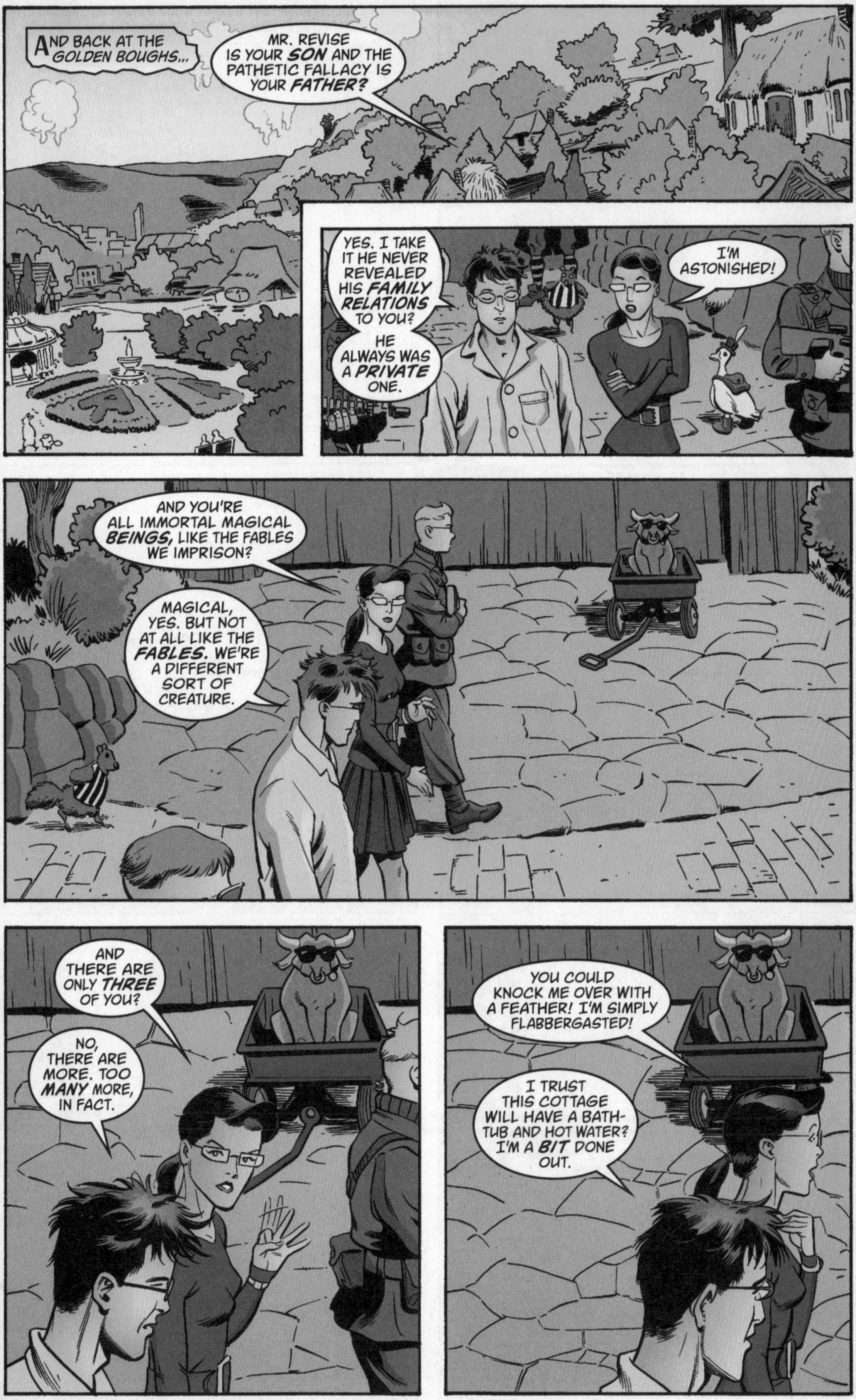
AND BACK AT THE GOLDEN BOUGHS...
MR. REVISE IS YOUR SON AND THE PATHETIC FALLACY IS YOUR FATHER?
YES. I TAKE IT HE NEVER REVEALED HIS FAMILY RELATIONS TO YOU?
HE ALWAYS WAS A PRIVATE ONE.
I'M ASTONISHED!
AND YOU'RE ALL IMMORTAL MAGICAL BEINGS, LIKE THE FABLES WE IMPRISON?
MAGICAL, YES. BUT NOT AT ALL LIKE THE FABLES. WE'RE A DIFFERENT SORT OF CREATURE.
AND THERE ARE ONLY THREE OF YOU?
NO, THERE ARE MORE. TOO MANY MORE, IN FACT.
YOU COULD KNOCK ME OVER WITH A FEATHER! I'M SIMPLY FLABBERGASTED!
I TRUST THIS COTTAGE WILL HAVE A BATH-TUB AND HOT WATER? I'M A BIT DONE OUT.

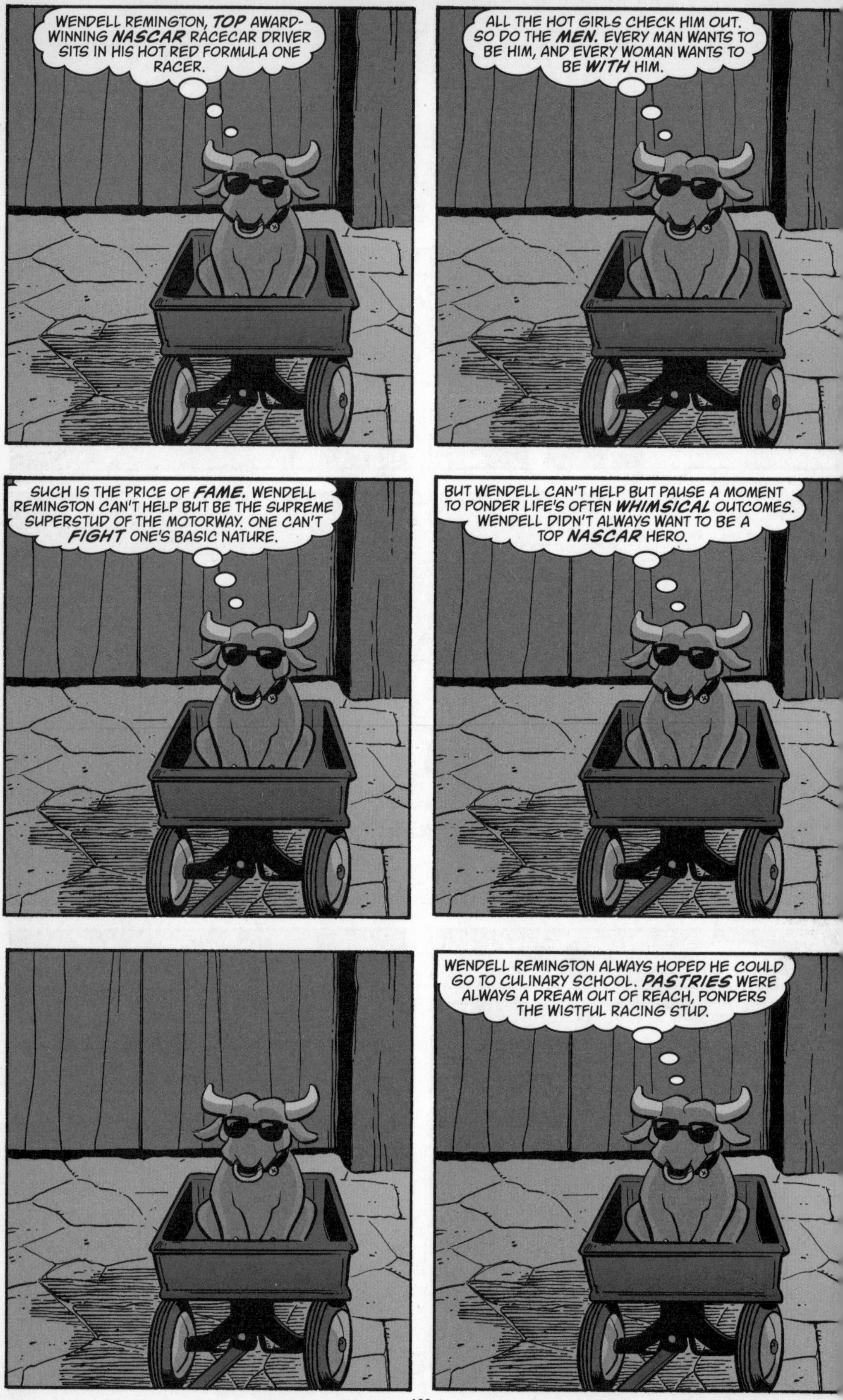

WENDELL REMINGTON, TOP AWARD-WINNING NASCAR RACECAR DRIVER SITS IN HIS HOT RED FORMULA ONE RACER.
ALL THE HOT GIRLS CHECK HIM OUT. SO DO THE MEN. EVERY MAN WANTS TO BE HIM, AND EVERY WOMAN WANTS TO BE WITH HIM.
SUCH IS THE PRICE OF FAME. WENDELL REMINGTON CAN'T HELP BUT BE THE SUPREME SUPERSTUD OF THE MOTORWAY. ONE CAN'T FIGHT ONE'S BASIC NATURE.
BUT WENDELL CAN'T HELP BUT PAUSE A MOMENT TO PONDER LIFE'S OFTEN WHIMSICAL OUTCOMES. WENDELL DIDN'T ALWAYS WANT TO BE A TOP NASCAR HERO.
WENDELL REMINGTON ALWAYS HOPED HE COULD GO TO CULINARY SCHOOL. PASTRIES WERE ALWAYS A DREAM OUT OF REACH, PONDERS THE WISTFUL RACING STUD.

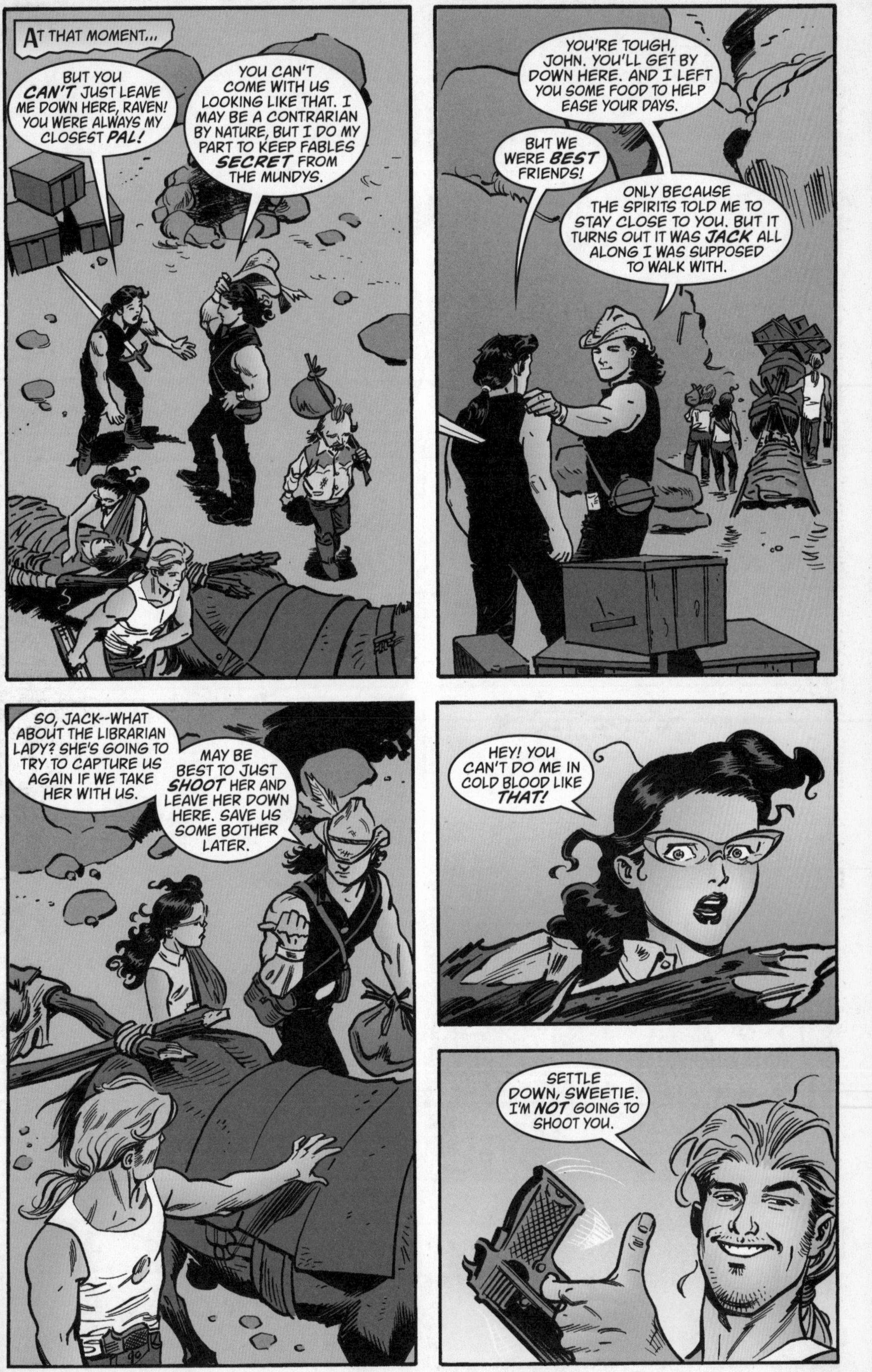
AT THAT MOMENT...
BUT YOU CAN'T JUST LEAVE ME DOWN HERE, RAVEN! YOU WERE ALWAYS MY CLOSEST PAL!
YOU CAN'T COME WITH US LOOKING LIKE THAT. I MAY BE A CONTRARIAN BY NATURE, BUT I DO MY PART TO KEEP FABLES SECRET FROM THE MUNDYS.
YOU'RE TOUGH, JOHN. YOU'LL GET BY DOWN HERE. AND I LEFT YOU SOME FOOD TO HELP EASE YOUR DAYS.
BUT WE WERE BEST FRIENDS!
ONLY BECAUSE THE SPIRITS TOLD ME TO STAY CLOSE TO YOU. BUT IT TURNS OUT IT WAS JACK ALL ALONG I WAS SUPPOSED TO WALK WITH.
SO, JACK--WHAT ABOUT THE LIBRARIAN LADY? SHE'S GOING TO TRY TO CAPTURE US AGAIN IF WE TAKE HER WITH US.
MAY BE BEST TO JUST SHOOT HER AND LEAVE HER DOWN HERE. SAVE US SOME BOTHER LATER.
HEY! YOU CAN'T DO ME IN COLD BLOOD LIKE THAT!
SETTLE DOWN, SWEETIE. I'M NOT GOING TO SHOOT YOU.

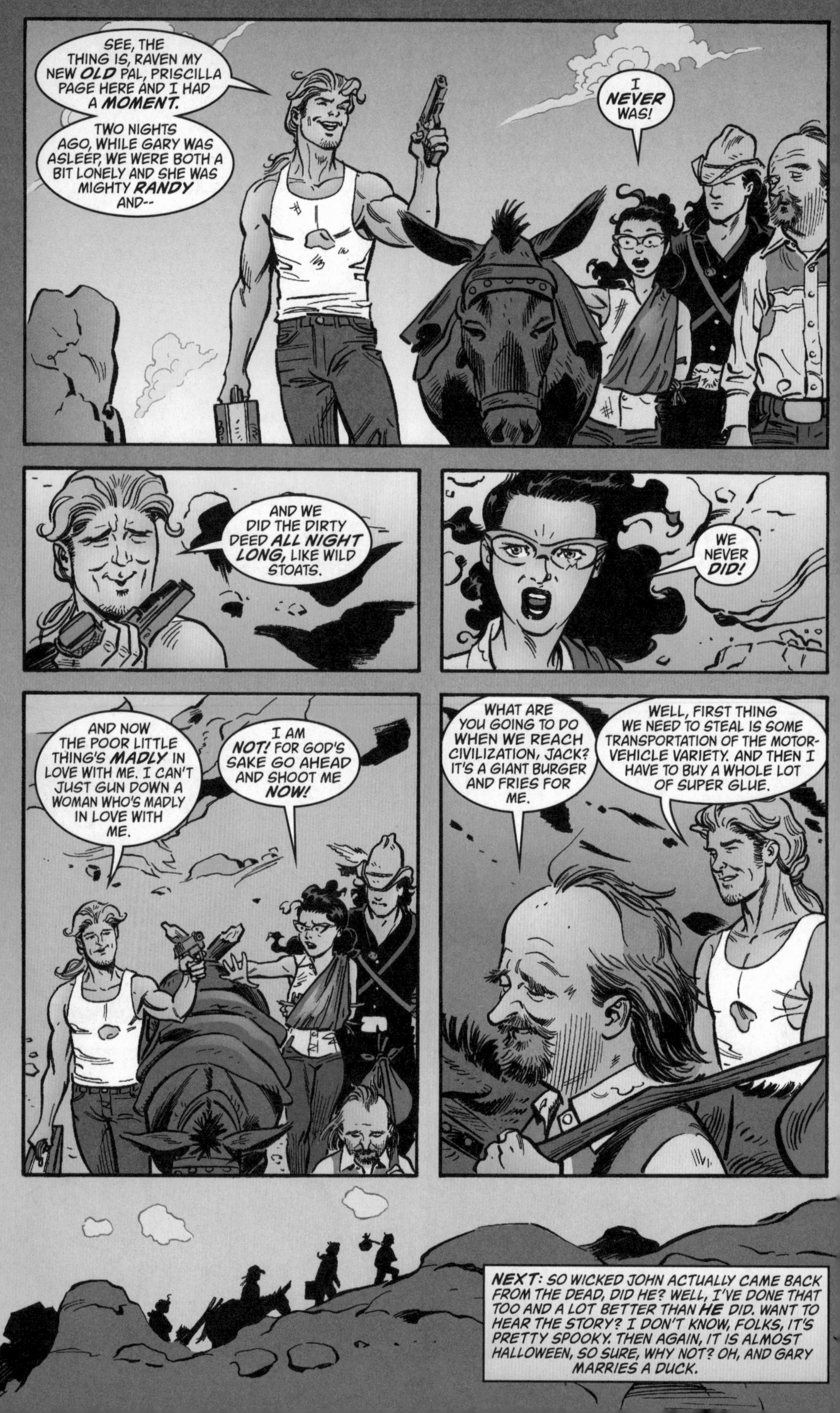

SEE, THE THING IS, RAVEN MY NEW OLD PAL, PRISCILLA PAGE HERE AND I HAD A MOMENT.
TWO NIGHTS AGO, WHILE GARY WAS ASLEEP, WE WERE BOTH A BIT LONELY AND SHE WAS MIGHTY RANDY AND--
I NEVER WAS!
AND WE DID THE DIRTY DEED ALL NIGHT LONG, LIKE WILD STOATS.
WE NEVER DID!
AND NOW THE POOR LITTLE THING'S MADLY IN LOVE WITH ME. I CAN'T JUST GUN DOWN A WOMAN WHO'S MADLY IN LOVE WITH ME.
I AM NOT! FOR GOD'S SAKE GO AHEAD AND SHOOT ME NOW!
WHAT ARE YOU GOING TO DO WHEN WE REACH CIVILIZATION, JACK? IT'S A GIANT BURGER AND FRIES FOR ME.
WELL, FIRST THING WE NEED TO STEAL IS SOME TRANSPORTATION OF THE MOTOR-VEHICLE VARIETY. AND THEN I HAVE TO BUY A WHOLE LOT OF SUPER GLUE.
NEXT: SO WICKED JOHN ACTUALLY CAME BACK FROM THE DEAD, DID HE? WELL, I'VE DONE THAT TOO AND A LOT BETTER THAN HE DID. WANT TO HEAR THE STORY? I DON'T KNOW, FOLKS, IT'S PRETTY SPOOKY. THEN AGAIN, IT IS ALMOST HALLOWEEN, SO SURE, WHY NOT? OH, AND GARY MARRIES A DUCK.

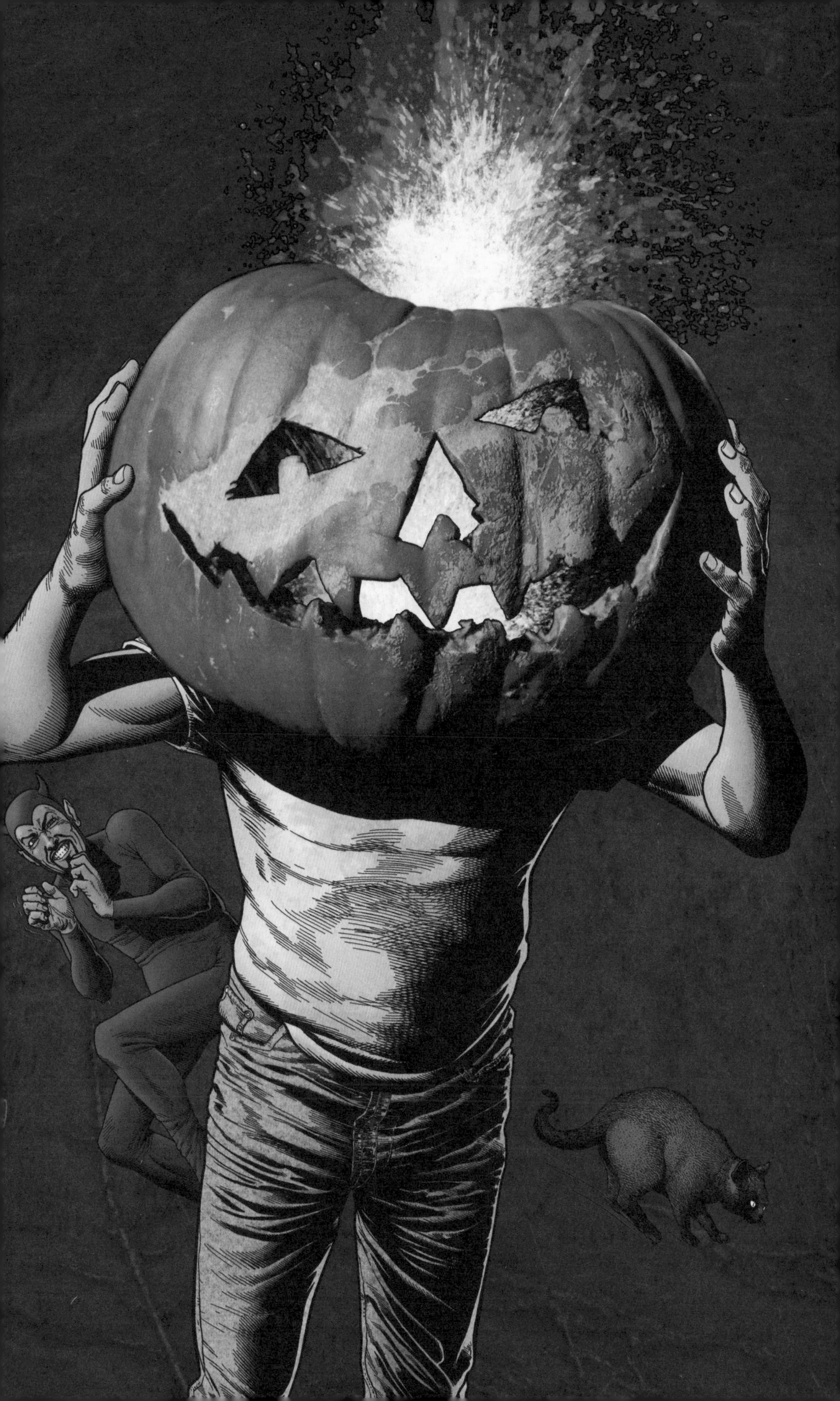

"You rubes!
Once I get my angel wings
I'm going to fly down here and
piss on every one of your
miserable peasant heads!"

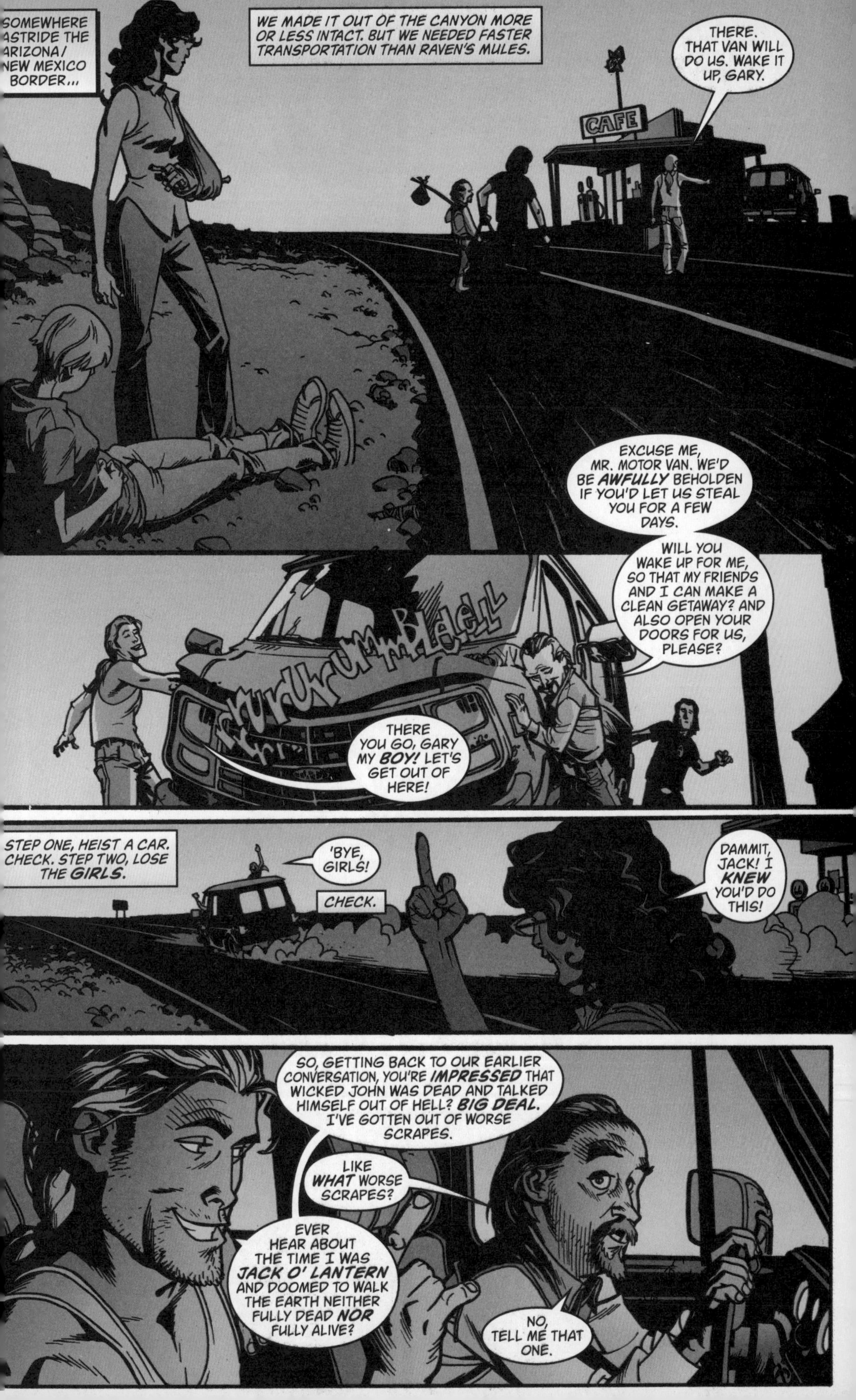

SOMEWHERE ASTRIDE THE ARIZONA/ NEW MEXICO BORDER...
WE MADE IT OUT OF THE CANYON MORE OR LESS INTACT. BUT WE NEEDED FASTER TRANSPORTATION THAN RAVEN'S MULES.
THERE. THAT VAN WILL DO US. WAKE IT UP, GARY.
CAFE
EXCUSE ME, MR. MOTOR VAN. WE'D BE AWFULLY BEHOLDEN IF YOU'D LET US STEAL YOU FOR A FEW DAYS.
WILL YOU WAKE UP FOR ME, SO THAT MY FRIENDS AND I CAN MAKE A CLEAN GETAWAY? AND ALSO OPEN YOUR DOORS FOR US, PLEASE?
THERE YOU GO, GARY MY BOY! LET'S GET OUT OF HERE!
STEP ONE, HEIST A CAR. CHECK. STEP TWO, LOSE THE GIRLS.
'BYE, GIRLS!
CHECK.
DAMMIT, JACK! I KNEW YOU'D DO THIS!
SO, GETTING BACK TO OUR EARLIER CONVERSATION, YOU'RE IMPRESSED THAT WICKED JOHN WAS DEAD AND TALKED HIMSELF OUT OF HELL? BIG DEAL. I'VE GOTTEN OUT OF WORSE SCRAPES.
LIKE WHAT WORSE SCRAPES?
EVER HEAR ABOUT THE TIME I WAS JACK O' LANTERN AND DOOMED TO WALK THE EARTH NEITHER FULLY DEAD NOR FULLY ALIVE?
NO, TELL ME THAT ONE.

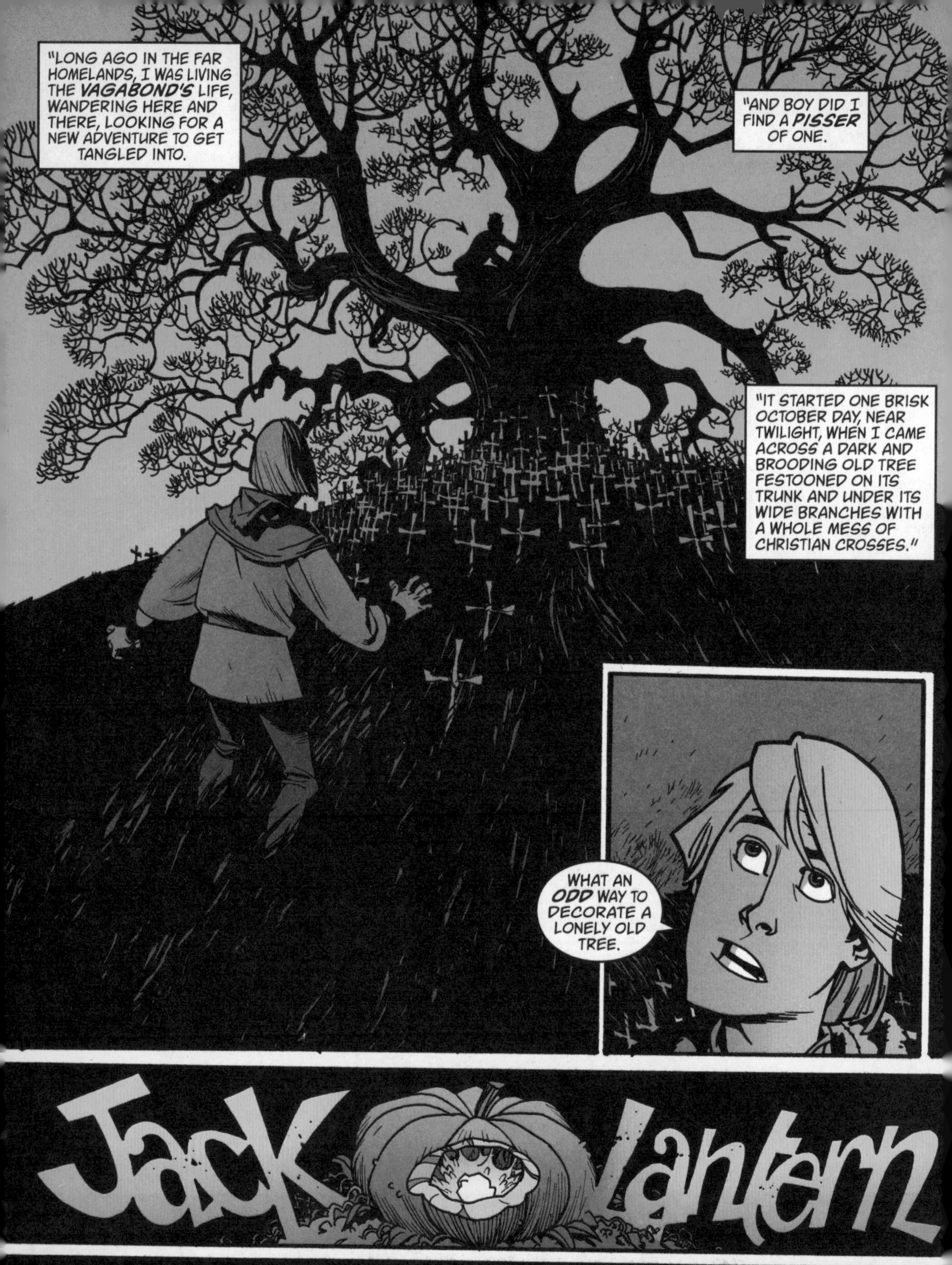
"LONG AGO IN THE FAR HOMELANDS, I WAS LIVING THE VAGABOND'S LIFE, WANDERING HERE AND THERE, LOOKING FOR A NEW ADVENTURE TO GET TANGLED INTO.
"AND BOY DID I FIND A PISSER OF ONE.
"IT STARTED ONE BRISK OCTOBER DAY, NEAR TWILIGHT, WHEN I CAME ACROSS A DARK AND BROODING OLD TREE FESTOONED ON ITS TRUNK AND UNDER ITS WIDE BRANCHES WITH A WHOLE MESS OF CHRISTIAN CROSSES."
WHAT AN ODD WAY TO DECORATE A LONELY OLD TREE.
Jack Lantern

In which we take a short time-out between our last epic arc and the next one to tell you a spooky little tale just in time for All Hallows' Eve.

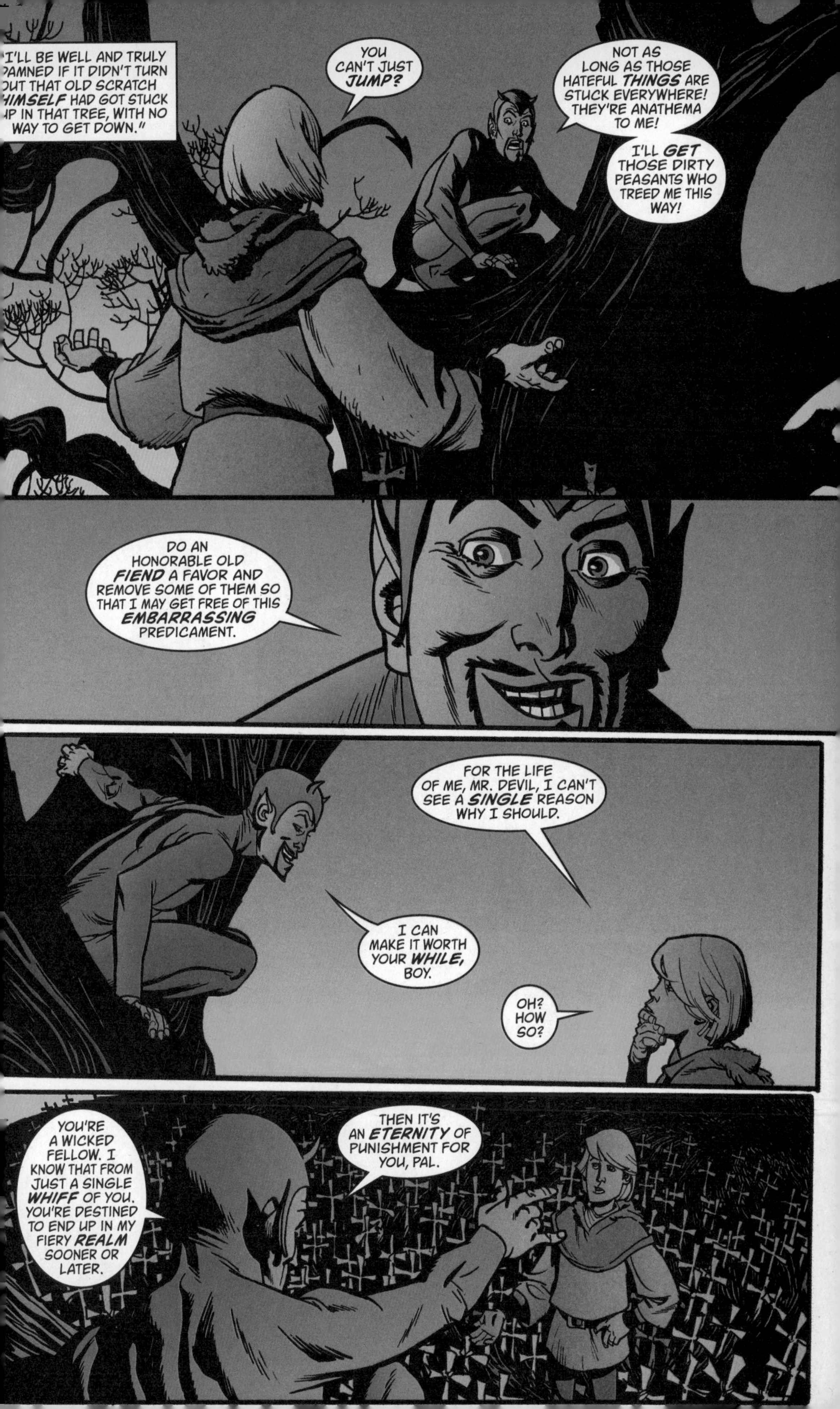
"I'LL BE WELL AND TRULY DAMNED IF IT DIDN'T TURN OUT THAT OLD SCRATCH HIMSELF HAD GOT STUCK UP IN THAT TREE, WITH NO WAY TO GET DOWN."
YOU CAN'T JUST JUMP?
NOT AS LONG AS THOSE HATEFUL THINGS ARE STUCK EVERYWHERE! THEY'RE ANATHEMA TO ME!
I'LL GET THOSE DIRTY PEASANTS WHO TREED ME THIS WAY!
DO AN HONORABLE OLD FIEND A FAVOR AND REMOVE SOME OF THEM SO THAT I MAY GET FREE OF THIS EMBARRASSING PREDICAMENT.
FOR THE LIFE OF ME, MR. DEVIL, I CAN'T SEE A SINGLE REASON WHY I SHOULD.
I CAN MAKE IT WORTH YOUR WHILE, BOY.
OH? HOW SO?
YOU'RE A WICKED FELLOW. I KNOW THAT FROM JUST A SINGLE WHIFF OF YOU. YOU'RE DESTINED TO END UP IN MY FIERY REALM SOONER OR LATER.
THEN IT'S AN ETERNITY OF PUNISHMENT FOR YOU, PAL.

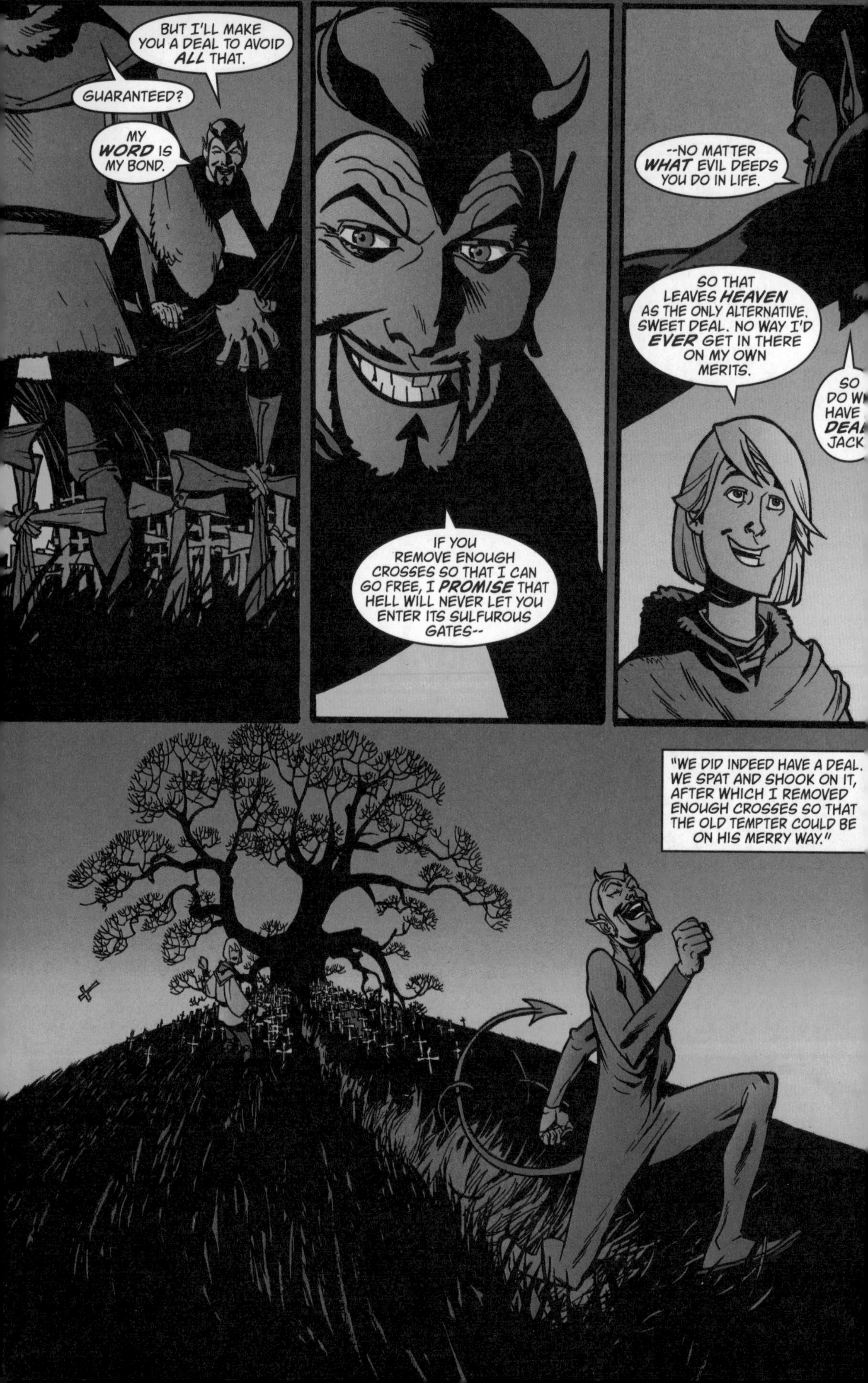
BUT I'LL MAKE YOU A DEAL TO AVOID ALL THAT.
GUARANTEED?
MY WORD IS MY BOND.
IF YOU REMOVE ENOUGH CROSSES SO THAT I CAN GO FREE, I PROMISE THAT HELL WILL NEVER LET YOU ENTER ITS SULFUROUS GATES--
--NO MATTER WHAT EVIL DEEDS YOU DO IN LIFE.
SO THAT LEAVES HEAVEN AS THE ONLY ALTERNATIVE. SWEET DEAL. NO WAY I'D EVER GET IN THERE ON MY OWN MERITS.
SO DO W HAVE DEA JACK
"WE DID INDEED HAVE A DEAL. WE SPAT AND SHOOK ON IT, AFTER WHICH I REMOVED ENOUGH CROSSES SO THAT THE OLD TEMPTER COULD BE ON HIS MERRY WAY."

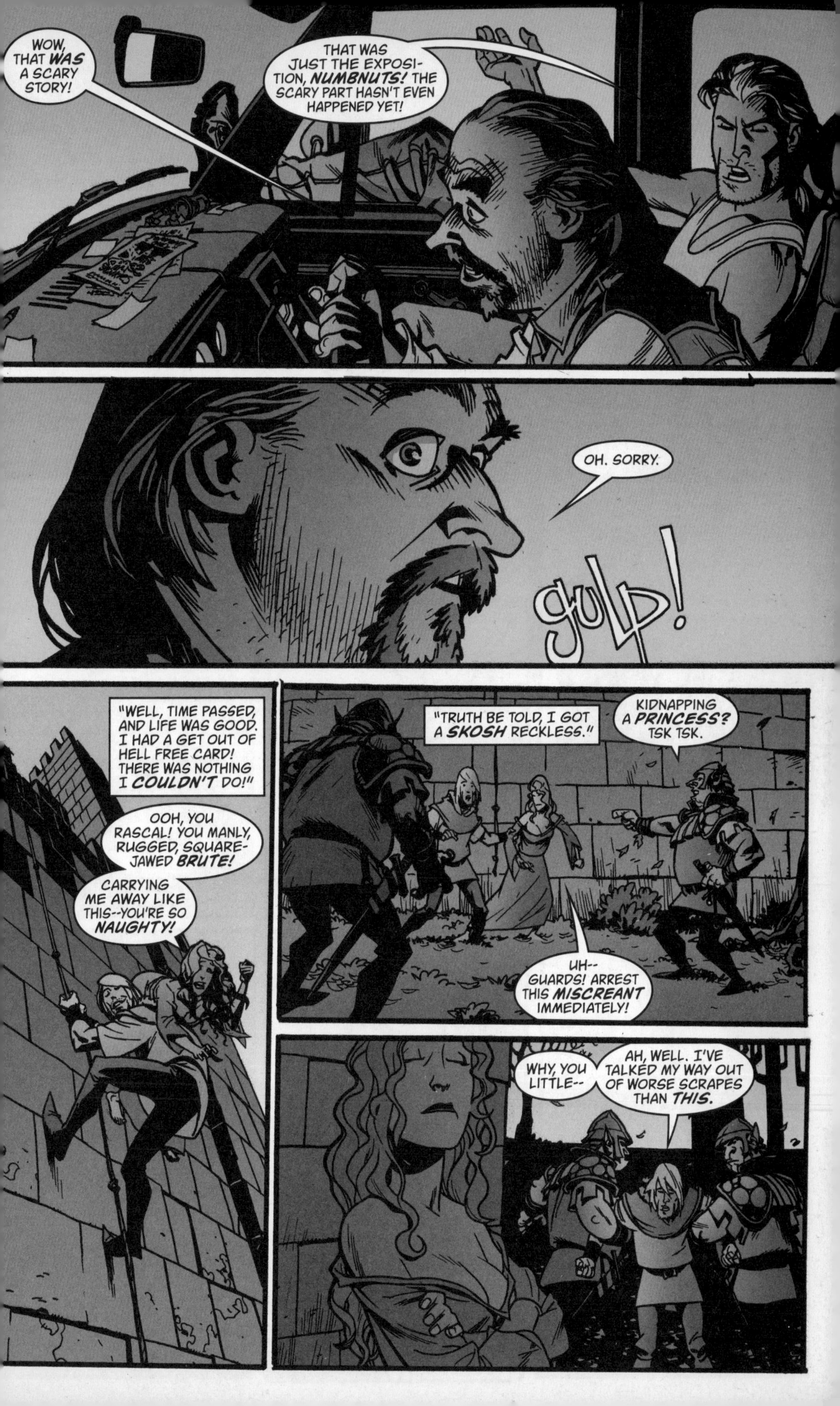
WOW, THAT WAS A SCARY STORY!
THAT WAS JUST THE EXPOSITION, NUMBNUTS! THE SCARY PART HASN'T EVEN HAPPENED YET!
OH. SORRY.
GULP!
"WELL, TIME PASSED, AND LIFE WAS GOOD. I HAD A GET OUT OF HELL FREE CARD! THERE WAS NOTHING I COULDN'T DO!"
OOH, YOU RASCAL! YOU MANLY, RUGGED, SQUARE-JAWED BRUTE!
CARRYING ME AWAY LIKE THIS--YOU'RE SO NAUGHTY!
"TRUTH BE TOLD, I GOT A SKOSH RECKLESS."
KIDNAPPING A PRINCESS? TSK TSK.
UH-- GUARDS! ARREST THIS MISCREANT IMMEDIATELY!
WHY, YOU LITTLE--
AH, WELL. I'VE TALKED MY WAY OUT OF WORSE SCRAPES THAN THIS.

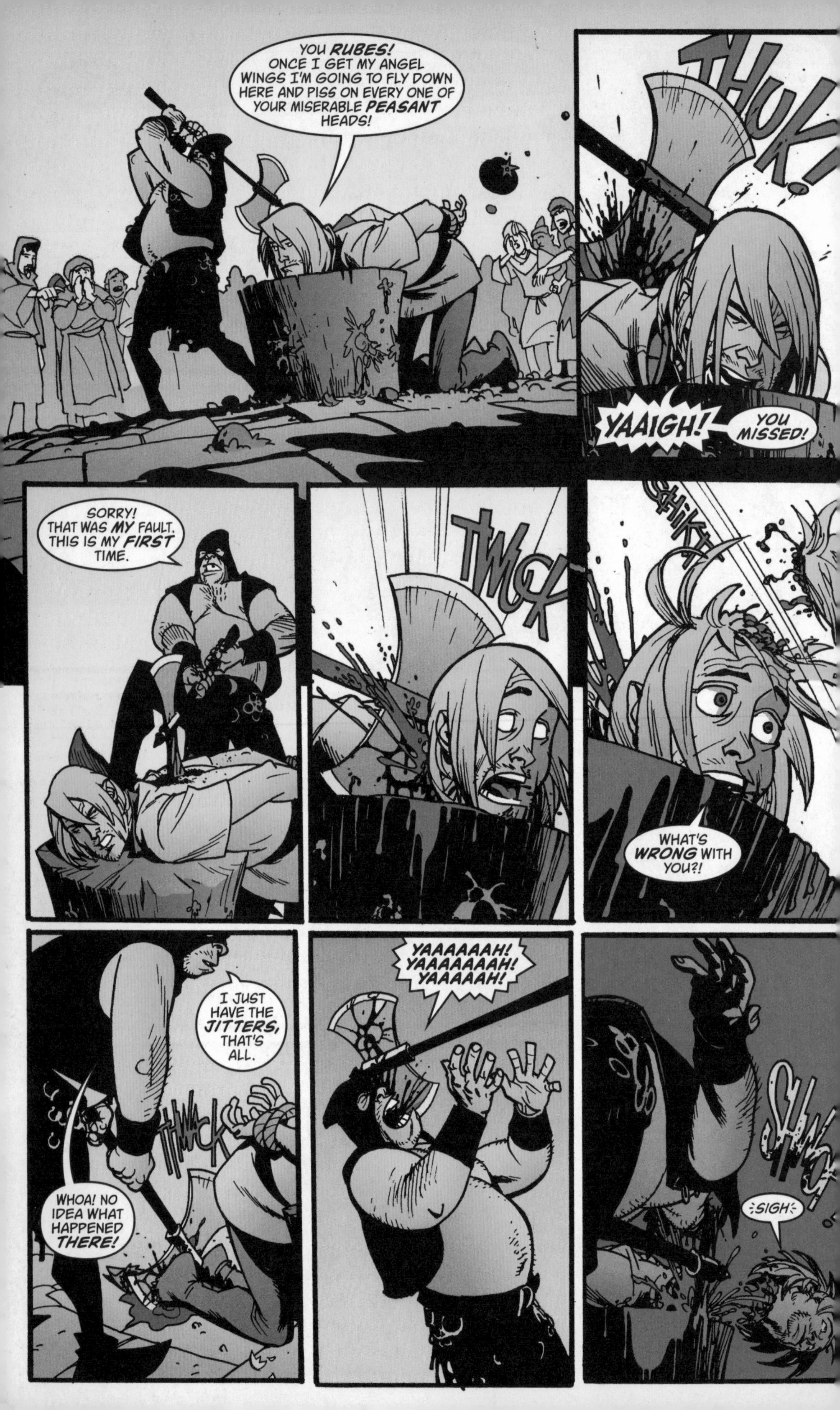

YOU RUBES! ONCE I GET MY ANGEL WINGS I'M GOING TO FLY DOWN HERE AND PISS ON EVERY ONE OF YOUR MISERABLE PEASANT HEADS!
THUK!
YAAIGH!
YOU MISSED!
SORRY! THAT WAS MY FAULT. THIS IS MY FIRST TIME.
TWOCK
CHIKT
WHAT'S WRONG WITH YOU?!
I JUST HAVE THE JITTERS, THAT'S ALL.
THWACK
WHOA! NO IDEA WHAT HAPPENED THERE!
YAAAAAAH! YAAAAAAAH! YAAAAAH!
SIGH

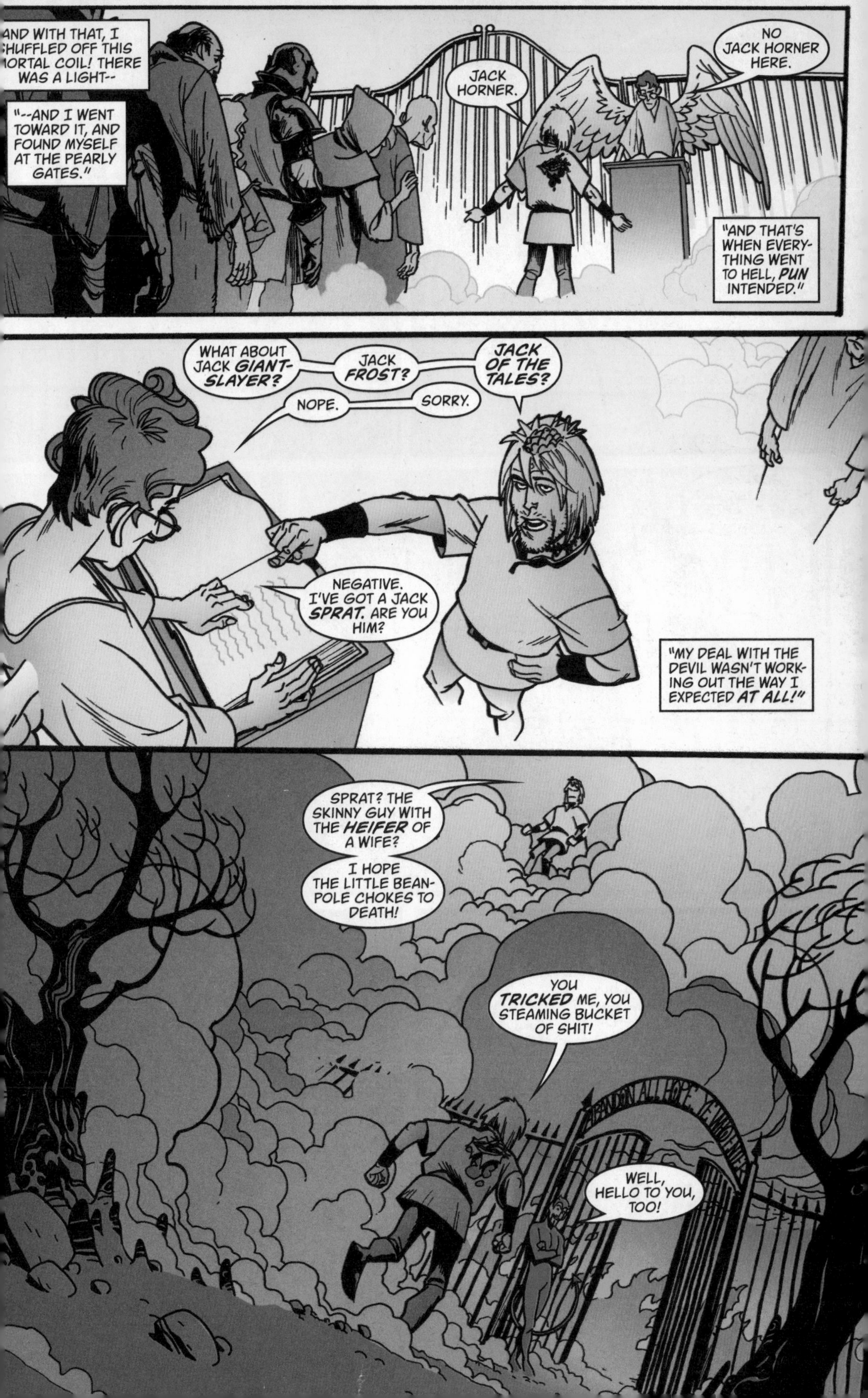
AND WITH THAT, I SHUFFLED OFF THIS MORTAL COIL! THERE WAS A LIGHT--
"--AND I WENT TOWARD IT, AND FOUND MYSELF AT THE PEARLY GATES."
JACK HORNER.
NO JACK HORNER HERE.
"AND THAT'S WHEN EVERYTHING WENT TO HELL, *PUN* INTENDED."
WHAT ABOUT JACK *GIANT-SLAYER?*
NOPE.
JACK FROST?
SORRY.
JACK OF THE TALES?
NEGATIVE. I'VE GOT A JACK *SPRAT.* ARE YOU HIM?
"MY DEAL WITH THE DEVIL WASN'T WORKING OUT THE WAY I EXPECTED *AT ALL!*"
SPRAT? THE SKINNY GUY WITH THE *HEIFER* OF A WIFE?
I HOPE THE LITTLE BEANPOLE CHOKES TO DEATH!
YOU *TRICKED* ME, YOU STEAMING BUCKET OF SHIT!
WELL, HELLO TO YOU, TOO!

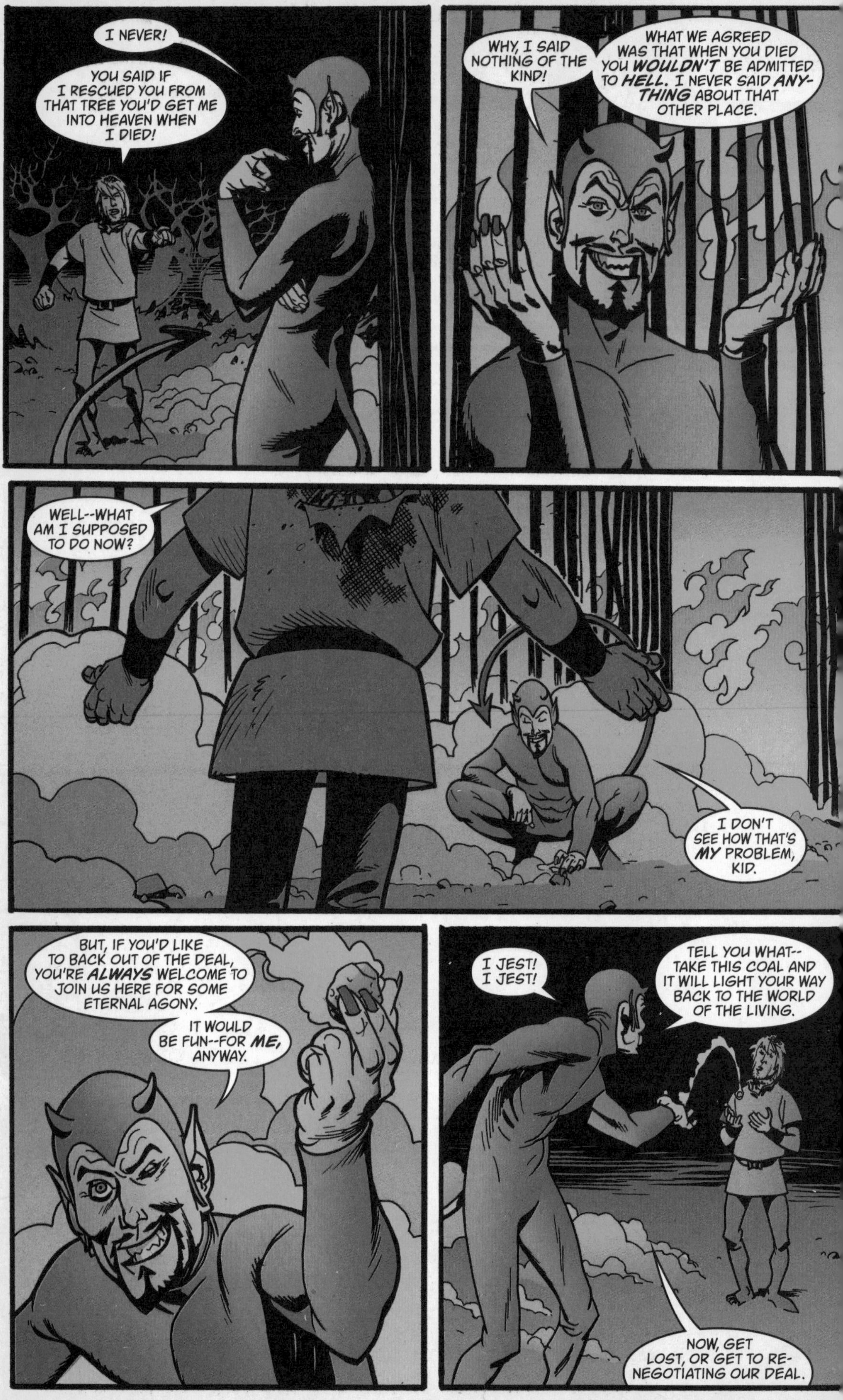
I NEVER!
YOU SAID IF I RESCUED YOU FROM THAT TREE YOU'D GET ME INTO HEAVEN WHEN I DIED!
WHY, I SAID NOTHING OF THE KIND!
WHAT WE AGREED WAS THAT WHEN YOU DIED YOU **WOULDN'T** BE ADMITTED TO **HELL.** I NEVER SAID **ANY-THING** ABOUT THAT OTHER PLACE.
WELL--WHAT AM I SUPPOSED TO DO NOW?
I DON'T SEE HOW THAT'S **MY** PROBLEM, KID.
BUT, IF YOU'D LIKE TO BACK OUT OF THE DEAL, YOU'RE **ALWAYS** WELCOME TO JOIN US HERE FOR SOME ETERNAL AGONY.
IT WOULD BE FUN--FOR **ME,** ANYWAY.
I JEST! I JEST!
TELL YOU WHAT--TAKE THIS COAL AND IT WILL LIGHT YOUR WAY BACK TO THE WORLD OF THE LIVING.
NOW, GET LOST, OR GET TO RE-NEGOTIATING OUR DEAL.

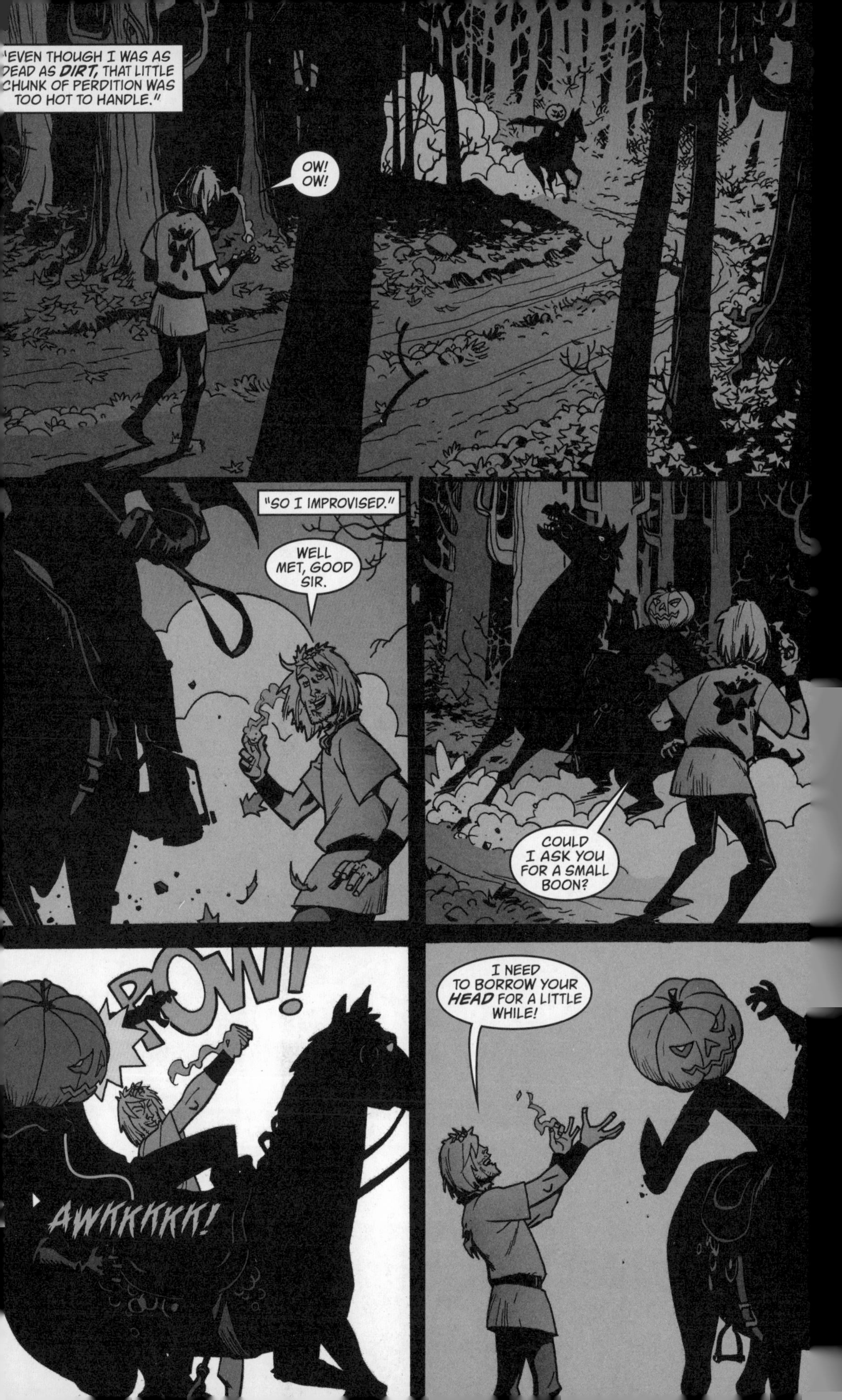
"EVEN THOUGH I WAS AS DEAD AS *DIRT,* THAT LITTLE CHUNK OF PERDITION WAS TOO HOT TO HANDLE."
OW! OW!
"SO I IMPROVISED."
WELL MET, GOOD SIR.
COULD I ASK YOU FOR A SMALL BOON?
POW!
AWKKKKK!
I NEED TO BORROW YOUR *HEAD* FOR A LITTLE WHILE!

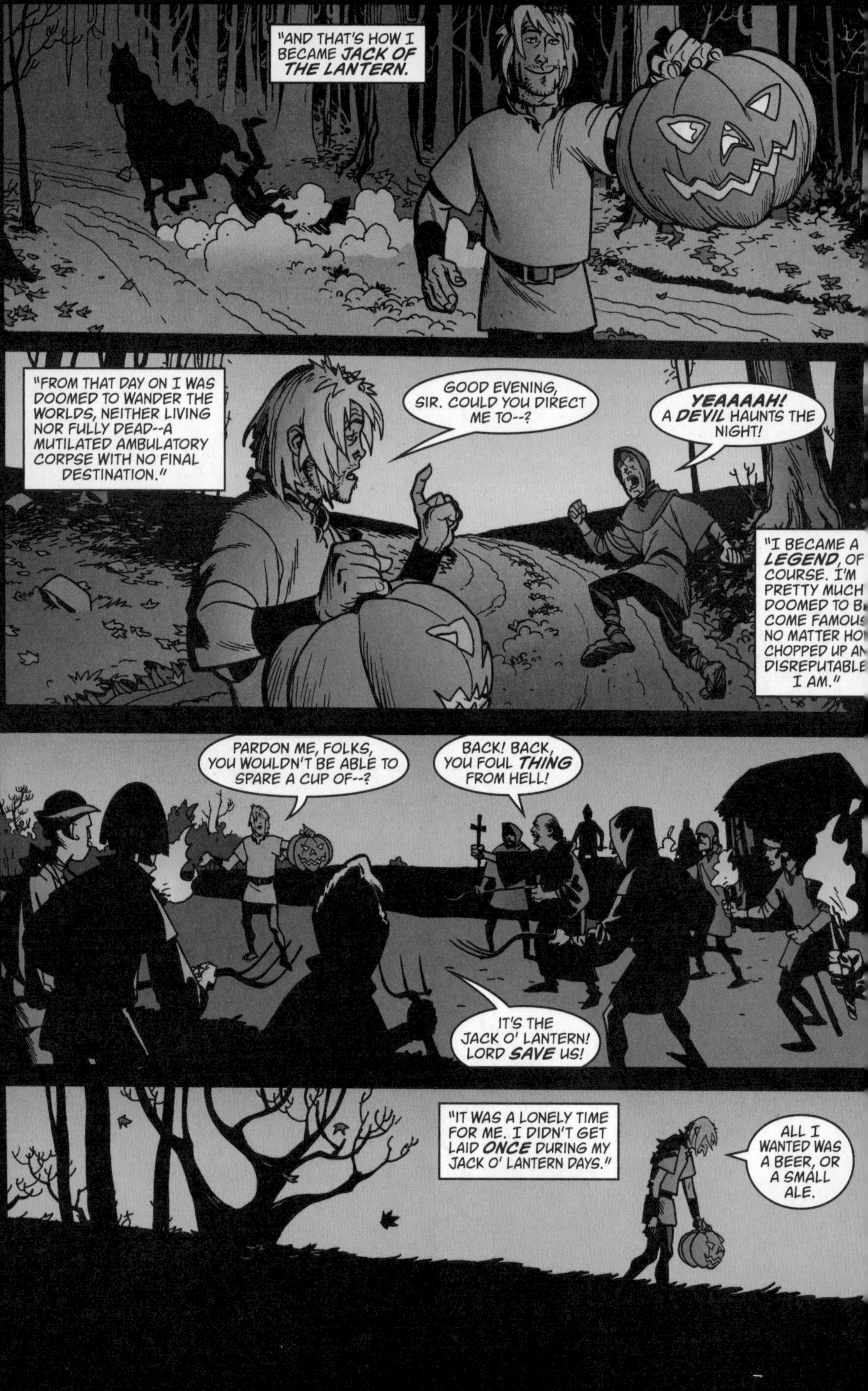

"AND THAT'S HOW I BECAME JACK OF THE LANTERN.
"FROM THAT DAY ON I WAS DOOMED TO WANDER THE WORLDS, NEITHER LIVING NOR FULLY DEAD--A MUTILATED AMBULATORY CORPSE WITH NO FINAL DESTINATION."
GOOD EVENING, SIR. COULD YOU DIRECT ME TO--?
YEAAAAH! A DEVIL HAUNTS THE NIGHT!
"I BECAME A LEGEND, OF COURSE. I'M PRETTY MUCH DOOMED TO B COME FAMOU NO MATTER HO CHOPPED UP AN DISREPUTABLE I AM."
PARDON ME, FOLKS, YOU WOULDN'T BE ABLE TO SPARE A CUP OF--?
BACK! BACK, YOU FOUL THING FROM HELL!
IT'S THE JACK O' LANTERN! LORD SAVE US!
"IT WAS A LONELY TIME FOR ME. I DIDN'T GET LAID ONCE DURING MY JACK O' LANTERN DAYS."
ALL I WANTED WAS A BEER, OR A SMALL ALE.

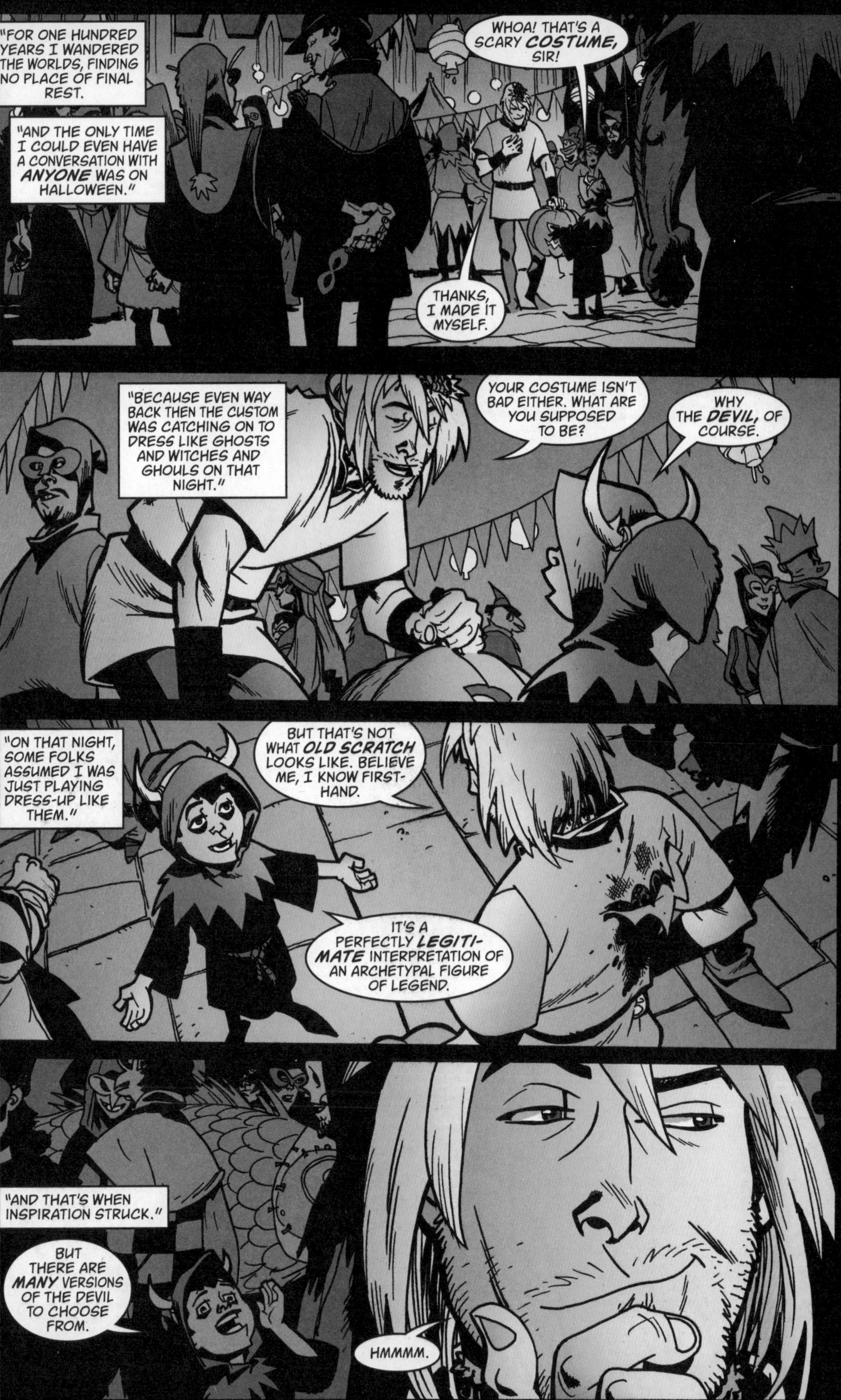
"FOR ONE HUNDRED YEARS I WANDERED THE WORLDS, FINDING NO PLACE OF FINAL REST.
"AND THE ONLY TIME I COULD EVEN HAVE A CONVERSATION WITH ANYONE WAS ON HALLOWEEN."
WHOA! THAT'S A SCARY COSTUME, SIR!
THANKS, I MADE IT MYSELF.
"BECAUSE EVEN WAY BACK THEN THE CUSTOM WAS CATCHING ON TO DRESS LIKE GHOSTS AND WITCHES AND GHOULS ON THAT NIGHT."
YOUR COSTUME ISN'T BAD EITHER. WHAT ARE YOU SUPPOSED TO BE?
WHY THE DEVIL, OF COURSE.
"ON THAT NIGHT, SOME FOLKS ASSUMED I WAS JUST PLAYING DRESS-UP LIKE THEM."
BUT THAT'S NOT WHAT OLD SCRATCH LOOKS LIKE. BELIEVE ME, I KNOW FIRST-HAND.
IT'S A PERFECTLY LEGITI-MATE INTERPRETATION OF AN ARCHETYPAL FIGURE OF LEGEND.
"AND THAT'S WHEN INSPIRATION STRUCK."
BUT THERE ARE MANY VERSIONS OF THE DEVIL TO CHOOSE FROM.
HMMMM.

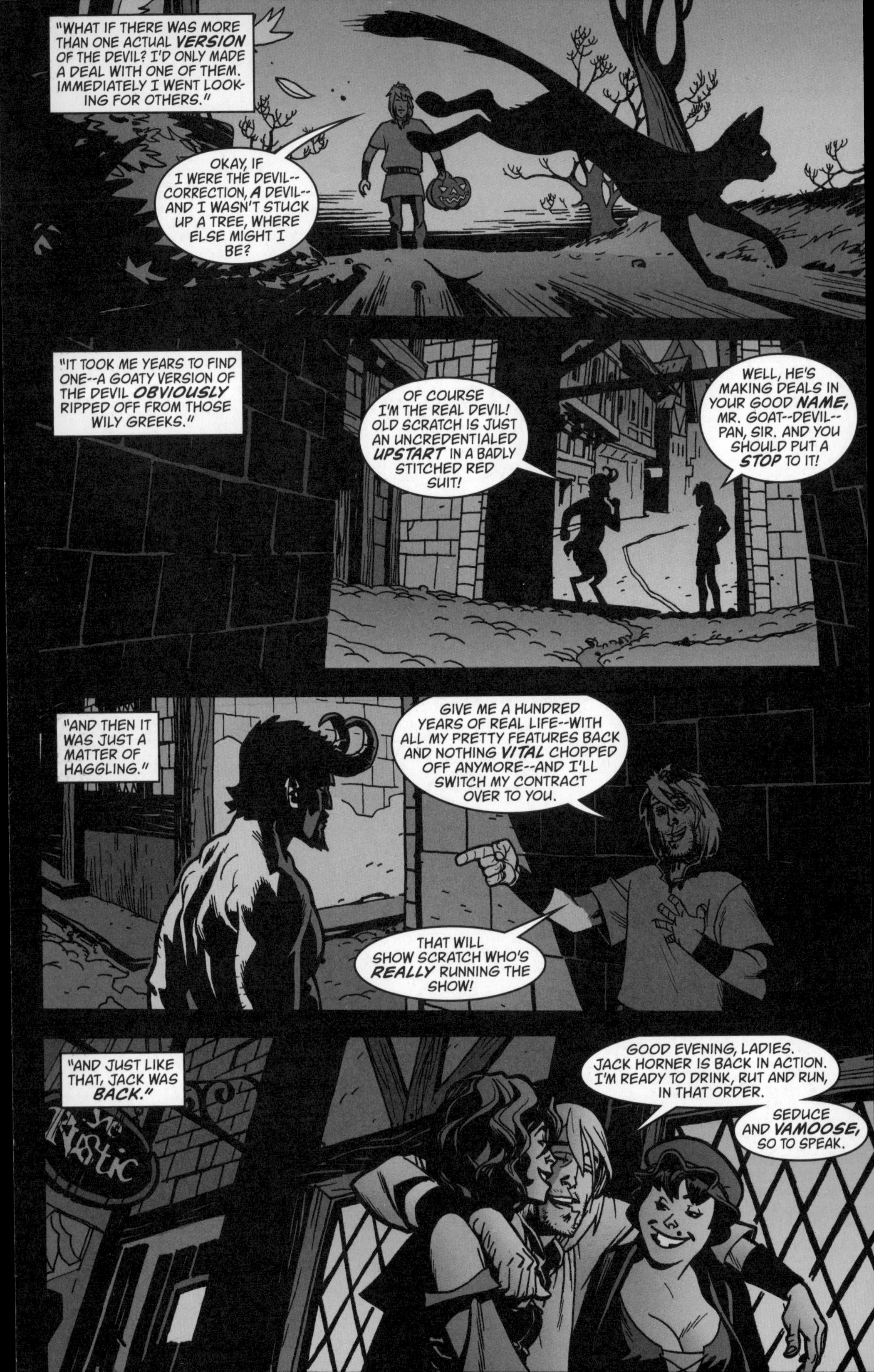
"WHAT IF THERE WAS MORE THAN ONE ACTUAL VERSION OF THE DEVIL? I'D ONLY MADE A DEAL WITH ONE OF THEM. IMMEDIATELY I WENT LOOKING FOR OTHERS."
OKAY, IF I WERE THE DEVIL-- CORRECTION, A DEVIL-- AND I WASN'T STUCK UP A TREE, WHERE ELSE MIGHT I BE?
"IT TOOK ME YEARS TO FIND ONE--A GOATY VERSION OF THE DEVIL OBVIOUSLY RIPPED OFF FROM THOSE WILY GREEKS."
OF COURSE I'M THE REAL DEVIL! OLD SCRATCH IS JUST AN UNCREDENTIALED UPSTART IN A BADLY STITCHED RED SUIT!
WELL, HE'S MAKING DEALS IN YOUR GOOD NAME, MR. GOAT--DEVIL--PAN, SIR. AND YOU SHOULD PUT A STOP TO IT!
"AND THEN IT WAS JUST A MATTER OF HAGGLING."
GIVE ME A HUNDRED YEARS OF REAL LIFE--WITH ALL MY PRETTY FEATURES BACK AND NOTHING VITAL CHOPPED OFF ANYMORE--AND I'LL SWITCH MY CONTRACT OVER TO YOU.
THAT WILL SHOW SCRATCH WHO'S REALLY RUNNING THE SHOW!
"AND JUST LIKE THAT, JACK WAS BACK."
GOOD EVENING, LADIES. JACK HORNER IS BACK IN ACTION. I'M READY TO DRINK, RUT AND RUN, IN THAT ORDER.
SEDUCE AND VAMOOSE, SO TO SPEAK.

F COURSE THERE WAS THE LIGHT PROBLEM THAT, UNDER E NEW DEAL, GOATY DEVIL GOT SOUL IN A HUNDRED YEARS."
NO, I DON'T WANT TO GET TO NOW YOU BETTER, LADY. I HAVE NLY 99 YEARS, SEVEN MONTHS AND THREE DAYS LEFT.
"BUT HE WAS A BETTER NEGOTIATOR THAN I EXPECTED AND WOULDN'T BUY OUT MY CONTRACT FROM THE OTHER GUY WITHOUT THAT ADDED PROVISO."
I CAN'T WASTE TIME WITH IDLE CHIT-CHAT.
RIP THAT BODICE AND LET'S GET DOWN TO BUSINESS.
"AS THE YEARS RELENTLESSLY TICKED BY, I WENT LOOKING FOR YET A THIRD DEVIL WHO MIGHT BE WILLING TO BUY MY DEBT FROM THE GOATY DEVIL DUDE."
In saying quite thou will abjure th' empyrean to stretch on my incarnadine shoal, and for thy agonies require but some fivescore fulgent years of blood and bone?
UH, YEAH, WHAT YOU SAID, LUCY-FUR.
and at my bawdy revels thou wilt me attend-- up to and including sensual back-rubs?

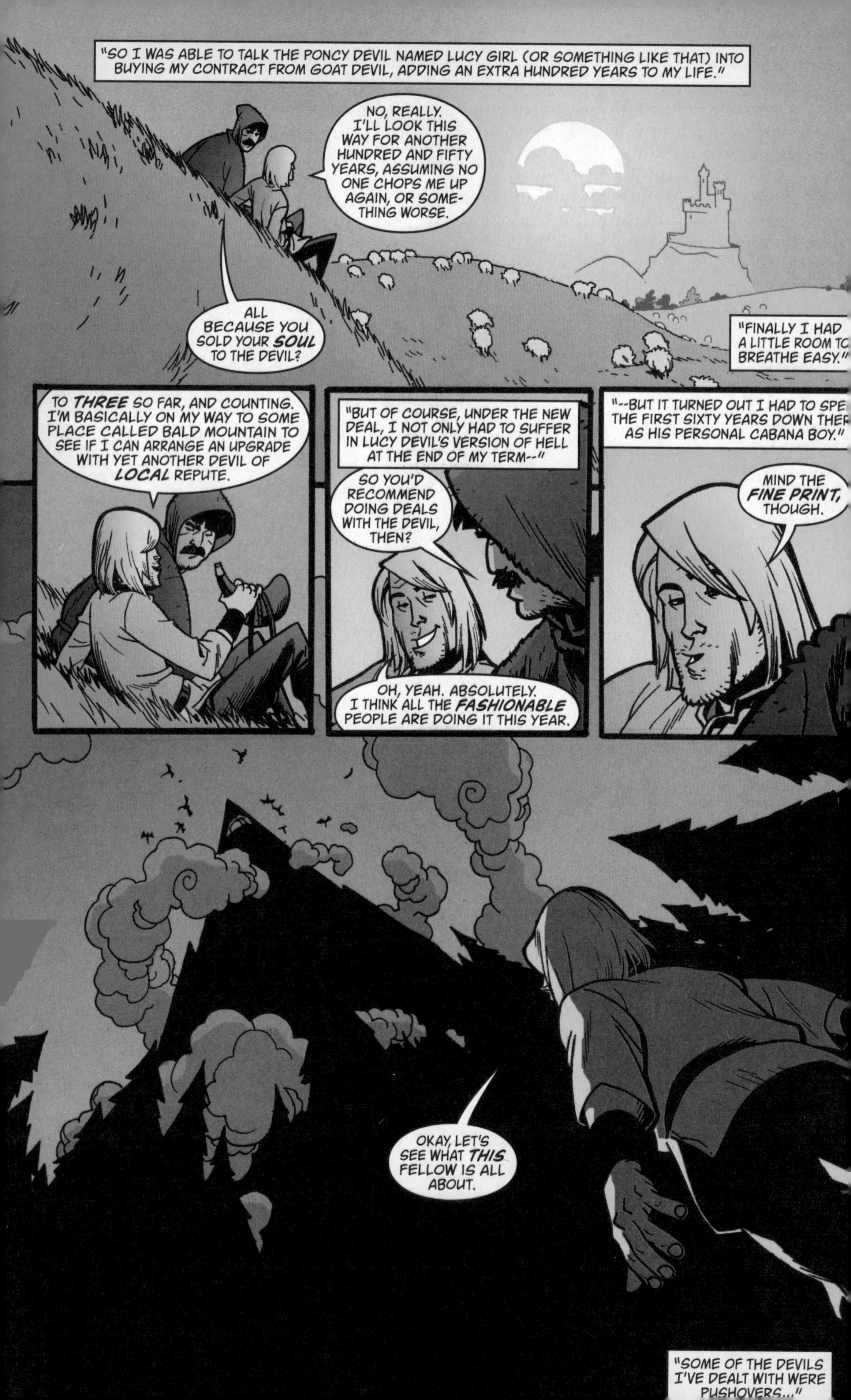
"SO I WAS ABLE TO TALK THE PONCY DEVIL NAMED LUCY GIRL (OR SOMETHING LIKE THAT) INTO BUYING MY CONTRACT FROM GOAT DEVIL, ADDING AN EXTRA HUNDRED YEARS TO MY LIFE."
ALL BECAUSE YOU SOLD YOUR SOUL TO THE DEVIL?
NO, REALLY. I'LL LOOK THIS WAY FOR ANOTHER HUNDRED AND FIFTY YEARS, ASSUMING NO ONE CHOPS ME UP AGAIN, OR SOMETHING WORSE.
"FINALLY I HAD A LITTLE ROOM TO BREATHE EASY."
TO THREE SO FAR, AND COUNTING. I'M BASICALLY ON MY WAY TO SOME PLACE CALLED BALD MOUNTAIN TO SEE IF I CAN ARRANGE AN UPGRADE WITH YET ANOTHER DEVIL OF LOCAL REPUTE.
"BUT OF COURSE, UNDER THE NEW DEAL, I NOT ONLY HAD TO SUFFER IN LUCY DEVIL'S VERSION OF HELL AT THE END OF MY TERM--"
SO YOU'D RECOMMEND DOING DEALS WITH THE DEVIL, THEN?
OH, YEAH. ABSOLUTELY. I THINK ALL THE FASHIONABLE PEOPLE ARE DOING IT THIS YEAR.
"--BUT IT TURNED OUT I HAD TO SPE THE FIRST SIXTY YEARS DOWN THER AS HIS PERSONAL CABANA BOY."
MIND THE FINE PRINT, THOUGH.
OKAY, LET'S SEE WHAT THIS FELLOW IS ALL ABOUT.
"SOME OF THE DEVILS I'VE DEALT WITH WERE PUSHOVERS..."

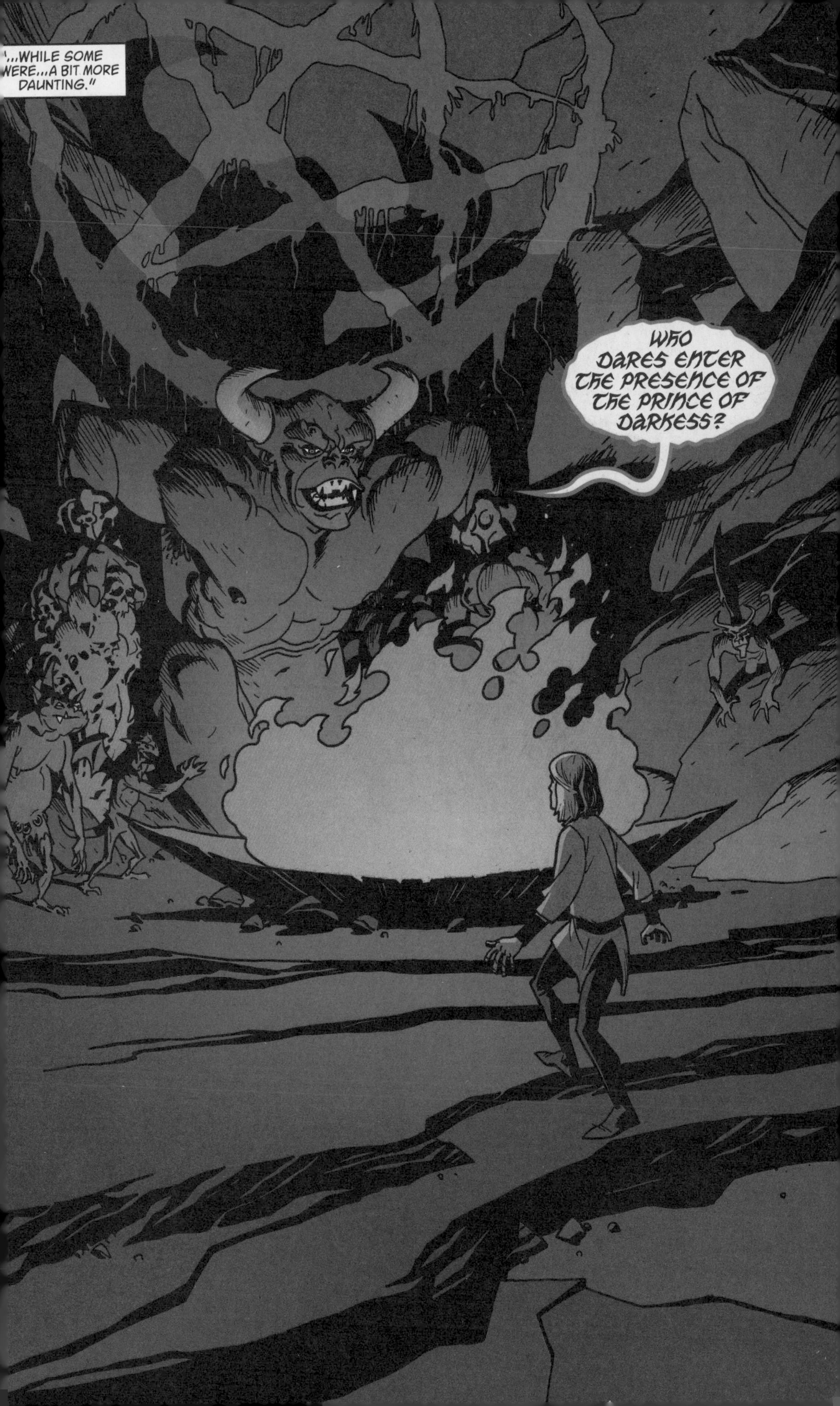
"...WHILE SOME WERE...A BIT MORE DAUNTING."
WHO DARES ENTER THE PRESENCE OF THE PRINCE OF DARKESS?

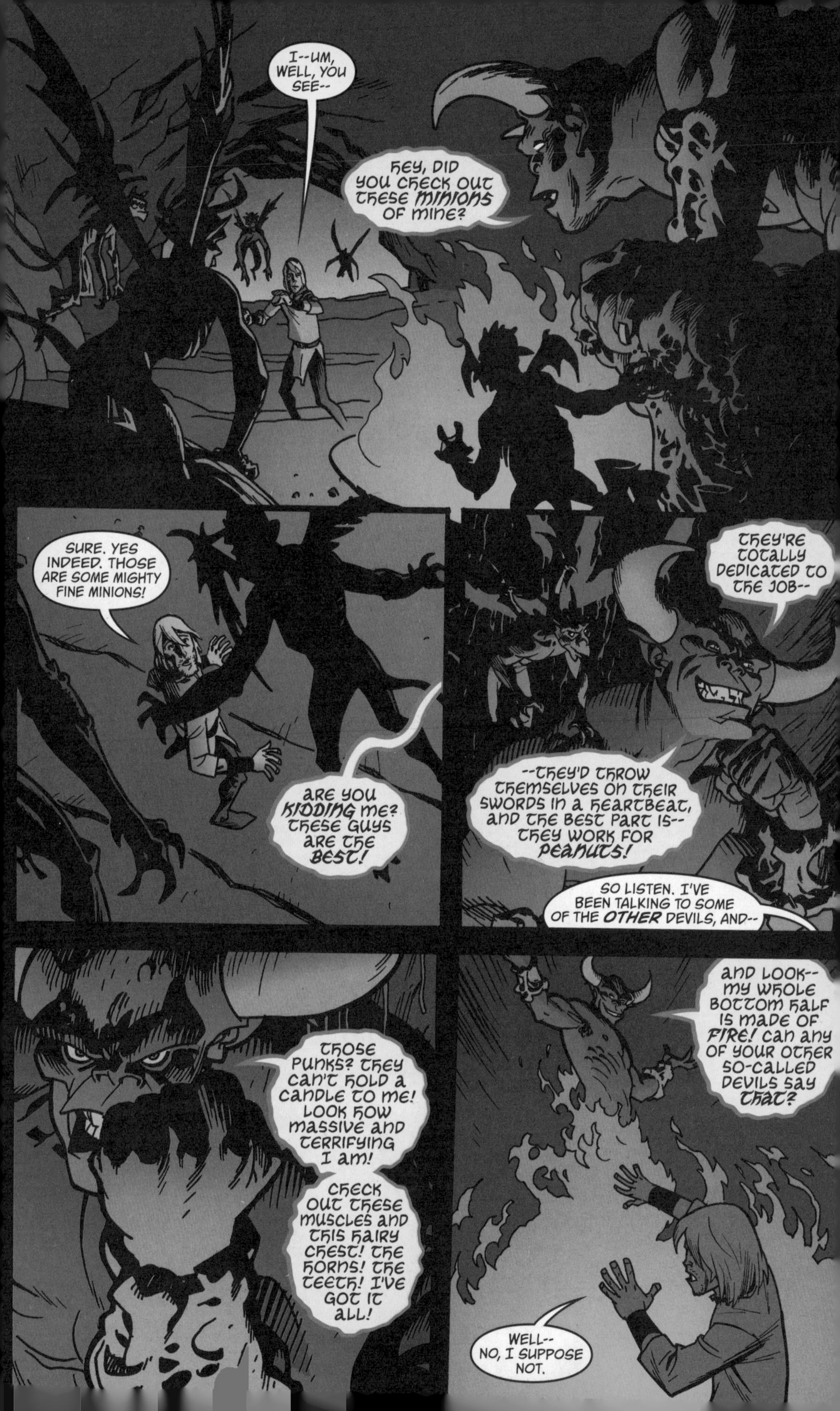

I--UM, WELL, YOU SEE--
HEY, DID YOU CHECK OUT THESE MINIONS OF MINE?
SURE. YES INDEED. THOSE ARE SOME MIGHTY FINE MINIONS!
ARE YOU KIDDING ME? THESE GUYS ARE THE BEST!
THEY'RE TOTALLY DEDICATED TO THE JOB--
--THEY'D THROW THEMSELVES ON THEIR SWORDS IN A HEARTBEAT, AND THE BEST PART IS-- THEY WORK FOR PEANUTS!
SO LISTEN. I'VE BEEN TALKING TO SOME OF THE OTHER DEVILS, AND--
THOSE PUNKS? THEY CAN'T HOLD A CANDLE TO ME! LOOK HOW MASSIVE AND TERRIFYING I AM!
CHECK OUT THESE MUSCLES AND THIS HAIRY CHEST! THE HORNS! THE TEETH! I'VE GOT IT ALL!
AND LOOK-- MY WHOLE BOTTOM HALF IS MADE OF FIRE! CAN ANY OF YOUR OTHER SO-CALLED DEVILS SAY THAT?
WELL-- NO, I SUPPOSE NOT.

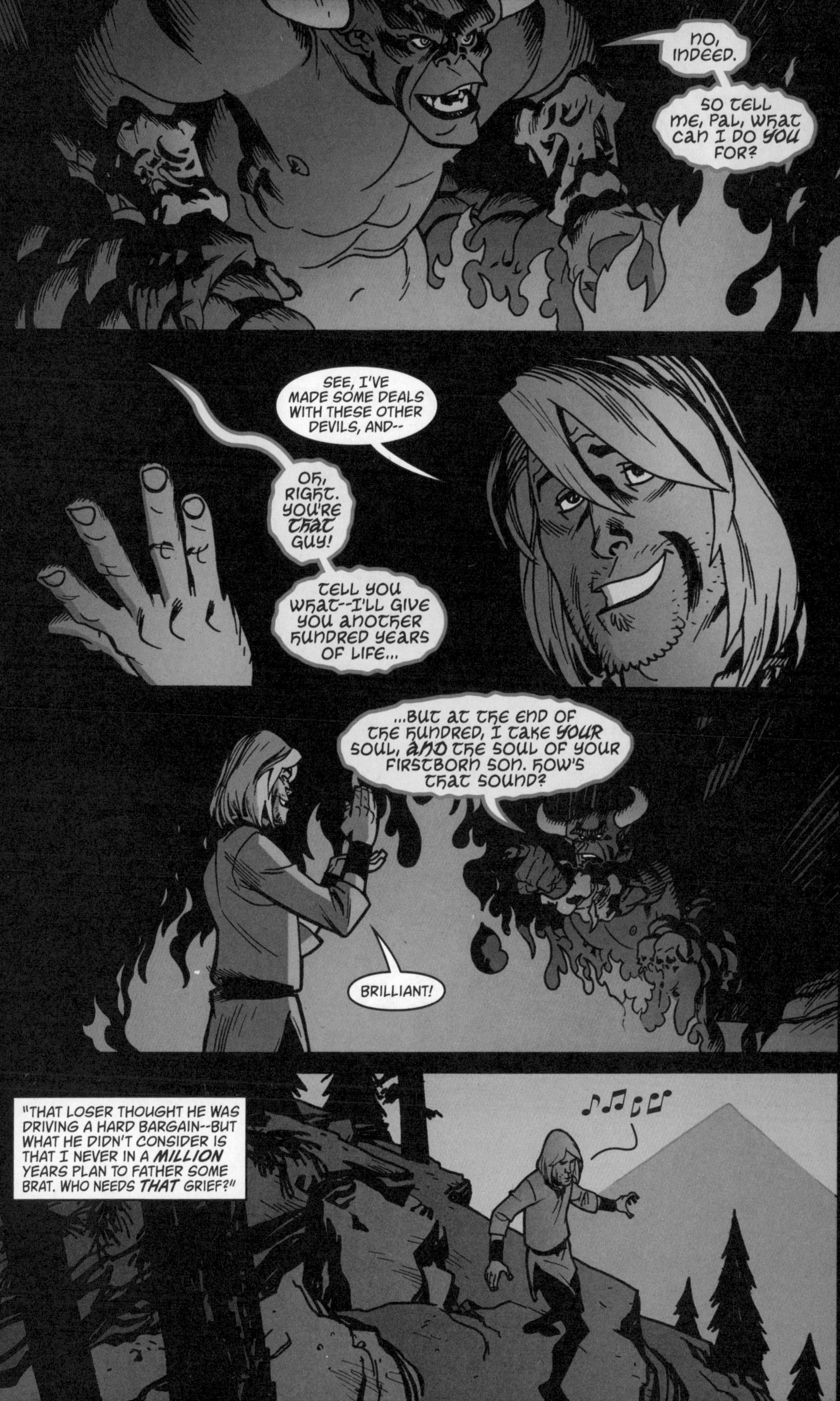

NO, INDEED.
SO TELL ME, PAL, WHAT CAN I DO YOU FOR?
SEE, I'VE MADE SOME DEALS WITH THESE OTHER DEVILS, AND--
OH, RIGHT. YOU'RE THAT GUY!
TELL YOU WHAT--I'LL GIVE YOU ANOTHER HUNDRED YEARS OF LIFE...
...BUT AT THE END OF THE HUNDRED, I TAKE YOUR SOUL, AND THE SOUL OF YOUR FIRSTBORN SON. HOW'S THAT SOUND?
BRILLIANT!
"THAT LOSER THOUGHT HE WAS DRIVING A HARD BARGAIN--BUT WHAT HE DIDN'T CONSIDER IS THAT I NEVER IN A MILLION YEARS PLAN TO FATHER SOME BRAT. WHO NEEDS THAT GRIEF?"

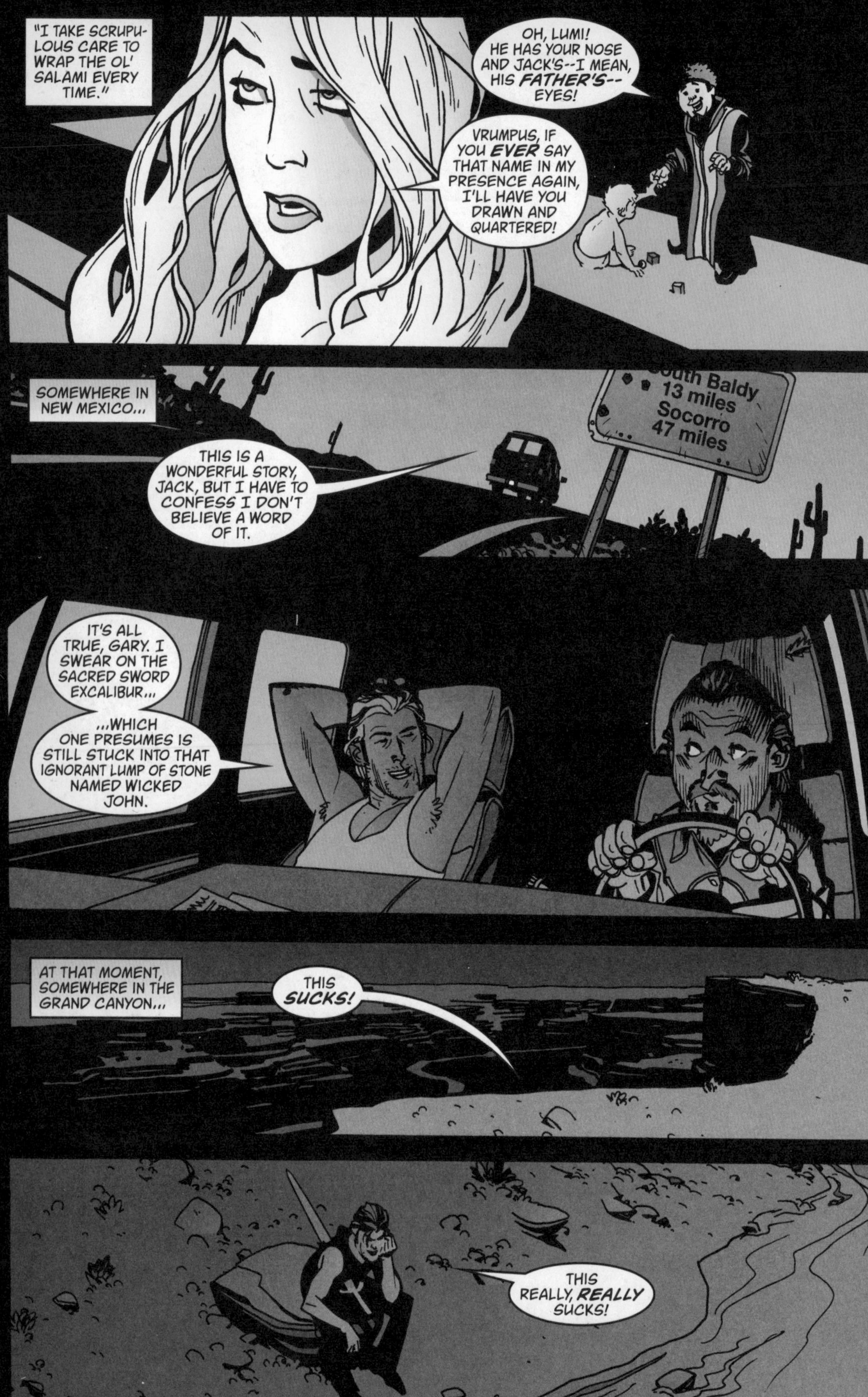

"I TAKE SCRUPULOUS CARE TO WRAP THE OL' SALAMI EVERY TIME."
OH, LUMI! HE HAS YOUR NOSE AND JACK'S--I MEAN, HIS FATHER'S-- EYES!
VRUMPUS, IF YOU EVER SAY THAT NAME IN MY PRESENCE AGAIN, I'LL HAVE YOU DRAWN AND QUARTERED!
SOMEWHERE IN NEW MEXICO...
South Baldy 13 miles Socorro 47 miles
THIS IS A WONDERFUL STORY, JACK, BUT I HAVE TO CONFESS I DON'T BELIEVE A WORD OF IT.
IT'S ALL TRUE, GARY. I SWEAR ON THE SACRED SWORD EXCALIBUR...
...WHICH ONE PRESUMES IS STILL STUCK INTO THAT IGNORANT LUMP OF STONE NAMED WICKED JOHN.
AT THAT MOMENT, SOMEWHERE IN THE GRAND CANYON...
THIS SUCKS!
THIS REALLY, REALLY SUCKS!

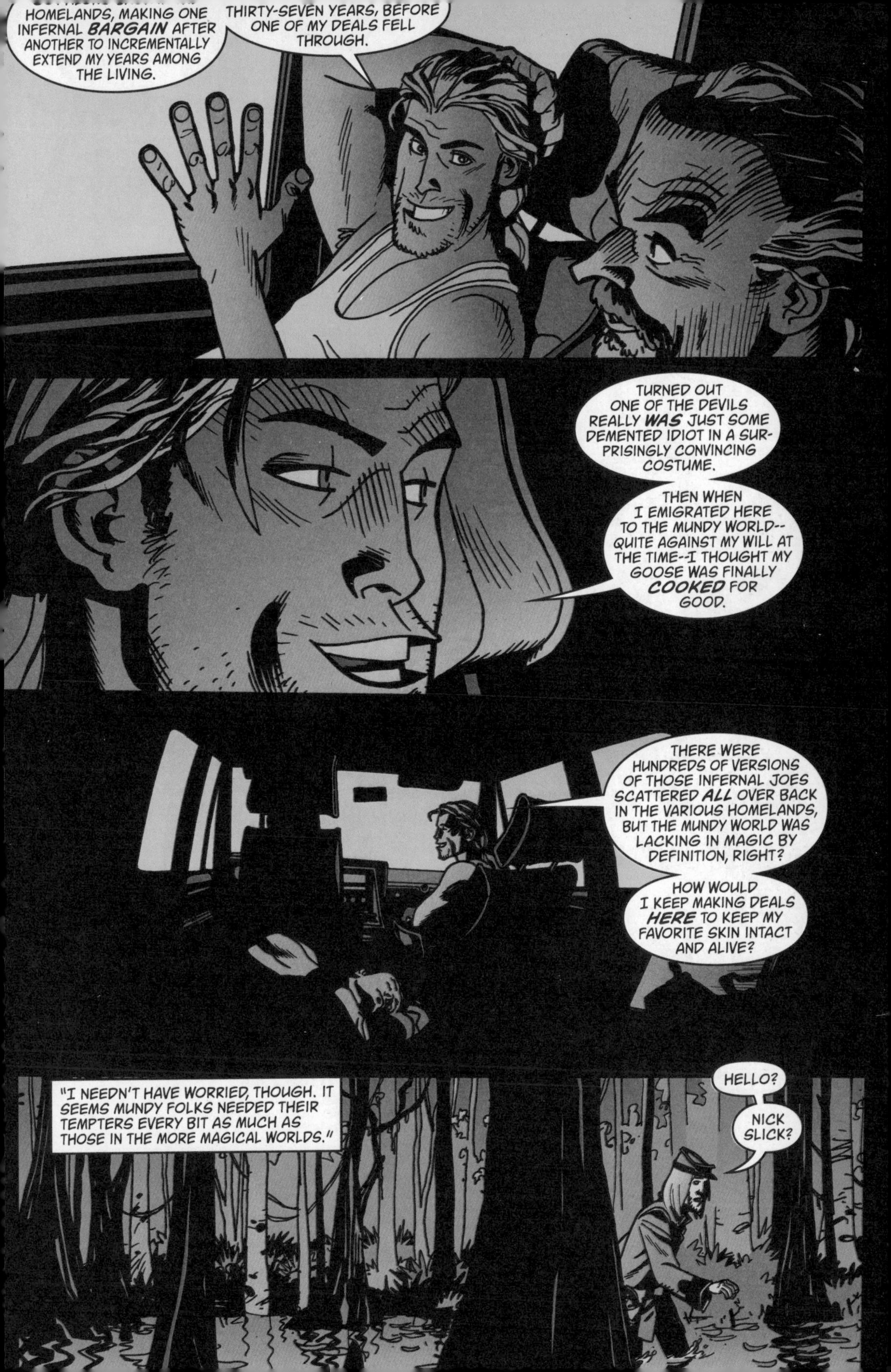
HOMELANDS, MAKING ONE INFERNAL BARGAIN AFTER ANOTHER TO INCREMENTALLY EXTEND MY YEARS AMONG THE LIVING.
THIRTY-SEVEN YEARS, BEFORE ONE OF MY DEALS FELL THROUGH.
TURNED OUT ONE OF THE DEVILS REALLY WAS JUST SOME DEMENTED IDIOT IN A SURPRISINGLY CONVINCING COSTUME.
THEN WHEN I EMIGRATED HERE TO THE MUNDY WORLD--QUITE AGAINST MY WILL AT THE TIME--I THOUGHT MY GOOSE WAS FINALLY COOKED FOR GOOD.
THERE WERE HUNDREDS OF VERSIONS OF THOSE INFERNAL JOES SCATTERED ALL OVER BACK IN THE VARIOUS HOMELANDS, BUT THE MUNDY WORLD WAS LACKING IN MAGIC BY DEFINITION, RIGHT?
HOW WOULD I KEEP MAKING DEALS HERE TO KEEP MY FAVORITE SKIN INTACT AND ALIVE?
"I NEEDN'T HAVE WORRIED, THOUGH. IT SEEMS MUNDY FOLKS NEEDED THEIR TEMPTERS EVERY BIT AS MUCH AS THOSE IN THE MORE MAGICAL WORLDS."
HELLO?
NICK SLICK?

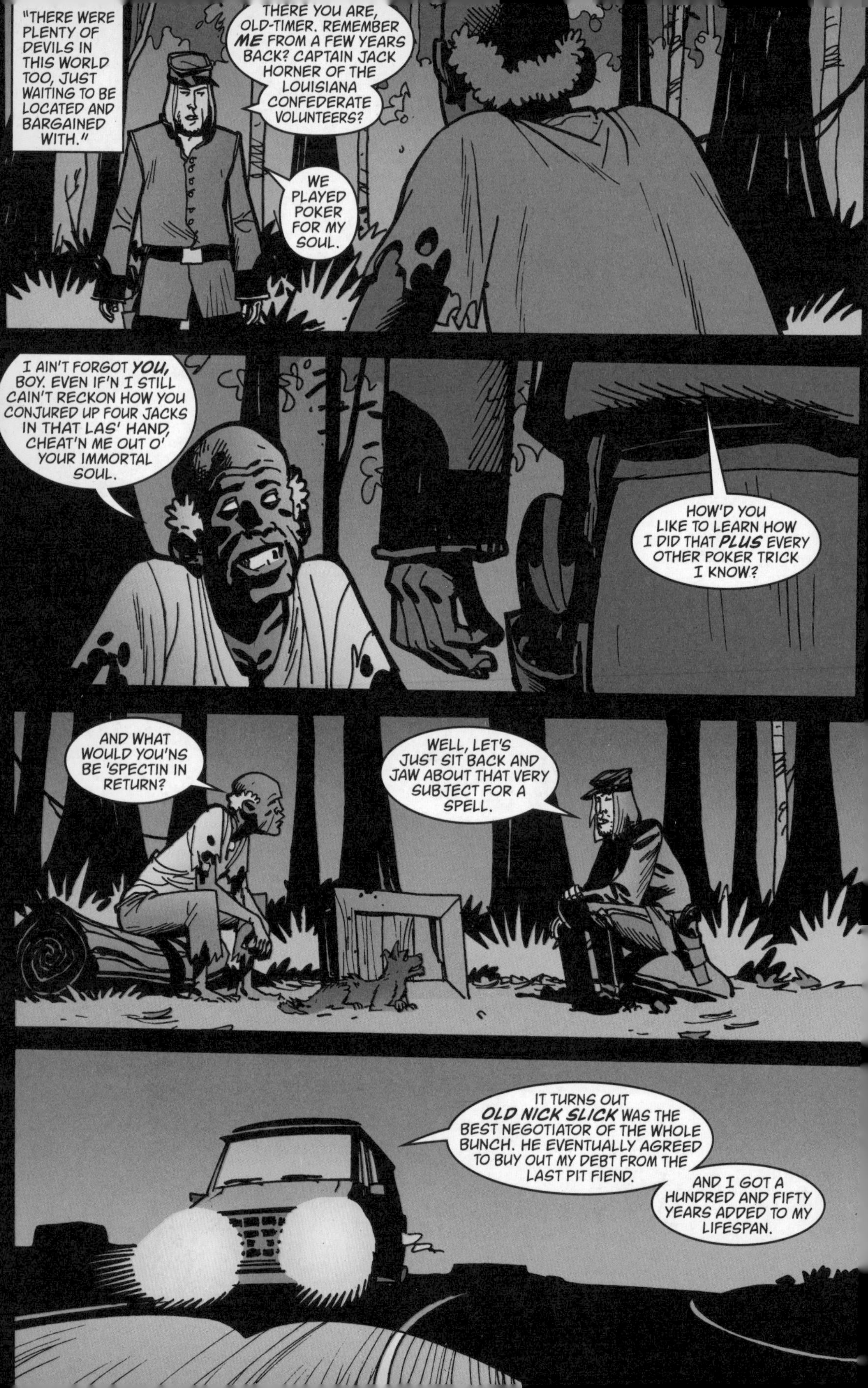
"THERE WERE PLENTY OF DEVILS IN THIS WORLD TOO, JUST WAITING TO BE LOCATED AND BARGAINED WITH."
THERE YOU ARE, OLD-TIMER. REMEMBER ME FROM A FEW YEARS BACK? CAPTAIN JACK HORNER OF THE LOUISIANA CONFEDERATE VOLUNTEERS?
WE PLAYED POKER FOR MY SOUL.
I AIN'T FORGOT YOU, BOY. EVEN IF'N I STILL CAIN'T RECKON HOW YOU CONJURED UP FOUR JACKS IN THAT LAS' HAND, CHEAT'N ME OUT O' YOUR IMMORTAL SOUL.
HOW'D YOU LIKE TO LEARN HOW I DID THAT PLUS EVERY OTHER POKER TRICK I KNOW?
AND WHAT WOULD YOU'NS BE 'SPECTIN IN RETURN?
WELL, LET'S JUST SIT BACK AND JAW ABOUT THAT VERY SUBJECT FOR A SPELL.
IT TURNS OUT OLD NICK SLICK WAS THE BEST NEGOTIATOR OF THE WHOLE BUNCH. HE EVENTUALLY AGREED TO BUY OUT MY DEBT FROM THE LAST PIT FIEND.
AND I GOT A HUNDRED AND FIFTY YEARS ADDED TO MY LIFESPAN.

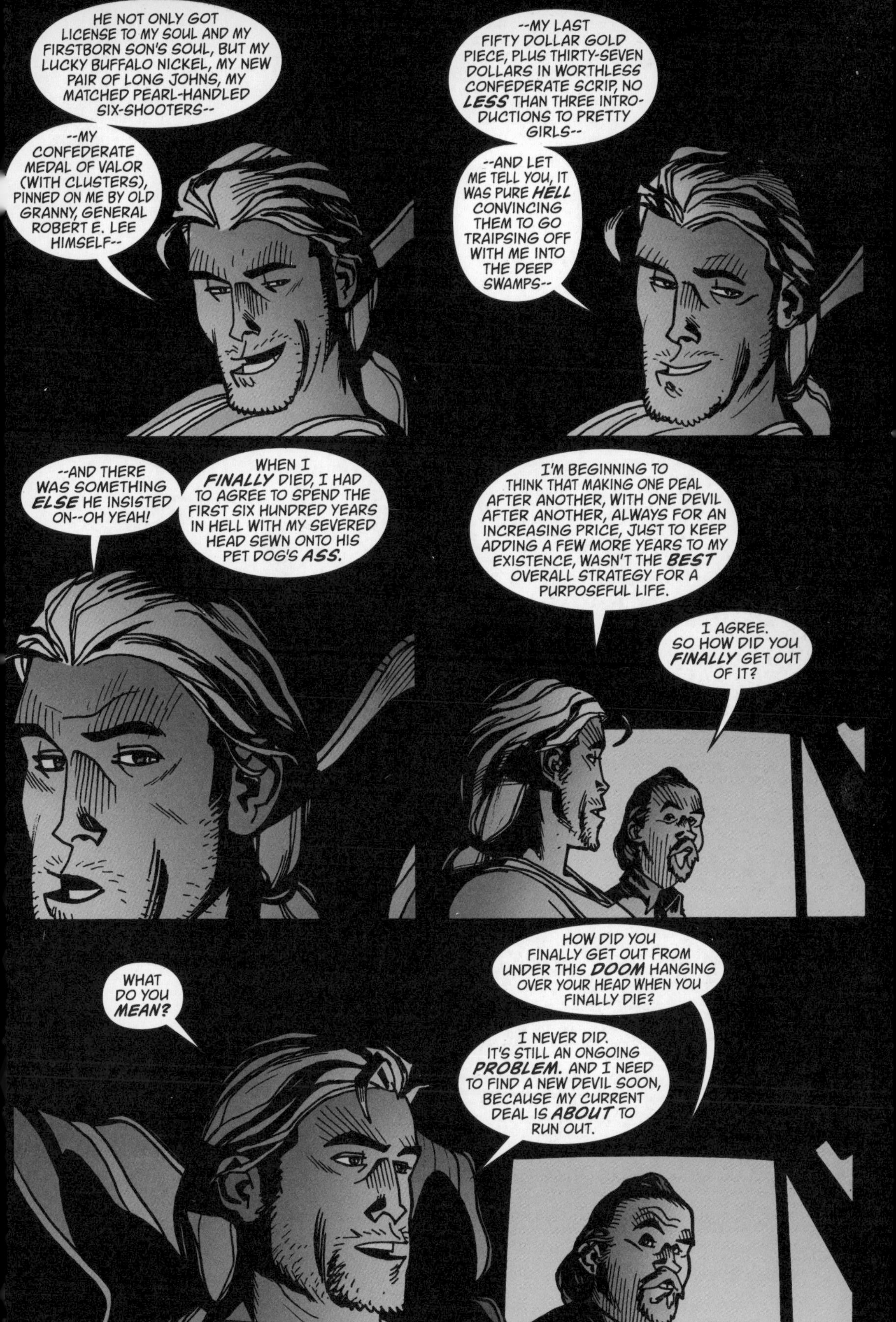
HE NOT ONLY GOT LICENSE TO MY SOUL AND MY FIRSTBORN SON'S SOUL, BUT MY LUCKY BUFFALO NICKEL, MY NEW PAIR OF LONG JOHNS, MY MATCHED PEARL-HANDLED SIX-SHOOTERS--
--MY CONFEDERATE MEDAL OF VALOR (WITH CLUSTERS), PINNED ON ME BY OLD GRANNY, GENERAL ROBERT E. LEE HIMSELF--
--MY LAST FIFTY DOLLAR GOLD PIECE, PLUS THIRTY-SEVEN DOLLARS IN WORTHLESS CONFEDERATE SCRIP, NO LESS THAN THREE INTRO-DUCTIONS TO PRETTY GIRLS--
--AND LET ME TELL YOU, IT WAS PURE HELL CONVINCING THEM TO GO TRAIPSING OFF WITH ME INTO THE DEEP SWAMPS--
--AND THERE WAS SOMETHING ELSE HE INSISTED ON--OH YEAH!
WHEN I FINALLY DIED, I HAD TO AGREE TO SPEND THE FIRST SIX HUNDRED YEARS IN HELL WITH MY SEVERED HEAD SEWN ONTO HIS PET DOG'S ASS.
I'M BEGINNING TO THINK THAT MAKING ONE DEAL AFTER ANOTHER, WITH ONE DEVIL AFTER ANOTHER, ALWAYS FOR AN INCREASING PRICE, JUST TO KEEP ADDING A FEW MORE YEARS TO MY EXISTENCE, WASN'T THE BEST OVERALL STRATEGY FOR A PURPOSEFUL LIFE.
I AGREE. SO HOW DID YOU FINALLY GET OUT OF IT?
WHAT DO YOU MEAN?
HOW DID YOU FINALLY GET OUT FROM UNDER THIS DOOM HANGING OVER YOUR HEAD WHEN YOU FINALLY DIE?
I NEVER DID. IT'S STILL AN ONGOING PROBLEM. AND I NEED TO FIND A NEW DEVIL SOON, BECAUSE MY CURRENT DEAL IS ABOUT TO RUN OUT.

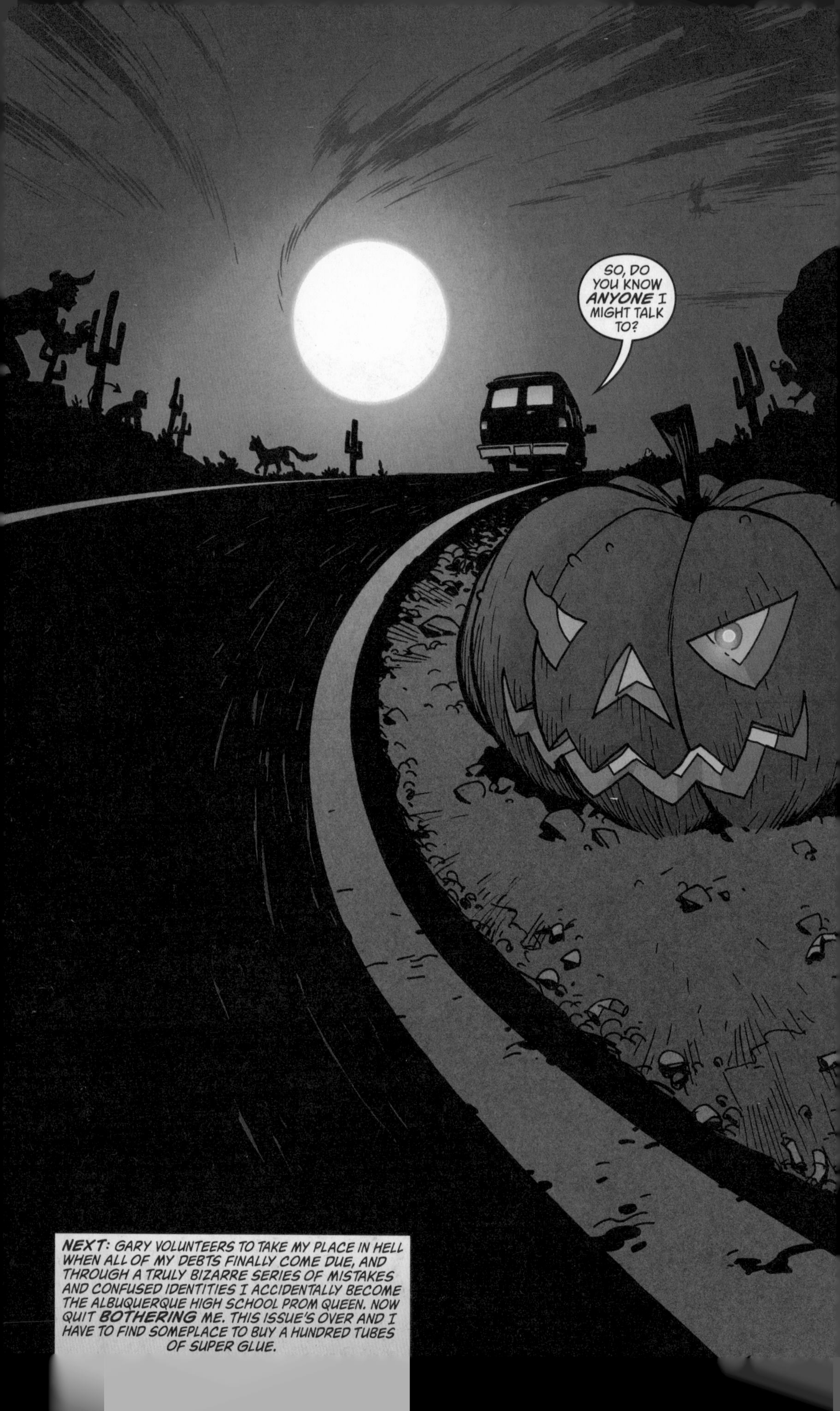
SO, DO YOU KNOW ANYONE I MIGHT TALK TO?
NEXT: GARY VOLUNTEERS TO TAKE MY PLACE IN HELL WHEN ALL OF MY DEBTS FINALLY COME DUE, AND THROUGH A TRULY BIZARRE SERIES OF MISTAKES AND CONFUSED IDENTITIES I ACCIDENTALLY BECOME THE ALBUQUERQUE HIGH SCHOOL PROM QUEEN. NOW QUIT BOTHERING ME. THIS ISSUE'S OVER AND I HAVE TO FIND SOMEPLACE TO BUY A HUNDRED TUBES OF SUPER GLUE.

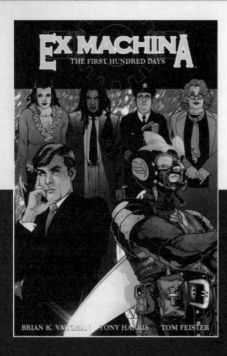